P9-CFM-872

The Solar Home

How to Design and Build a House You Heat with the Sun

Mark Freeman

STACKPOLE
BOOKS

Copyright © 1994 by Mark Freeman

Published by
STACKPOLE BOOKS
5067 Ritter Road
Mechanicsburg, PA 17055

All rights reserved, including the right to reproduce this book or portions thereof in any form or by any means, electronic or mechanical, including photo-copying, recording, or by any information storage and retrieval system, without permission in writing from the publisher. All inquiries should be addressed to Stackpole Books, 5067 Ritter Road, Mechanicsburg, PA 17055.

Printed in the United States of America

10 9 8 7 6 5 4 3 2

First edition

Cover design by Kathleen D. Peters

Line drawings by Lisa Falconer-Otey

Library of Congress Cataloging-in-Publication Data

Freeman, Mark, 1927–
    The solar home : how to design and build a house you heat with the
sun / by Mark Freeman. — 1st ed.
        p.   cm.
    ISBN 0-8117-2446-8
    1. Solar houses—Design and construction—Amateurs' manuals.
I. Title.
TH7414.F74   1993
690'.8370472—dc20   93-43602
                                                                          CIP

The Solar Home

To Frank Trerise

Without Frank, there would have been no Fiddlers Green, and without Fiddlers Green, there would have been no book.

CONTENTS

Part Three: Solar Living

ACKNOWLEDGMENTS

THE FOLLOWING PROFESSIONALS were helpful in answering questions and giving advice; any errors are mine, however, and not theirs: Ray Bates and his crew from Peabody, Bates, and Company; David Owen of Owen Associates; John, Doug, Charley, and the rest of the gang at Curtis Lumber; the folks at Quaker Electric and at Adirondack Glass; Bill Brown, Sheetrocker extraordinaire; Jack Jamieson, stonemason; and others I've probably forgotten.

Thanks for all their help to passive solar homeowners Mary Ann and Jim Potter of Queensbury, New York; Helen and George Johnson of Greenwich, New York; Hank and Bonney Hughes of Santa Fe, New Mexico; Bob and Sarah Michaels of Ottawa, Ontario, Canada; and others.

Thanks also to the following people, who were amateur builders when we started but are amateurs no longer: Patty Freeman-Lynde, Polly Freeman, Bob Carty, Al Cederstrom, and lots of others who helped with construction, for an hour or for a week. Most of all, I owe a great debt to my wife, Anne, who not only shingled roofs but also read copy, and who is the world's best speller.

INTRODUCTION

WE MOVED INTO FIDDLERS GREEN, our passive solar house, on Christmas Eve 1986. Since that date, we have never paid a nickel to an oil company, electric company, or any other company to heat our home. That's really all you need to know to decide whether you want to live in a solar house. If consuming less fuel—either because you believe America is too dependent on fossil fuels or because you'd just as soon keep the money you've been paying your fuel or power company—is not important to you, then you probably shouldn't read any further. Granted, solar heat is vastly more friendly to the environment than other forms, and it has other advantages, but the fact that it's free is what most of us like best about it.

We do have a backup heating system: a small woodstove in the basement. We don't buy wood; we cut it on our property. Our demand doesn't keep up with the supply furnished by our five acres of woodlot; two acres would probably be enough. We burn about two and a half cords every winter—slightly more in a mild winter, slightly less in a cold one. (This paradox, one of many associated with solar heating, will be explained later.) It takes us less than forty hours to cut, split, and stack a year's wood supply. Even if we used oil heat as a backup, we would burn less than three hundred gallons of fuel a year.

In case you think there is something unique about our situation, here's another case to consider: Helen and George Johnson live in a passive solar house about ten miles from us. The design and construction of their house are somewhat different, but the size is very nearly the same. They also have no backup heat other than wood, and they also burn about two cords a year. We've heard similar stories from people in many other locations.

Burning wood provides about 20 percent of our heat. Most of the rest comes from the sun, although some heat—perhaps more than we think—

comes from other sources, such as electric lights, cooking, and the warmth of human bodies. If you don't think human bodies give off much heat, remember that party you went to in the dead of winter? Thirty people attended, and your host finally had to open some windows. We're still learning new things about our house that fascinate and amuse us; the latest is that though snow doesn't melt off our roof much, when we get a dusting, the first part of the roof to emerge is an oval exactly over our bed.

Fiddlers Green is in the foothills of the Adirondacks, about six hundred feet above sea level, just north of the forty-third parallel of latitude. It gets cold here, and it snows a lot. The average number of degree-days per year here is 7,500. (One degree-day is recorded on a day when the mean daily temperature is 64 degrees F—one less than 65 degrees. A week of days averaging 30 degrees produces 245 degree days.) We don't know the exact figures for insolation (how much sunshine the location gets), but it is often cloudy in winter. Our house has approximately sixteen hundred square feet of floor space, not counting the full basement, and most of the ceilings are very high, which makes the solar heating work better (another paradox). According to a local oil dealer, if it were a conventional house, newly constructed and well insulated, it would cost on the average a thousand dollars per year to heat. (Since he sells oil for a living, his estimate is probably conservative.) We pay nothing.

If you decide to build a passive solar house, you should know that the motto of a great many Americans is "Don't confuse me with the facts; I've made up my mind." Some of your friends and relatives will tell you that they know for a fact your plan can't possibly work. Ignore them. Half of them will tell you that you'll freeze in winter; the other half, that you'll roast in summer. When I ask people what they do when it gets too hot in their house, they always reply, "We open a window." They seem astonished to find that we can do the same thing.

Neither dire prediction will come true, but that won't convince them. I once gave a relative an entire tour of the house, explaining every facet of the solar and wood heating systems. I took her from the top of the house to the basement, exploring every corner. When I got through with my explanation, I asked if she had any questions.

"Yes," she replied. "Where's the furnace?"

There isn't any furnace; there isn't any electric heat; there isn't any cost.

Not everything in this book will apply to you. For example, you may have to or want to hire a licensed electrician to do the wiring of your house and won't need the chapter on that subject, or the electric company or inspector in your area may do things quite differently from the procedures outlined here. Building codes may be very different. You may not need a septic tank or a well, because even in a fairly rural area you may be able to be hooked up to municipal services. In most cases, if you can skip some portion of the advice in this book, you're fortunate. Others will need it.

> **NOTE:** Once, my brother-in-law decided to apply new wallpaper. He bought prepasted paper and read the directions, which began, "Remove paper from special cardboard container. Place container in bathtub and fill container with water." This seemed to him like total nonsense, so he ignored it and did as he thought best. An hour later, festooned with paper like Laurel and Hardy, he went back and reread the directions. At the end were these words: "Please, try our way first."

We won't tell you always to try our way first, but please don't dismiss our advice lightly. It comes from people who've been there. In some cases, what we suggest is what we didn't do but later bitterly wished we had. If you have an "expert" adviser who disagrees with us, do two things: Ask yourself whether he wants to sell you something, and get another opinion. Presuming that you have already purchased this book, we have nothing else we want to sell you. We are not beholden to any manufacturer of building materials, and we have no ax to grind except our belief that life in a passive solar dwelling is comfortable, inexpensive, good for the environment, and good for the human spirit.

Throughout this book, the term "I" refers to the author, Mark Freeman. The term "we" usually means Mark and Anne Freeman but sometimes refers to the author and his friends and coworkers who built Fiddlers Green.

Part One

Design

Design Considerations
for Any Dwelling

DESIGN AND CONSTRUCTION are totally interrelated. Don't try to design
your house until you've read not only part 1, but also part 2 and probably part 3 as well.

Even professionals sometimes forget two very important rules of
design and construction:

RULE 1: Walls have thickness! They cannot be represented by
a pencil line on a plan; they take up space.

RULE 2: Two-by-fours aren't 2 inches by 4 inches! They are
about 1½ inches by 3½ inches, and not always perfectly that,
while 2x12s, often used as rafters, are anywhere from 11 to 11½
inches wide, although most are about 11¼. Trying to build a perfect house with imperfect materials will drive you mad. Strive
only for near-perfection. On the other hand, ¾-inch plywood or
⅝-inch Sheetrock is always exactly that. Lumber yards call 2x4s
or 6x6s dimension lumber. We call them planks. Boards are thinner than planks, usually 1 by something.

When you buy a contractor-built house, what you get is average: The house is designed for the average family, average climate, and average pocketbook. It will be made of average materials—materials chosen, in many cases, because they are convenient for the builder's crew to use, not because they are the best value for the money.

You could hire an architect and tell him all of the characteristics you want built into the house. Then you could hire a contractor to transform the architect's drawings into reality. Even if you could afford all that, you would be surprised: At least a few of your dreams would have been left out of the finished product, and some of the architect's and builder's ideas would have crept in.

When you design and build your own house, you can have it exactly the way you want it. Well, not exactly. You will find as you go along that compromise is necessary. For example, you may find that the window at the peak that you designed in the shape of a five-pointed star is going to cost as much as all the rest of the windows together and is very likely to leak. Therefore, you may compromise on this point, but it will be your choice; if you don't want to, you don't have to.

The house you design and build will be tailormade to suit your family and your lifestyle. The first thing you have to do, therefore, is to make a thorough analysis of these, as they are now and as you expect them to become. Take several weeks and put everything you think of down on paper, then revise it. Usually this is done primarily by a couple, but everyone who is going to live in the house should participate to some extent. You may be surprised by what comes up in this process, but with luck you will still be living together when it is over.

Here are a few but by no means all of the areas to be discussed:

• Family members: number, ages, sexes, sizes. For example, depending on family members' sizes, you may want sinks and counters higher or lower than standard.

• Comfort. Do you want all the rooms always 68 degrees? Or 78 degrees? Do you enjoy awakening to a 55-degree house, or do you want some rooms warmer and some colder?

• Sleeping habits. What are family members' feelings about privacy and space? Some people get claustrophobic in small spaces; some hate too much openness. Some open plans don't have doors on bedrooms. This works fine for a mature couple, but most people with children don't like the arrangement. If nothing else, it precludes running off in mid-argument and slamming the bedroom door.

• Bathroom habits. Do you want tubs, showers, or both? How frequently will they be used? Do you want toilet and sink areas compartmentalized away from the tub or shower? Is a hot tub or sauna a necessary part of your lifestyle? You aren't confined to traditional bathroom arrangements. You can have a shower stall in one corner of the bedroom; we know of people who do and who love it. Or a lavatory, as in European hotels.

• The future. How large will the family be eventually? Will Tiffany get a pony or Jason take up drums? Are there likely to be temporarily permanent guests, like an in-law?

• Avocations and vocations. Some questions are obvious. Will anyone be working in a home office? Many people have planned to use the spare bedroom as their office and later regretted not having designed a real office into the house. Do you garden or plan to do much outdoor work? A mudroom, greenhouse, or combination of the two may be in order.

• Cooking and eating. What kinds of cooks are there, or will there be, in the family? Do you need just a freezer and a microwave, or do you want a huge kitchen with fireplace, complete with roasting spit? How often do you entertain, how many people, and in what ways? Do you need a formal dining room?

• Family activities. Are there or will there be musicians, and if so, what kind? A grand piano may require slightly more attention to the load-bearing capacity of floor joists. A lot of practicing may even justify special soundproofing in one room (or a slightly heated room over a thoroughly detached garage). If truly high-fidelity sound reproduction is important to you, at least one room should be specially designed for it. Should there be an artist's studio, with north light? A darkroom? Built-in projection facilities?

• Animals. Are there or will there be pets, and if so, how many and what kind? Will they spend all, some, or none of their time indoors?

• Machines. Will there be boats? How many, what kind, how big, and where stored? Cars? Trucks? Lawn tractor or similar equipment? Will there be a complete wood- or metalworking shop?

All this only scratches the surface. I can't guess if you go in for mime or want a full-size indoor putting green.

There are some design considerations that are not personal. The design must be adapted to the site, or vice versa, and to the climate. Local building suppliers and contractors in the North persist in selling homeowners sexy designs that look great and function well in Arizona but are not suited to a cold climate. No matter what anyone tries to tell you, a flat roof is impractical in snow country.

As you are going through this process, you will find that you automatically become much more aware of every house you enter. Do you like the Joneses' downstairs powder room off the living room, or the Smiths' huge center island in the kitchen? Don't be swayed by stylish magazines or influential friends. Be sure it's what *you* want. You might be surprised to find that many of your guests would prefer, for reasons of privacy, to walk upstairs to the bathroom off the guest bedroom.

You can get ideas from motels, hotels, and public buildings, as well as from private homes. Remember that you don't have to be traditional or conventional. I know of a beautiful house that has a master bedroom suite tucked away up a staircase all by itself, where both the bathroom and the bedroom have large arched openings with no doors. I know of another that has a large room, totally brick and tile, containing a wooden hot tub and a row of showers like those in a gym.

You may not like either of those ideas, but you may have some unconventional idea that suits you. Real estate agents will tell you that it will make the house harder to sell, but I say go for it! If ease of resale is very important to you, you'll have to consider building a house that suits most buyers, rather than one that just suits you. Often, however, what agents believe most buyers are looking for has more to do with what agents like than what buyers like. You never know what a potential buyer will or won't want in a house.

When you finally have all of everyone's needs and desires sketched into the house, you will probably have to scrap half of it. In 1993 the average cost of construction in the United States was about seventy dollars per square foot. (The cost varies greatly from one part of the country to another and may have increased considerably by the time you read this.) While yours will be vastly less than that, because you are going to do the work yourself, you can't afford a building the size of the Taj Mahal, which is what you probably have designed by now. So the compromises begin, but remember, they are your compromises, not those forced on you by an outsider.

DRAWING THE PLAN

After you have a rough idea of what you want in a house, you can sketch it out on paper. This may be quite satisfactory for a while, especially if someone in the family is artistic, but sooner or later you will need scale drawings. In addition to reams of graph paper, just about the only satisfactory medium for this, you'll need sharp pencils, high-quality erasers, a good surface like a draftsman's drawing board, a protractor, a ruler, and probably a T-square. An artist's or draftsman's supply store can furnish these, as well as templates for common household items such as tubs, toilets, sofas, beds, and even grand pianos. A set of these in the scale you're using is handy, but you can improvise by cutting your own out of cardboard and using quarters and matchboxes for various round or square items.

At this point you should familiarize yourself with the local building code. In most localities it can be obtained from the town or county code enforcement office. Don't fret too much about it, however; it is unlikely that you would design a house embodying serious violations of the code, and inspectors sometimes permit slight departures from it.

Draw to scale each room and the house as a whole. Plans that are drawn as though someone were looking down directly on each floor or room are called *floor plans;* those that show the sides in the same one-dimensional way are *elevations.* You will need a floor plan for each story, even the basement, and elevations from the outside of the east, west, north, and south sides, including additions. Now you will probably go back to your friends' homes and annoy them again by measuring doors, windows, and other features. At some point you will want to draw, separately, a wiring diagram, even a rough one, and a plumbing plan.

Sketch out all the plans roughly at first, then refine them. Don't leave out any detail; that's how you find out there won't be room to carry an armload of wood past the water heater. Don't forget *Rule 1.* Plan all windows and doors carefully. How will they look from the outside; from the inside? There are certain standard sizes for doors, but windows come in all sizes, shapes, and kinds. All windows in the same wall should be at the same height; if they are different sizes, it is probably better to have the sills at the same height, rather than the tops. Think about which way doors will swing and what they will hit or cover up when open.

The building code probably requires that exterior and interior doors on your house be of a minimum width and height and that all rooms have at least two possible exits. If there is no building code in your area, look at the code for some other place and see if it contains sensible ideas you want to incorporate. Especially if you have children, do you really want a bathroom that has one door and no window, which means that you couldn't get into it in an emergency? Even if there is no code requirement, do you want to go without smoke alarms?

Now you're ready to adapt your house plan to the special requirements of a passive solar house.

2

Special Design Considerations for Passive Solar Construction

PRESUMABLY BY NOW everyone knows how solar heating works. On a global scale, the greenhouse effect may be overheating our planet, but it can also be used to heat our houses. If enough of us use the greenhouse effect instead of oil for home heating, we can put less carbon dioxide into the atmosphere and ameliorate the effect on the planet. That's another solar paradox.

Here's a quick refresher course on the greenhouse effect. Light energy from the sun passes through a transparent medium, like glass, plastic, or air. When it strikes a surface, it is transformed into heat energy, which passes through glass much less readily than light. A black or nearly black surface changes most of the light to heat, while a light-colored surface reflects much of the light. For the homebuilder, once sunlight has been changed to heat, the challenge is to keep as much of this heat as possible in the house through the use of insulation, heat sinks, and a few other tricks such as shutters.

The term *passive,* when applied to solar construction, means that there is no fancy gadgetry. The sun shines through the windows and heats the house. There are no electric eyes, automatic fans, solar panels, or photovoltaic cells. Those are the trappings of *active* solar construction,

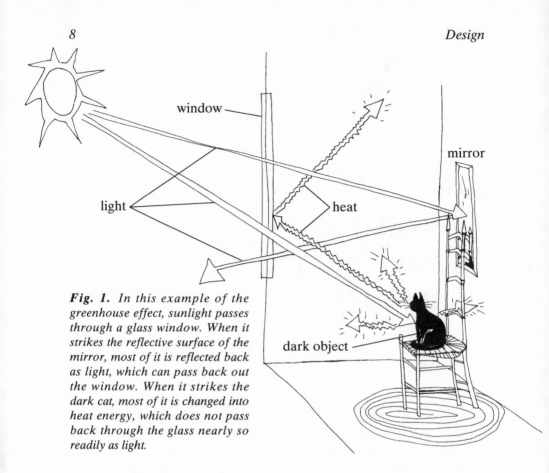

Fig. 1. *In this example of the greenhouse effect, sunlight passes through a glass window. When it strikes the reflective surface of the mirror, most of it is reflected back as light, which can pass back out the window. When it strikes the dark cat, most of it is changed into heat energy, which does not pass back through the glass nearly so readily as light.*

which is almost always done by high-tech, high-pressure, and high-priced companies. Sometimes it even works.

Actually, most solar house designs are a mixture of active and passive. They have a couple of gadgets, but not so many that if the electric power goes off the heating system ceases to function. Fiddlers Green, for example, has two ducts, two fans, and one thermostatic switch.

Everything you need to know about passive solar construction can be put into one paragraph: Be sure that your site has a good southern exposure. (If you live south of the equator, always read "north" where it says "south" in this book, and vice versa.) Put all or almost all of the windows on the south side. Superinsulate the house, with special attention to the vapor barrier, and provide a fairly substantial amount of heavy material to act as a heat sink. That's all there is to it!

Americans love electronic complexity. When strangers want to know about our solar home, they always want to hear about the Mickey Mouse parts, the "bells and whistles," the thirty-five tons of sand under the greenhouse, the duct snaking through the sand bed, the thermostatic switch. When we tell them, essentially, the information in the preceding paragraph, they nod but they don't comprehend. We know people who live in solar houses in Santa Fe and in Ottawa, as well as several others within a few miles of us. Each house is different, but they are all super-insulated and have almost all the glass on the south side. Bonney in Santa Fe has a solar water heater but few other gadgets. Bob in Ottawa has more high-tech gadgets than we do; Mary Ann, nearby, has fewer. None of us has many.

Your design will have to incorporate these three features: south windows, superinsulation, and heat sink. Since heat sink may be the most technical of the three (although it's not very high-tech), let's take that up first.

HEAT SINKS AND AIR CIRCULATION

A heat sink is a volume of dense material you can sink heat into. Certain kinds of material absorb a lot of heat energy when the building is warm and release it slowly as the ambient temperature drops. The ones most commonly used in solar construction are masonry (bricks, cement blocks, and concrete), rocks of various sizes, sand, and water. Generally speaking, the denser the material, the better the heat sink, but other factors like availability and ease of handling will affect your choice of material. For example, per pound, water is a better heat-absorbing material than granite, but per cubic foot, rock is better. In other words, a heat sink using water will take up more space in your house than one using rock.

You should design a lot of heat-absorbing material into your house and plan ways for the heat to get to it. Here are a few solutions:

Fiddlers Green has a full basement. The basement walls and floor, which are all heavily insulated on the exterior, are made of reinforced concrete. The north wall is ten inches thick; the others are the standard eight inches. The house also has a very massive chimney, eight feet wide at the base, four feet wide at the top, and three feet thick throughout. The chimney is not on an exterior wall but is within the house for most of its height. There is an attached greenhouse or sunspace, with concrete knee walls and a floor of flagstone over concrete. Under that floor is a bed of sand, some thirty to forty tons, with a duct snaking through it. Finally, inside the house is an extensive area of slate flooring. All of these materials act as heat sinks. (See figure 2.)

The sun shines directly on the greenhouse floor, the slate, and the lower part of the chimney. Heat reaches the sand bed from the greenhouse floor above it by conduction and from the basement via a fan blowing air into the duct, which takes a winding course through the sand and back into the basement. Heat reaches the basement via another fan

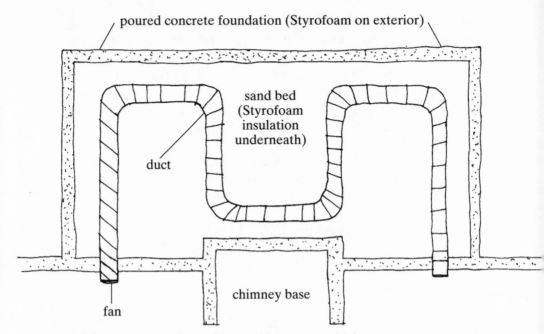

poured concrete foundation (Styrofoam on exterior)

sand bed (Styrofoam insulation underneath)

duct

fan

chimney base

Fig. 2. *One method of circulating air through a sand bed under a greenhouse: A fan moves air from the basement, through a winding duct in the sand bed, and back into the basement. The process is dual: When the sand bed is warmed by the sun shining on the slate floor above, the basement is warmed; when the woodstove in the basement is in use, the air entering the duct is warmer than the air leaving it, and the sand is warmed. In all such systems, the heat exchange is slow and is seldom more than a few degrees.*

and duct from the highest part of the house. Of course, when we're using the wood stove in the basement, heat is produced there. Air flows throughout the house at all times, so the ambient temperature is the same in every part of the house. (See figure 3.)

Helen and George Johnson's Solargreen has two sand beds, one under the greenhouse and another under the wood stove, which is on the first floor. Both sand beds employ ducts and fans to blow warm air into the basement, and there is a duct designed to return air from the top of the house to the bottom. (See figures 4 and 5.)

Potters' Solarwood has a two-story greenhouse that extends across the entire south side of the house. Two ducts, one on each end, take warm air from the highest point in the greenhouse to the basement. The duct openings and fans are manually controlled. (See figure 6.)

Rocks ranging from huge boulders to gravel are used in many passive solar designs. Bob's house in Ottawa has no basement, but rather a

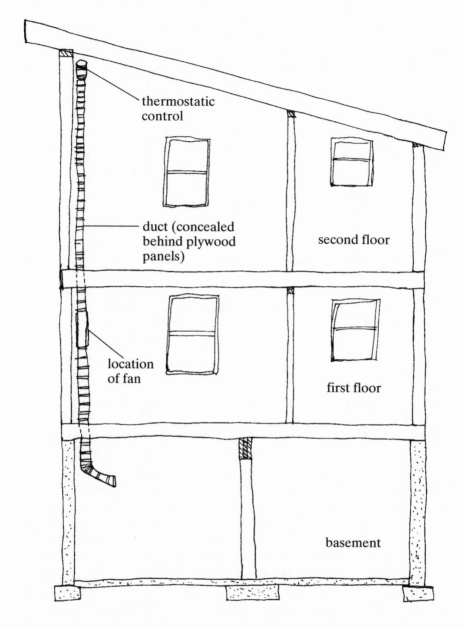

Fig. 3. *One technique for circulating air in a passive solar house: Warm air rises by gravity to the highest point, which is at the south end of an upstairs bedroom. When the temperature at this point reaches 75 degrees, the thermostatic switch turns on the fan, which pumps air to the basement. At 72 degrees, the fan goes off. In summer, the thermostat may be set higher if desired. An open design permits air to circulate freely throughout the building.*

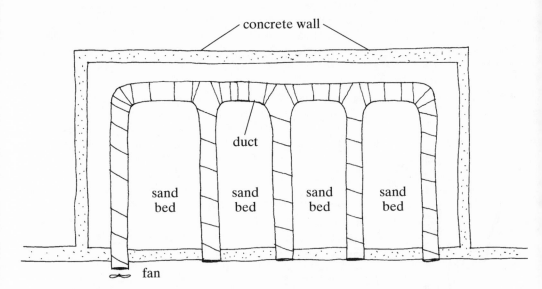

Fig. 4. *This system for blowing air through a warm sand bed under a greenhouse uses an unusual arrangement of branching ducts. Compare this with figure 2.*

bed of large rocks. Air is blown from the house through the rock bed and back into the house. This design is attractive in that no duct is used; the warm air simply percolates among the rocks. (See figure 7).

There are many other ways to build a heat sink into your house. Water is relatively inexpensive. Some solar designs involve numerous steel drums, painted black, filled with water, and placed where the sun will shine on them. To us, this seems less attractive than slate or concrete, and there are always the dangers of leakage or bacteria buildup, but many successful solar houses do use water for heat storage. (See figure 8.)

You may think of other ways to incorporate heat sinks into your design and to allow air to flow readily from one part of your house to another. Warm air rises to the highest point possible. Imagine a model of your house, with water at the lowest point. Now mentally turn it upside down. Would the water flow readily to one point? It should. Now turn it back right side up, and install a duct and fan to blow the warm air back from that point to the basement (or lowest point).

A solar house should have an "open plan," with large openings between rooms and few doors to shut. Even bedrooms and bathrooms can be doorless; clever design can ensure privacy. Any doors should be left open as often as possible.

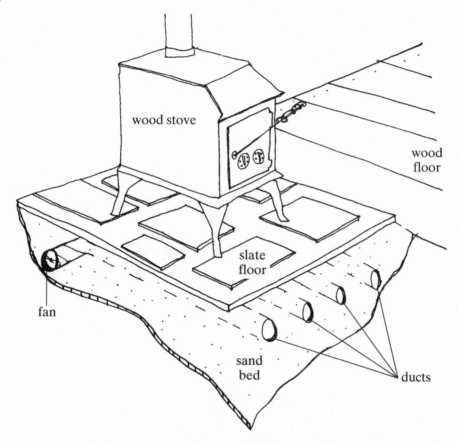

Fig. 5. *This somewhat unusual arrangement can be used to store heat from the wood stove. Although heat generally rises, it also radiates in all directions. When the stove is in use, radiant heat warms the slate floor under the stove on the first floor and passes into the sand bed under it, which is in the basement. A fan blows air through the ducts in the bed, with warm air emerging in the basement. Compare this with figure 4; the two systems function together.*

PLACEMENT OF GLASS

Putting all or almost all of the windows and doors on the sunny south side is not as difficult as designing heat sinks, but it does take a little design juggling. Most solar houses are long along the east-west axis and narrow in the north-south dimension, for reasons that will become clear to you when you begin juggling. Ideally, the north wall should be totally unbroken, with no door or window. The ideal site would have a hill behind the house to the north, so the view in that direction wouldn't be too great

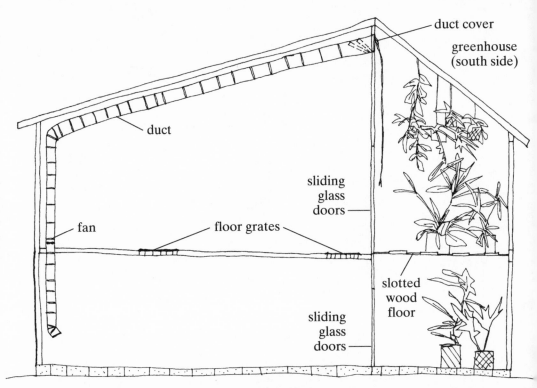

Fig. 6. *A two-story greenhouse takes up the entire south side of this solar home. Deck flooring allows heat to rise from the lower story of the greenhouse to the upper story and then to the top of the house. Ducts run from there to the basement. The duct covers and the fans are manually controlled. Warm air blown to the basement rises through grates to the first floor.*

anyway, but many people can't bear to have an entire side of the house with no opening.

A common practice in solar construction is the use of clerestory windows, which are, in modern terms, windows high up in a higher-than-normal wall. It is difficult to design a solar home without them. Bear in mind, however, that it is convenient to be able to reach windows, both on the inside and the outside, to wash them, to open or close drapes or shutters (or the windows themselves), and simply to install them to start with. Again, clever design can get around this problem, but you may sometimes wish you had a library ladder on wheels as a permanent living room fixture.

Two ideas worth considering are making the south side of the house longer than the north, so that the east and west sides slant in from front to

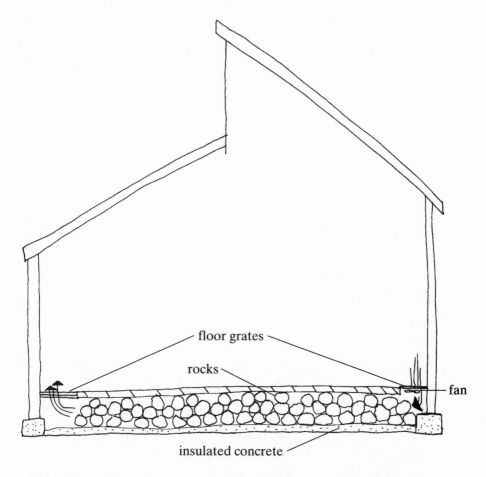

Fig. 7. *In this house rocks are used as a heat sink. There is no basement; warm air generated by passive solar heating is blown through a "crawl space" filled with large rocks. A thermostat turns on the fan when the temperature of the rocks falls below 65 degrees and turns it off when it reaches 68 degrees. There are no ducts; the air passes between and among the rocks.*

back, or having a sort of semienclosed courtyard to the south. The second is probably more practical, in terms of construction costs. All corners are expensive, but corners that are not 90 degrees are very expensive. All construction materials and techniques are designed with the idea that there will be only right angles in the house, and few of those. We know a couple who built and now live in an octagonal house. It is very nice. They are very determined people, and very wealthy.

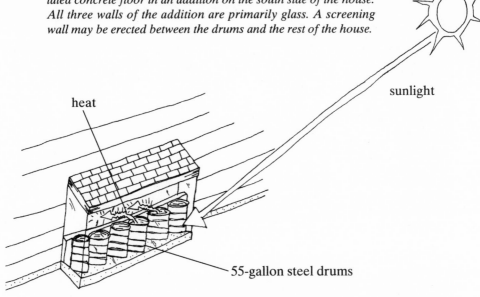

Fig. 8. *Water is a cheap and efficient heat sink. These ordinary steel drums, painted black and filled with water, rest on an insulated concrete floor in an addition on the south side of the house. All three walls of the addition are primarily glass. A screening wall may be erected between the drums and the rest of the house.*

sunlight

heat

55-gallon steel drums

Making the south side longer than the north may not turn out to be feasible, but it is not too difficult to make the south side higher than the north, and most solar houses are designed this way, which is why most feature clerestory windows.

Earth berming is another frequent feature of passive solar design, in which the north side (and sometimes the roof) is totally or partially buried in a hillside. The Hughes house in Santa Fe uses this technique. Before you go too far with this design feature, however, talk to a knowl-

N

Fig. 9. *One way to collect more solar energy is to design a building with a long south wall and a shorter north wall, like this. Unfortunately, corners that are not 90 degrees are both difficult and costly to construct.*

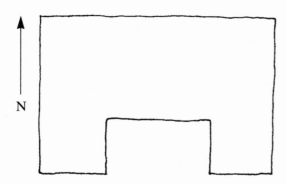

N

Fig. 10. *A design involving a courtyard on the south side of the house would collect sunlight in the early morning and late afternoon as well as at midday. While each additional corner adds to the cost, this design, having 90-degree corners, might be cheaper than that shown in figure 9 and would offer a warm and pleasant space for outdoor living.*

edgeable local excavation and foundation contractor. There are some difficulties and drawbacks involved in this type of design, not the least of which is that the north concrete wall may have to be thickened and buttressed to withstand the strain.

Of course, all the parts of your design will interact with one another. For example, if you have no windows on the north and many windows on the south, that will determine to some extent how you use insulation. It will make it easy to design a very thick north wall, with no breaks in the insulation or vapor barrier; this will lead naturally to placing almost all closets, cupboards, and bookcases against that wall. To complete the cycle, these storage areas will further increase the insulation value of the north wall.

INSULATION AND VAPOR BARRIER

Most books on this subject will, at this point, engage in a lengthy discussion of R-values, which everyone talks about and nobody understands. R-value is a *relative* measure of how fast heat will travel through a material. For example, standard fiberglass insulation is said to have an R-value of 3.5 per inch. For comparative purposes, concrete block has a value of 0.2 per inch. "Experts" suggest an R-value of 20 for walls and 30 for roofs or ceilings.

R-values are useful, but they are only as good as the people installing the insulation and the overall job. What you want is walls and ceilings that will hold in as much heat as possible, and this is a function of many factors besides the R-value of the material. Insulation that is crammed in too tightly, has gaps, or becomes wet loses most of its insulating value. What you really want for insulation is as much as you can possibly get. Follow the suggestions in this book and you'll have enough.

As a practical matter, it is easy to design an eight-inch-thick wall, as you will see. Ten inches would be possible, but it probably isn't necessary. Most heat escapes through the ceiling; your highest ceilings or the roof should have about twice the insulation of the walls. If you design a full attic, you can insulate above the ceilings to your heart's content and solve most of your condensation problems at the same time. Unfortunately, you will discover that attics do not mesh well with most solar designs, and few of us can afford to build into our dwellings some seven thousand cubic feet of space that is used for nothing but storage.

Most house construction today involves a plastic (polyethylene) envelope, completely surrounding the interior, inside the insulation. The purpose of this vapor barrier is to prevent leakage of air and the moisture it contains. In contractor-built houses, considerable attention is paid to insulation, but much less to the vapor barrier. In typical construction, the carpenters install the vapor barrier reasonably well. Then the plumbers and electricians come along and hack huge holes in it. You can do a great deal to prevent this during construction (one of our friends literally bribed electricians and plumbers to make the smallest holes possible), but protection of the vapor barrier begins with design.

Design your house to require as few breaks as possible in the polyethylene shield. Though you have to have electrical and plumbing fixtures somewhere, try to keep them away from exterior walls and, even more, off the ceiling. This does not mean the interior ceilings, those that have another room above them, but the ultimate ceiling—the one that contains the insulation. Instead of putting light fixtures in ceilings, consider track lighting on the walls. Though local building codes will probably force you to have electric outlets on exterior walls, they should not prevent you from carrying all your plumbing pipes up interior walls, which is the only sensible place for them in a cold climate anyway. In terms of design this may mean, for example, that you can't stand at the kitchen sink and look out through a window, unless it's a window into the living room. Certainly it's nice to look at a view while you work at the sink; however, "you pays your money and you takes your choice."

In most cases you will find that design that makes sense for a solar house makes sense for any house. For example, if you have chosen a good site, the best view is to the south, so putting most of the windows on that side is doubly sensible. To give another example, very few people want to stand at the bathroom sink and look out over the landscape. Although frequently that view is more attractive than looking into a mirror, for practical purposes most of us choose the mirror.

At about this point, you should construct a three-dimensional scale model of cardboard or similar light board. This is the only way you can really find out what your house will look like and how it will function. Houses and people are three-dimensional, but plans are only two-dimensional. You can even set the finished model of your passive solar house in the sunlight at various angles to see exactly how the sun will shine in the windows at various times of the year. If you are talented, the model will make a great conversation piece when displayed in the finished house.

When you're sure your plans are completely settled, draw them in final form as clearly and neatly as you can. Then take them to an expert who can turn them into blueprints. You may not want to pay the fee a licensed architect will charge, or you may not be lucky enough to find one who is willing simply to draw up blueprints, but an engineer or draftsman can do the job.

In many jurisdictions, blueprints have to be approved by a state or county engineer, who will want to be sure that your specifications (specs) are sturdy enough. You'll need some help with this from local experts like building materials suppliers or contractors, who know facts like the minimum allowable sizes of joists or rafters to span a given distance.

After your design has been turned into blueprints, you are ready to build your house, hiring contractors to do the parts of the work you will not do yourself.

3

Site Selection

MOST PROSPECTIVE HOME BUILDERS do not give sufficient consideration to the location of the house. In some cases, as when a piece of land is inherited, the house must be adapted to the site. In most cases, however, you should give at least as much thought to the site as to the design of the house.

SITE CONSIDERATIONS FOR A PASSIVE SOLAR HOUSE

The selection of the correct site for your solar home is absolutely crucial. Fortunately, it's not very difficult. The only absolute requirement is that it have a southern exposure.

Buy a cheap compass. Every time a real estate agent (or owner) shows you a piece of land, set the compass down on a flat, nonmagnetic surface and find out which way is south. That's the direction your house will face, and it cannot be obstructed by a nearby hill, another building, or tall trees you are unable or unwilling to remove.

Don't depend on anyone else, especially anyone who wants to sell you land, to tell you which way is south; they won't know or, to put it politely, will be inaccurate. Use a compass. If the house cannot face due south, 10 or 15 degrees off is acceptable, but no more, especially to the west. The ideal setting is south-southeast by south, or about 170 degrees (180 degrees is due south). If your house faces slightly east of south, it will receive winter sun early in the morning, when it is most needed. If it faces 20 degrees or more away, passive solar heating will not function nearly as efficiently.

When you're on a potential site, look around. In winter the sun will rise somewhat south of east and set somewhat south of west. The farther north you live, the more this will hold true. Note whether these directions, especially the direction of sunrise, are blocked by obstacles you can't remove, like hills, or trees that are on someone else's land. Low hills some distance away are no problem, but high hills quite near are. Ideally, you should view the site on December 21, when the sun is lowest in the sky. If it seems reasonably suitable then, it will be suitable the rest of the year. It may not always be practical to visit the site then, but try to see it on a sunny day between November and January. Locations that look great in June can be pretty dark in December.

Most solar houses are in rural settings, on sites of an acre or more, where the owner can control what is built between him and the sun. It is possible to have a solar house in the city, but it's hard to predict what will be erected to the south of you, blocking your heat source, in the future. A good city location is a spot just north of a cemetery or city park. The north side of a residential street, across from one- or two-story buildings, may be safe if zoning laws prohibit taller construction, but zoning laws can change.

A hill sloping to the south is an ideal location. The house should be built just below the top of the hill, so that cold north winds will be blocked by the hill and the trees, if any, on the top. If there aren't any trees, you should plant quick-growing species, like poplars, as soon as possible or you should build a bit farther down the hill or find another site. Such a hill need not be too steep; even a slight slope will give you all the protection you need. Building a house into the side of a very steep hill admittedly helps to keep it warmer in winter and cooler in summer, but it adds to the cost of construction, cuts down on the amount you can do yourself, and may create dampness and strength problems in the north wall.

One major advantage a sloping site has over a flat one lies in its microclimate. Land sloping to the south catches the sun's rays at a more direct angle. A rule of thumb is that every degree of slope is the same as a move seventy miles south; if your site slopes at 7 degrees, you will experience the climate of a spot approximately five hundred miles south of you. This will, of course, not affect the angle at which the sun shines in your windows, but it will affect how cold it is outside your house. We have good friends and fellow gardeners who live a quarter mile from us, under the same hill but on the north side. Our growing season is a month longer than theirs.

A flat field, although not as good as a south slope, is satisfactory. Here a good hedge of tall trees to the north is a must. You may read elsewhere that deciduous trees (to the south) will provide shade in summer without blocking insolation in winter. This is only partly true. Any tree (or anything else) that blocks the sun in winter should be removed. This doesn't mean you can't have trees south of your house. Since the run rises well north of east and sets well north of west in summer, but moves much farther south and lower in the sky in winter, any kind of trees northeast or northwest of the house will provide shade in summer without blocking the sun's rays in winter.

One advantage a flat site has over a sloping site is that it is easier to construct a driveway and to locate a garage, whether attached or not, on the north side, which is an ideal location. Many solar houses on flat land have the main entrance on the north side of the house.

Most mistakes you make in the design and construction of your house won't be critical, but a serious mistake in site selection may be. Don't let anyone, least of all yourself, talk you into buying an unsuitable piece of land.

SITE CONSIDERATIONS FOR ANY HOUSE

Anyone building a house, solar or otherwise, will have a number of questions about the site. You may want to know about taxes, schools, churches, fire protection, police protection, public transportation, highway maintenance, and hundreds of other items. Like us, you may prefer to live on a little-traveled dirt road. You may have no personal stake in the school bus route, or you may have six school-age children. Such matters depend on your particular household and lifestyle.

If you are going to do all or most of the construction yourself, find out about zoning laws and building codes in the area. Learn how local banks feel about lending money to do-it-yourselfers, especially those who plan to build a solar home with or without what banks call backup heating. Both banks and building codes have come a long way since the 1970s, when it was almost impossible to get either money or inspector approval for the sort of home described in this book.

If you can possibly avoid getting a bank mortgage, do so. Banks make all kinds of conditions; you will probably have to sign a contract stipulating that you will have the house totally finished by a certain date, or else. If you have an accident during construction and wind up with your leg in a cast, tough! One of the advantages of doing it yourself is that you can pay for the materials as you go along; the bills won't all come due at once. You may be able to get the house 75 percent finished, then get a home equity loan, rather than a mortgage. Banks are not always as fussy about the heating system of a house on which they are giving out a home equity loan.

Before buying a piece of property, have a perc test done, even if it's a rough one you do yourself. Perc tests determine how fast water will percolate through the soil. If the answer is "very slowly," the authorities won't let you build there, and you wouldn't want to anyway, since your septic tank wouldn't work. To do your own rough test, dig four good-sized holes at various points around the house site, with special emphasis on the future location of the septic tank. Pour a gallon of water into each hole and time how long it takes the water to disappear. If it seems to you inordinately long, check with local authorities or your potential excavation contractor. Do this in normal dry weather, not immediately after a rain or at the end of a long drought. If you have seen the site only in dry weather, be sure you see it after a three-day rain or during the spring thaw. You don't want a swimming pool for a basement.

Another thing you should do yourself is check for ledge or bedrock where your basement will be. If you must, sneak onto the property without the agent or owner, carrying a sledgehammer, several ten-foot lengths of steel pipe, and something to stand on, like a tall stepladder or a pickup truck (if you can drive to the house site). At what will be the four corners of the house and in the center, try to drive the pipe straight into the ground. (You can do this while you're waiting for the water to percolate out of the holes.) If it hits something, it may be a boulder. Move a few feet and try again. If there seems to be an obstacle five feet down or so in most places, you probably have bedrock, and some local geologist could have told you that to start with. (In most areas, the county agricultural agent can show you a soil map covering your site, which will indicate, among other things, ledge or bedrock.)

You will also want to know what sort of water supply you can count on. In most areas you will be hiring a well driller. You'll want to talk to others who have employed him and to neighbors about their well-drilling experience. Probably yours will be similar to theirs, but there is always the possibility of luck, good or bad, when drilling a well. If your site is sloping, it is usual to locate the well above the house and the septic tank below; local law will probably require that they be a certain number of feet apart. If there's a clean, reliable year-round stream or pond on the property, you may not need a well. If your site has city water and city sewerage, you can avoid those worries.

Finally, access is important, both for the lumber truck to deliver materials to your site and for the power company to deliver electricity to it. You may also want to investigate phone connections, although anywhere you can get power you can probably get a phone. Two things you will need immediately are electric power and a rough driveway to the site.

Construction people will tell you that there are no problems that can't be overcome. There are ways to install septic tanks in hardpan, ways, like blasting, to get around bedrock, ways to deal with a feeble supply of bad-tasting water. You can carry all the construction materials to the site on your back, and you can use a portable generator to make electricity. All such solutions cost you—in money, time, energy, or all three. You will probably have to make some compromises, but if you can find a site that doesn't have any major problems or drawbacks, grab it, even if the taxes are a lot higher. Taxes have a way of changing.

4

Designing Foundation, Basement, Garage, and Stonemasonry

THE OVERALL DESIGN of your house will determine the design of its component parts, which means that this is the time to decide its dimensions. If the house is 20 by 60 feet, then the foundation is 20 by 60. If there is a sunspace addition on the south side that is 10 by 20, then there is an addition to the foundation at that spot that is 10 by 20. Don't design too many such additions; remember, corners cost money. In the real world, as opposed to this book, you will not design the foundation, then the living room, then the kitchen; you will keep working back and forth until all parts are in harmony.

FOUNDATION AND BASEMENT DESIGN

You will need a rough plan, preferably on graph paper, of the overall dimensions of the foundation, indicating whether there will be a basement or crawl space under the house, and where; where a chimney will rest; where the garage will be; and the like. Later on an expert, like your foundation contractor, can help you with specs: which walls will need buttressing, how big the footings (thicker, rougher, sub-foundation foundations) should be, how much rebar (steel reinforcing rods) the concrete will need.

We strongly urge you to have a full basement. It is possible to build a solar house with a partial basement or crawl space underneath (we've seen one), but it isn't easy, and doing without a basement will not cut the cost as much as you think. You have to build many tons of heat sink into the house somewhere; where better than the basement?

In many parts of the country, houses built on a poured slab are the norm. This is one example of a construction technique that is practical for the contractor but not for the homeowner. I don't believe that a passive solar house on a poured slab is a good idea. It certainly isn't feasible for a do-it-yourselfer. In such construction, all plumbing connections and some other vital items are embedded in the slab, which means that later on if you have a minor leak, the first tool you'll need will be a jackhammer.

A full basement is a good place for your laundry, for your wood-stove, for wood storage, for everything-else storage, for the water pump, water heater, water softener if any, for a cold cellar for vegetables, for a wine cellar, for the electric panel box, for a workbench, or for the kids to skate on a rainy day. It is the logical place for the rocks, sand, water, or whatever serves as a heat sink. It is a good place to park your car. If you don't put these things in the basement, you have to design space for them somewhere else. Construction costs are usually computed as so much per square foot; square feet in the basement cost less than square feet in the main house. Finally, it is much, much easier to wire and plumb a house with a full basement than one without.

Having said that, let me add that our house does not have a totally full basement: The area under the greenhouse or sunspace does not have a foundation as deep as that of the main house, and the "basement" under the greenhouse is completely filled with sand.

Designing a full basement is not very difficult. It will be, essentially, one big room. If part of it is partitioned off as a garage, you need to decide how much space this will require. Remember *Rule 1*. You should allow about 5 inches on your plan for a simple 2x4 partition between the garage and the basement. Why 5 inches? The 2x4 is $3^{1}/2$ inches wide, the fireproof Sheetrock is $^{5}/8$ inches thick, and there is Sheetrock on each side of the wall. Leave another quarter inch to be on the safe side. You will find that when you nail or screw things together, there is usually a tiny air space. In other words, if you nail three 2x4s together, the resultant piece will be a bit more than $4^{1}/2$ inches thick.

You will of course design into the basement the space for the heat sink material. You will plan where ducts will be to blow air from other areas into the basement and back, and to circulate it through the rock or sand bed, if that is the plan. You may design a space for a wood stove. In many solar houses, the basement is the nerve center of the heating system. Like the main house, the basement should have an open plan in order to allow air to circulate freely.

If the basement has a chimney, a laundry room, or any other major feature, draw these in. Draw in doors and windows. Our friend the architect told us we didn't need any basement windows; our foundation contractor told us to draw in as many as possible, and he was right. I wish we had more. A standard size for basement windows is 32 by 18 inches. Exterior doors vary; 36 by 78 inches is common. An easy way to find out such things is to go measure them in a modern house.

You will need to draw in the basement stairs, after deciding where in the house you want the top of them to come. At "Fiddlers Green" the basement stairs are in the northeast corner, and under them, insulated from the rest of the house, is a combination cold cellar, pantry, and wine cellar.

Sketch in every object that will be in the basement: washing machine, dryer if any, water heater, pump and tank, freezer, workbench, and so on. You will probably move these around, but you should at least get an idea of how much space they take up and whether it will be possible to walk between them. It is surprisingly easy to design a basement in which you can't walk between the stairs and the washing machine.

Part of the problem of designing is that paper is two-dimensional but rooms are three-dimensional. Draw not only a floor plan but also an elevation for each wall. Remember that all items will take up three-dimensional space—sometimes, as in the case of stairs, quite a lot of space. Allow a space about 3 by 10 feet for the stairs; this will be covered in more detail in chapter 23.

Your foundation contractor will probably build your basement with eight-foot walls. You might think you could save money by persuading him to make them shorter, or you might decide to make them shorter if you build the foundation yourself. Don't. The floor, which will be poured *after* the walls, will use up about eight inches of that height. There will probably be a *girder* (see chapter 12), which will take up another ten inches or so. By the time you've put in plumbing, you'll be ducking under the drain pipes if you are over five foot eight.

The posts or pillars to support the girder will have to be indicated on your plan. A footing will be poured under the location of each post.

GARAGE DESIGN

Even Americans who have garages seem to leave the car outdoors. I always wonder why. In winter, if you leave the car in a slightly heated garage, it starts more easily, the windshield doesn't have to be scraped, and you don't freeze for the first five minutes of the ride. If you change your own oil or perform similar tasks, a garage is a must. In summer or a milder climate, it keeps the sun off your car and gives you a place to work where flies don't bite. A basement garage or other attached garage also enables you to get into the car without walking through rain or snow. Any kind of garage probably pays for itself in the increased longevity of vehicles stored there.

A basement garage is the best, but it has two major drawbacks. The first is that it's hard to fit a two-car garage into the average basement. If you have two cars, you can solve this problem by keeping one of them somewhere else. It is not unthinkable to keep your major vehicle in the basement and another, like a pickup truck, in a small, simple, unattached garage.

The second drawback is that it's impossible to have a remote-controlled overhead door, unless you cut into the insulation and Sheetrock on the ceiling, which creates a fire hazard among other difficulties. You need extra headroom for the electric motor, more than your basement offers. The cost of having all the basement walls ten feet high is more than most people would want to pay for the convenience of a remote-controlled door.

Basement garages were very dangerous before building codes required that they be separated from all the rest of the house with fire-resistant Sheetrock. Even with this, never park a car with a leaky gas tank or similar problem inside any building, least of all your dwelling.

An attached garage is better in most ways than a separate one, but it also poses problems. Any outbuilding attached to a solar house would ideally be on the north side. Here it provides additional insulation without blocking insolation. If the site slopes south, however, it's difficult to drive up to a garage on the north side. Ultimately, where—if anywhere—you can put an attached garage depends on the nature of the site.

The big advantage of a totally separate garage is that you can put it anywhere. Anywhere, that is, where you can drive to it and it doesn't block the view or the sun's rays and isn't too far from the front or back door. One thing we tend to forget about cars is that they don't just carry people—they carry fifty-pound bags of dog food, ten concrete blocks, five gallons of paint, and the like. Bear that in mind in planning the garage location.

Wherever the garage will be, designing it is fairly simple. Measure the length, width, and height of your car. Then allow plenty of room for opening doors and getting out. Are you likely ever to have a larger car, a van that is higher, a long sedan as you get older and richer? It's a lot easier to make the garage big enough now than to enlarge it later. Are you going to keep two cars in the garage? Do you want space for a lawn tractor or similar equipment? A reasonably roomy one-car garage might be 12 by 20 feet. This allows for the car and a few lawn mowers and other bulky tools, automotive supplies, snow shovels, and the like. It is even possible to keep a car and a garden tractor in this size garage and drive either one out first, if you drive carefully and park carefully.

Overhead doors come in standard widths: 9 feet, 11 feet, and so on. Nine feet is not too big an opening for the average driver to put the average car through. An overhead door may be 78 or 84 inches high. Use the 84-inch one.

If your garage is not in the basement, you will have to design it just like a little house, although you can avoid foundations in a nonattached garage if you're willing to settle for a dirt floor and post-and-beam construction. In any case, it will need walls, a roof, windows, and a door or two. (See the chapters on these subjects.) Whether your garage will have insulation and wiring, maybe even plumbing, will almost certainly depend on whether it's attached or separate; heating a separate building is probably not practical.

CHIMNEY AND FIREPLACE DESIGN

A solar house with backup electric heat and no fireplace might have no chimney at all, but such a design is very unlikely. Electric heat is the most expensive kind in most of North America. It is, however, much less costly to install than an oil or gas furnace, it takes up less space, and it makes less dirt. Just try never to use it.

Chimneys cost lots of money. You will probably pay an expert to build one, and it will be the second most expensive item you contract out, exceeded only by excavation and foundation taken together. Nonetheless, I urge you to have a fine large brick or stone chimney. First of all, you're quite likely to want to burn wood. More important, the chimney will function as a heat sink. Chimneys are massive. A good-sized one weighs many tons. If you have no chimney, you'll have to add that much rock or sand to the design or suffer some loss of efficiency. Finally, a massive brick or stone chimney adds wonderfully to the beauty and charm of both the exterior and the interior.

Most experts will try to talk you out of a fireplace. The accepted wisdom is that you will lose more heat from a fireplace than you gain. This need not be true. Chapter 25 tells you how to gain much more heat from a fireplace than you lose. I must admit, however, that though we do get heat and pleasure out of our fireplace on chilly spring or fall days, we rarely use it in the dead of winter. A fireplace makes a charming focal point for a living room, even with no fire in it. And if you don't have a mantel, where will you hang your stockings?

Unless you are going to build the chimney and fireplace yourself, consult your stonemason to help you complete your design. The most important factor in designing a chimney into your home is to get it inside the house, not on an exterior wall. If half your chimney is outdoors, then half of whatever heat it holds will go outdoors. It's actually worse than that, because the chimney will conduct heat from indoors to outdoors faster than your insulated walls will. Put the chimney into any partition wall: between the living room and kitchen, living room and bedroom(s), or living room and sunspace.

The minimum length and width of the chimney will be determined by the number of flues in it. You should not use the same flue for any two sources of flue gases, like a woodstove and a fireplace. A woodstove flue will probably be eight inches in diameter, a fireplace flue ten. Oil or gas furnaces may not need such large flues. The chimney will need to be much larger than the flue or flues; each flue will be surrounded by insulation. You might as well design a massive chimney; it won't cost all that much more than a tiny one.

The minimum height requirement for a chimney is that it be two feet taller than the highest part of the roof it penetrates, but it is a good idea to have it much higher in order to make it draw better. If a higher section of roof is less than ten feet away, the chimney should be at least two feet higher than that point. Chimneys often taper as they rise; that is, one might be 3 by 8 feet at the base but only $2^1/2$ by 4 at the top. This makes an attractive effect, and the shelf thus created is an ideal support for a mantel. The chimney will require a large, strong footing. If you have a basement, it should start at basement level; the support that would otherwise have to be poured under the chimney from the basement to the first floor would cost nearly as much as just building the chimney all the way down.

About all you need to know in order to design your fireplace is how big a log you want to put into it. Your stonemason probably will not build it from scratch but will use a metal form in one of several standard sizes. It will be lined with firebrick, and the final effect will be very attractive.

Properly designed fireplaces will draw well even if they are not very deep. Fireplaces in New England colonial houses were very shallow. A fireplace 38 inches wide at the opening (narrowing toward the rear), 20 inches deep, and 30 inches high will comfortably handle 30-inch logs.

> **NOTE:** It is absolutely essential in a tightly sealed house like yours that your fireplace have a duct that brings in air from outdoors. Many building codes now stipulate this. Otherwise you will have to open a window every time you have a fire, or the fireplace simply will not draw. The duct should open into the fireplace from a wall near the back; it should not be in the hearth floor where ashes can fall into it. Since your chimney is on an interior wall, you will have to design a fairly long duct to the outdoors. The air in the duct will be cold, not hot.

The design plan should indicate the size, shape, and finish material of the hearth. Make it big enough; sparks will surely leap out of your fireplace onto it. With an oversize hearth completely surrounded by slate flooring, you can go to bed and sleep peacefully with a fire burning and the screen in place.

Most fireplaces have a trap in the floor to allow the ashes to go down to a pit inside the chimney in the basement. Nobody seems to have thought about whether this is truly useful. Sooner or later the pit will have to be cleaned out, unless you plan to sell and move, leaving the buyer a full chimney. It is usually easier to take the ashes from the fireplace directly outdoors than to clean out the pit.

You may or may not want to have a cap on your chimney. Caps are heavy and expensive and may adversely affect draft. There is usually, year-round, a current of air moving up your chimney, which prevents rain from coming down. In extremely wet weather, however, when no fire is burning, there can be a buildup of water at the bottom of the chimney, where it can mix with ashes, creosote, or both and seep into the basement. So far, this has not been a serious problem for us, but it's one more reason to keep the chimney swept. A clean chimney allows a stronger updraft.

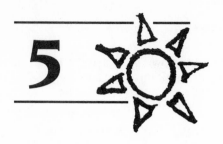

Designing Kitchen, Bathrooms, and Laundry

BATHROOMS, KITCHENS, AND LAUNDRIES require a great deal more planning than living rooms or bedrooms. The obvious factor that they have in common is plumbing, and planning where plumbing will go can be very tricky. This chapter deals with areas of your house that have water piped to them and waste water piped away from them. In addition to more conventional facilities, you might have a hot tub in a bedroom or solarium, you might have a sauna, or you might decide to have a sink and toilet in one area of your house (real estate agents call this a "half bath") and a shower stall somewhere else (real estate agents don't have a name for that).

HOW PLUMBING WORKS
Most people already have some grasp of how plumbing functions, but perhaps a brief refresher course is in order. Water comes from a city water supply, a well, or some other source, like a spring. It enters the house through the basement wall (unless there is no basement) via a "main," a large-diameter pipe. Outside the basement, it must be buried below the frost line, usually about four feet underground in very cold climates, to prevent freezing.

If the source is not a city water supply, often the water goes first to a pressure tank. A pump builds up the pressure in the tank so that water will run briskly even out of second-floor faucets. Modern drilled wells, pumps, and pressure tanks are reasonably foolproof; usually the householder does not have to worry too much about them. If they do break down, the person who installed them will probably be the one who repairs them.

From the tank the water flows through small-diameter supply pipes. Some goes to a heater, which could be electric, gas, or solar. Solar heaters usually only preheat the water before it flows to a gas or electric heater. From this point on, two sets of pipes, hot and cold, run to all facilities, with a few exceptions such as toilets.

Every facility that water flows to (except outdoor faucets) needs a drain pipe. Drain pipes are much larger in diameter than supply pipes, with the largest coming from toilets and the smallest coming from bathroom sinks ("lavatories"). Drain pipes run to a city sewage system, septic tank, or, occasionally, a cesspool or dry well. Because gases come back up from these, traps and vents are necessary. Traps always remain full of water and prevent sewer gases from entering the house. Drain systems also have to be vented to allow the gases to dissipate harmlessly into the atmosphere at a fairly high point on the house. Since sewer gases contain methane, they not only smell bad but also are flammable.

EFFICIENT ARRANGEMENT OF ROOMS

Bathrooms and kitchens usually are located near each other; they either back up to or are directly above one another. It is a convenient plumbing arrangement to have a kitchen sink on one side of a wall and a bathroom on the other, or to have a bathroom on the second floor just above one on the first floor. Obviously, if rooms that use plumbing are scattered all over the house, then pipes—both supply pipes and waste pipes—will have to be run all over the house. The nearer together the baths and kitchen are, the more you can combine piping, which will save money on materials. If will also save money on labor if you aren't doing the work yourself.

Unfortunately, at some point in your designing you will discover that a house that has a kitchen and a laundry room backed up to each other downstairs and two bathrooms directly over them lacks some of the charm you wanted in your dream house, and you will have to effect some compromise between efficiency and charm and convenience.

It is often practical to put bathrooms, which usually have few windows, on the north side of a passive solar house. The design might have two baths back-to-back or over each other. Some modern houses have no window in the bathroom, but a vent and fan. Aside from the fact that such an arrangement means a hole in your roof that permits heat to escape, a bathroom with no window is dark and gloomy at best. You can solve this problem with a bathroom that is on one or the other end of the house and therefore can have east or west windows, a bathroom that has a north window (let's hope it's the only one in the house), or one that has a skylight. We have seen all three of these arrangements in solar houses, and we recommend the east or west windows.

BATHROOM SPACE AND CONVENIENCE

It is common today to have a bathroom partitioned as in a motel, so that one person can use part of it while another is bathing. Some people like more privacy than this; others feel claustrophobic in small spaces. Don't rule out making a mockup of a sink or toilet space to see how you feel when in it.

It is inconvenient to walk up and down stairs in the middle of the night to use the bathroom. For older people it can be downright dangerous. There's a great deal to be said for having a bathroom on the same floor as, and not far away from, any bedroom.

DRY WELLS AND GREYWATER

If there are two or more bathrooms, it is a convenient and comfortable arrangement to have them clustered together—perhaps two back-to-back upstairs and one directly underneath—and the kitchen and laundry on another plumbing "circuit" entirely. If you use this idea, you may be able to have the kitchen and laundry drain into a dry well or cesspool rather than into the septic tank. The only waste that really has to go to a septic tank is the waste from toilets. *Greywater* is the usual term for waste water that does not include human waste. It isn't necessary that this go into the septic tank; moreover, it is undesirable, because detergents and grease in greywater interfere with the bacterial action of a septic tank. You'll probably have to have your septic tank and/or drain field ("leach field") dug up and pumped out some day, but you certainly want to delay that awful hour as long as possible.

A dry well is simply a large hole in the ground lined with good drainage material and covered sturdily so that no one can fall through into it. Greywater percolates through the gravel and dissipates harmlessly into the surrounding soil. You can probably persuade the inspector to permit this arrangement. If you can't, you can either run all your drains to one septic tank or have two septic tanks, a very expensive proposition. Of course, if you have city sewerage, you don't have a problem.

> **NOTE:** True greywater would be the ideal liquid with which to water your garden. I say "would" because if your building code permits you to do this, it's one of the most progressive in the country.

A FEW THOUGHTS ON LAYOUT

You probably don't need a great deal of help in the actual layout of the kitchen and baths. There are plenty of glitzy magazines to consult for that. Look at some of the considerations in chapter 1 again, and make sure the rooms suit *you*. Someone else may want a fireplace in the kitchen, a "keeping room," or an island for the sink, but do you? Do you want a counter, not a wall, between the kitchen and living room or dining room, so you can take part in all the conversation while getting dinner? Will most of the dining in the house be done in a dining area of the kitchen? An old-fashioned pantry is nice, but it cuts down considerably on the size of the kitchen. A cold cellar in the basement might be a good substitute.

There are plenty of books on the placement of stove, sink, refrigerator, microwave, and other appliances, and plenty of time-and-motion studies to tell you the most efficient kitchen layout. For many of us, the kitchen is not a factory but the heart and soul of the house. Most Americans eat most of their meals in the kitchen. Make it big enough and friendly enough. There's a lot to be said for eating breakfast at big, sunny windows in winter, looking out at the birds at the feeder.

Most ranges have hoods, or at least vents, over them. These devices are just one more hole in the house that lets heat out. You may not be able to avoid one because of code requirements or for practical reasons, but there are tightly sealed houses that don't have them, particularly if the range is toward the center of the room and not under a low ceiling.

LOCATION OF PIPES

This book deals primarily with the nitty-gritty, like the placement of plumbing pipes. You will probably design your plumbing so that pipes are, for the most part, within walls. There are other possibilities: You can run some of them into closets, or you can simply build enclosures for them. Old houses that were plumbed long after they were built often have long, narrow boxes in the corners of walls, or have the toilet elevated on a "stage" to provide a place for the pipes to run underneath.

You will be surprised at how much space pipes take up. Bathroom partitions are often built on 2x6s to allow room for drain pipes, but the largest drains and vents won't even fit in this size wall. On the first floor, of course, most pipes will be under the floor—in other words, in the basement—but even if you don't have any plumbing on a second floor, vent pipes have to go to the top or a point near the top of the house.

A common solution to this problem is to run pipes inside exterior walls. We urge against this, for several reasons. The first is that the pipes may freeze and burst, then thaw and leak. Pipes in partitions never freeze, unless the house is abandoned and unheated in the winter. It is true that vent and drain pipes are less likely to freeze up solid than supply pipes, but you probably won't find it convenient to run supply pipes in one wall and drains in another.

Even if your climate makes it unlikely that pipes will freeze, it's still better not to run them through exterior walls. For one thing, this will dissipate heat from your hot-water pipes to the outdoors, and you may have to wait a long time to get water hot enough for shaving on cold mornings. There's a more important reason, however. If you build the house yourself, you will make the exterior walls and roof much more resistant to the passage of heat than a professional would. Holes you cut in the walls or roof, especially holes in the vapor barrier, let heat out.

Which brings us to a trick with vent pipes. Usually they go through the roof. If you ever, perhaps as a kid, crawled around on a roof, you probably noticed one or more big pipes that weren't chimneys. If you crawled close to one, you discovered a bad smell emanating from it. If your vent pipes don't smell bad, your septic tank is not working correctly.

Most building codes don't say that the vent pipe has to go through the roof, just that it has to reach the exterior so many feet above the toilet or sink. Try to persuade your building inspector that the rule can be satisfied if the pipe emerges from an exterior wall, high up. If you have to cut a hole in your house, a hole in the wall will let out many times less heat than a hole in the roof. In a passive solar house, the back (north) wall will have few or no windows and may have a hill behind it; vent pipes protruding six inches or so from this wall will not be unsightly.

LAUNDRIES

Most homeowners who have a clean, dry basement put the clothes washer down there. One caution is in order, however: Sometimes drainpipes in the basement don't drain very well, because they aren't far enough above the septic tank or dry well. If you think this is going to be a problem, put the washer up on a platform. It make look a little odd, but you'll be glad you did.

You notice there was no mention of a dryer. In a home generally designed to be in harmony with the environment, a dryer is an abomination. The sun is right out there to dry your clothes. Summer or winter, you can hang them on the line and they'll dry fresh and clean. Unless, of course, you live in one of those awful developments where clean clothes on a line are considered unsightly but a junk car in the front yard is OK.

If you have a dryer, you'll pretty much have to vent it outdoors, which means that in the dead of winter you'll be pumping heat out a hole in the house you worked so hard to make leakproof. You can vent it indoors through appropriate filters, but this is frowned on by manufacturers, particularly of gas dryers, for safety reasons. It also puts a lot of moisture into a house you're trying to keep moisture out of.

Before starting to design the rooms that contain plumbing, you should read chapters 19 and 20 in addition to this chapter.

6

Designing Other Rooms

THE DESIGN OF BEDROOMS, a living room, and similar areas for a solar house doesn't differ greatly from their design for any house. The normal design of a solar house—a vast expanse of windows and doors and a relatively high wall to the south, a few windows and doors on the east and west, and almost no openings in the low north wall—precludes certain arrangements and facilitates others. You will quickly learn to take advantage of it.

BEDROOMS
Most solar builders will choose to have bedrooms run the width of the house (from north to south), which means that there will be a great deal of glass on the south end of the bedroom, and few or no windows to the north. With this arrangement, it is sensible to put a large closet at the north end of the bedroom. You may also decide to have a bathroom north of the bedroom, in which case the bathroom will have a window to the east or west.

One easy, cheap, and attractive way to get enough glass on the south side of a bedroom is to incorporate a sliding glass door into the design. This gives downstairs bedrooms a direct opening to a deck or patio. In upstairs bedrooms, the door can lead to a balcony, which is neither difficult nor expensive to construct. Bedrooms like this will be sunnier than most, which is pleasant, but you may find drapes a necessity on nights with a full moon or for privacy.

The placement of furniture in a room with several floor-to-ceiling windows may require some juggling. Not only is it undesirable to block the windows with a bureau, for example, but anything exposed constantly to sunlight will fade. Most people know that this is true of fabrics; it is even true, to a lesser extent, of wood finishes.

On the other hand, few pleasures in life compare with arising on a spring morning and looking out your big bedroom windows at the world, or even going out on your balcony in the middle of a moonlit winter night to survey the stars and the snowscape.

LIVING ROOMS AND FAMILY ROOMS

By now you're probably beginning to get the picture. What was said above about bedrooms is equally true of living rooms, family rooms, or whatever you choose to call them. They will probably run the width of the house, which means that the north wall will be blank, with the possible exception of an entrance door, and the south wall will be mostly glass. It is sensible to plan closets, bookcases, and cupboards all across the north wall. In addition to all their other advantages, these will add further to the R-value of the north side of the house.

Chances are that the ceiling of the living room will be higher than normal, at least on the south side, which gives an elegant effect. Sliding glass doors on that side will lead to the sunspace or outdoors. A focal point of the room may be a fireplace or a woodstove with glass doors. Since we recommend that chimneys be built into an interior wall, you might want to take advantage of this arrangement to have a fireplace in the kitchen or a bedroom.

If you're serious about using fireplaces or woodstoves, you'll need a lot of wood. It has to be stored somewhere, and the nearer to the place where it will be burned, the better. Indoors is better than outdoors, but that is not always practical. If you want to build a wood storage area into a cupboard, put it as close as possible to the fireplace. Firewood is very dirty stuff to carry across your heirloom rugs and past your white couch.

One advantage of having a full basement is that you can construct a rumpus room or playroom down there. Since a properly constructed, properly insulated and sealed basement will be as warm and dry as any other part of the house, finishing it should not present any problems.

OTHER ROOMS

Real estate brokers say that a conventional dining room contains the least-used space in a modern home. Few families today entertain at sit-down dinners more than four times a year; fewer still have servants. If you have a dining room, it certainly will adjoin the kitchen, but chances are you'll settle for a large kitchen with a corner devoted to dining, and the occasional formal dinner will be held in what is ordinarily the living room.

One of the greatest joys of designing your own house is that you can have that special room you've always dreamed of. If you're a serious photographer, a darkroom is certainly possible. One solar house we know features a long, narrow darkroom along the north wall, with an opening to project movies and slides onto an inconspicuous screen built into the living room. Other possibilities are a woodworking room, a weight and fitness room, an office, or anything else you want. While windows are nice, if you have to have a room without them on the north side or down in the basement, one of these rooms could be put there.

Dual-purpose rooms are seldom satisfactory. It might be a better idea to put that home office in the basement, rather than combining it with a guest bedroom. Every time you have overnight guests, you'll have to clean up the office and put everything away, and you run the risk that they will fool with your computer or spill cosmetics on your desk. Again compromise may be necessary, but here is one final argument: The IRS, at present, says that if anybody sleeps in your office, even one night out of 365, it does not qualify for a home-office deduction. Presumably this does not include nodding off over the typewriter.

Many solar house owners are serious gardeners, and a greenhouse, described in the next chapter, would be useful, as would a cold cellar or root cellar. This cellar may be separate from the house or built into a corner of the basement. In that case, panel insulation will be left off the exterior walls and floor for this part of the basement. The room will be separated from the rest of the basement by heavily insulated partitions, and the ceiling in this part of the basement will be insulated. Such a room will have a constant winter temperature of about 40 degrees. In summer, it will not be the 45 degrees you would like, but it will be 10 to 15 degrees cooler than the ambient temperature. At least in winter, a cold cellar functions as a very large walk-in refrigerator.

The above are a few suggestions for taking advantage of the limitations imposed by passive solar house design. Your ingenuity will suggest many more.

7

Designing a Sunspace or Greenhouse

OUR ANCESTORS KNEW about solar heating: Many Victorian houses had an attached room with many windows, called a sunporch; very rich Victorians had an attached greenhouse, called a conservatory. The majority of passive solar house designs adopt and refine this idea. Unfortunately, get-rich-quick entrepreneurs who have jumped on the solar bandwagon commonly offer such rooms, to be attached to an existing house for a high price, as the solution to all the homeowner's heating problems. But a solar house is an integrated whole; you can't get its benefits by tacking on a solar "Band-aid."

A greenhouse, sunroom, or whatever it is called can certainly be part of your design. We'll refer to it hereafter as a sunspace. If you're a gardener, it's the place to grow plants indoors. It's a good location for a hot tub, or it can serve as a second living room, a pleasant place to entertain on a sunny winter afternoon. It can be a mudroom, an intermediate zone where muddy boots and wet parkas are shed before going into the house proper. It can combine several of these functions. Before you go too far in designing a sunspace, however, first read chapter 16, Windows and Exterior Doors.

In winter, a sunspace provides heat to the house in the daytime and is colder than the main house at night. Usually, sliding glass doors and

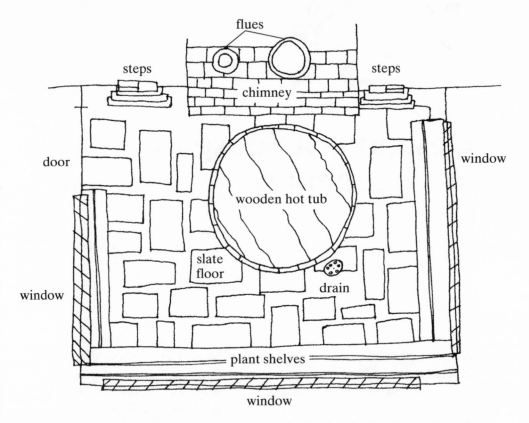

Fig. 11. *This typical greenhouse, attached to the south side of a passive solar house, features a slate floor, which serves as a heat sink. Huge windows and a glass door admit light from three sides. The massive chimney, between the main house and the greenhouse, stores heat and transmits it in both directions.*

wall vents close off the sunspace at night or on dark days. A sunspace must have southern exposure, which means that it can be an extension on the east or west end of the house or an addition to the south side.

The south side is probably the most popular, for several reasons. Construction is much cheaper and heating more efficient, since the north wall of the sunspace is the south wall of the house. Here, the other three walls of the sunspace are mostly glass. When the sunspace is an east or west extension, however, it must have a heavily insulated north wall, and it receives sun from only two sides, not three. But there is a major drawback to having the sunspace on the south wall: If it is south of the living room, the sunspace will shut off much of your view.

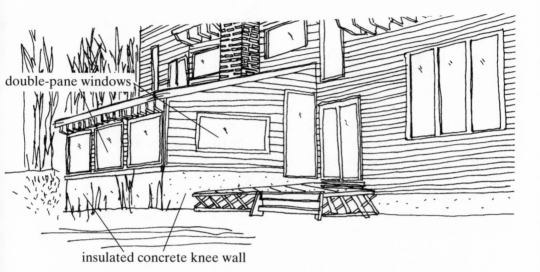

double-pane windows

insulated concrete knee wall

Fig. 12. *This is an exterior view of the greenhouse shown in figure 11. Heat that is generated in this area in the daytime enters the house through two sliding glass doors and two vents; at night these are closed. The sunspace has three 4-by-6 thermal windows on the south side and two 3-by-6 thermal windows on the east. Figure 30 gives another view.*

Almost every passive solar house we know has a sunspace or a greenhouse, and every one is on the south side of the house. In one case, the entire south side of the house, two stories high, is a greenhouse with sliding glass doors and vents as described here. In another, the greenhouse is a small addition on the southeast corner, but it also has doors, vents, and a ducted sand bed underneath, like Fiddlers Green. In a third, a greenhouse forms a large part of the west side of the front of the house. It has a slate floor several feet lower than the main floor and is unique in being completely open to the rest of the house.

The roof of a sunspace addition affords wonderful access to living room clerestory windows, and you will appreciate this not only in installing these high windows but also in cleaning them, replacing them, or covering them with shutters. Such a roof usually slopes to the south and is therefore a good location for a solar water heater or for sunbathing on February days. This is not a joke; the angle formed by the sunspace roof and the south wall of the house will be wonderfully warm on sunny days in late winter.

We recommend fairly conventional building techniques similar to those used for the south side of the main house. Since the walls are mostly glass, there is not much room for insulation and therefore not much reason to make the walls extremely thick, although you may want to build them out of 2x6s. It is possible to make the walls entirely of glass, as in a greenhouse, but that's neither easy nor desirable. Very large windows with small spaces between them on three (or two) sides of the sunspace will be all you'll need. There is a trade-off: the more glass, the warmer in the daytime (if the sun is shining) and the colder at night. If the nighttime temperature is so low in the sunspace that water freezes, it's not such a good place for plants or a hot tub.

Conventional greenhouses have glass in the roof, but most sunspaces attached to passive solar homes do not. Such an arrangement has the advantage of letting in more sun in the day, but this is outweighed by the disadvantage of letting out more heat at night. It also heats up the sunspace in summer. Most devices for shuttering skylights or ceiling glass are awkward, and some don't work very well. Finally, it's a great deal easier to construct a roof that doesn't leak if there are no windows in it.

If the sunspace has large but otherwise conventional windows, its size will be pretty much determined by the size and number of windows. A 12-by-24 sunspace, for example, might have three 4-by-6 thermal windows across the south side and one or two 3-by-6 ones on the east and west ends. If the sunspace is to function as a mudroom it will need an exterior door, and it should probably have one in any case. It is a good idea to have two doors, one on the east and one on the west, if the room will be used as a greenhouse or a mudroom. You may be able to find doors with plate-glass inserts at a secondhand building supply store, or you can cut down on the number of windows and have sliding glass doors at one or both ends. Bear in mind, however, that glass on the east or west side will usually let out more heat than it provides.

A greenhouse should probably have vents to the outdoors, complete with fans. We know of several that do not, but humidity can become quite high, which is another reason it should be possible to shut the greenhouse off from the main house.

Like most aspects of solar construction, designing the openings between the house and the sunspace involves trade-offs. The larger and more numerous the openings, the more daytime heat you gain and the more nighttime heat you lose, since heat will pass through closed doors and vents. Being able to open about 25 percent of the wall between the two rooms is about right, provided that vents are placed at the highest possible point. You can save money by using cheaper, less-efficient metal-framed doors between the two rooms, since the temperature in the sunspace will seldom go below 50 degrees.

You may choose not to extend the basement below the sunspace, and the floor of the sunspace may be two or three steps down from the main house. Under the sunspace is a good location for a bed of sand, gravel, or rocks, penetrated by air ducts, to serve as a heat sink. In any case, the foundation of this part of the house will be insulated just as the rest of the foundation is. For the floor, many people choose slate or tile, which are impervious to water and are good absorbers of solar energy. The floor should have a drain.

For the rest of the design, you're on your own. Depending on intended use, you may want to design in plumbing, special wiring, benches for plants, cupboards, or other features. You will certainly never regret having added such a room to your overall plan.

Part Two

Construction

8

Why You Can and Should Do It Yourself

MOST PEOPLE THINK building a house is beyond their powers. Raising African violets is difficult; baking really good bread is difficult; building a house is easy, provided that you have certain assets: time, patience, self-confidence, and the ability to read and assimilate information.

WHY YOU CAN DO IT YOURSELF

Look at it this way: If you have enough brains to read and understand this book, then you're at least as smart as the average plumber, electrician, or carpenter. Though these people aren't stupid, they're not outstandingly more brilliant than you.

What they have is know-how, skill that they acquired, almost always, on the job. You will acquire some of that skill as you work your way through building your home, which means that the roof will probably be better built than the floor. Don't worry, the floor will be built well enough, and the mistakes won't show or cause the house to fall down. Your house will be more attractive and sturdier than most contractor-built houses.

What have you got that the average house carpenter hasn't? First of all, time. You'd better have—building a house yourself takes lots of time. At first you'll be surprised how fast the rough framing goes. Then you'll be surprised how much more there is to do after that's finished, even though the house looks, on the outside, just like a house.

The chief difference between you and the average carpenter is that he can do a given job much faster than you can. In the time it takes you and your crew of amateurs to get one wall built and raised, pros could do four. They probably wouldn't do them any better, and maybe not as well.

Pros are faster because they know all the shortcuts. Sometimes, however, shortcuts result in inferior work. In the aftermath of Hurricane Andrew, many Florida homeowners learned a tragic lesson: The contractors who built their houses took too many shortcuts.

You will check and recheck everything, going from book to plan to work again and again to be sure you have it just right; a pro won't. Most of the time he'll get it exactly right the first time, but occasionally he won't. If he makes a mistake, he'll figure that the sheathing will cover it.

You will probably use better and sturdier materials than the pros, because you will discover quite early on that materials are incredibly cheap, compared to labor, and most of your labor will be free, or at least inexpensive. A contractor chooses materials that have two qualities: They're the cheapest available that still meet the specifications, and they will allow his crews to work rapidly. For example, he will use preformed roof trusses. You won't, because you don't own a crane.

You'll need at least two people who have a long uninterrupted block of time available. There are a lot of things one man or woman alone can do in building a house, but most jobs take two. A crew of three to four amateurs, two of whom have all summer free, can build a three-bedroom house between April and October—that is, they can get it to the point at which the owner can move in and be reasonably comfortable while he puts the finishing touches on it.

You could do the job faster if you could get the outside contractors, like excavators and stonemasons, to start on time and work steadily. But chances are that you won't be able to. All over the world, good craftsmen are in great demand. Every single one of them will promise a finish date that he can't deliver. You might as well know that now.

That's why it's fortunate that you are going to do as much as you can, including the plumbing and wiring, yourself. In building, everybody wants the other guy to do it first: The plumber wants the electrician to be finished, the electrician wants the Sheetrock man to be done, the Sheetrock man wants the whole house done before he starts. (Sheetrock is one of those trade names everybody uses; the generic term is something like "gypsum plaster board.") If you do it yourself, you won't have to wait for somebody else to finish one job before you can start the next.

Home building used to take place only in the warmer months; now contractors keep their crews working all winter. If worst comes to worst, you'll be surprised how much you can get done in January, especially if the house is "closed in," as carpenters say. With luck, however, it won't come to that.

Besides time, you'll need patience. The ideal house carpenter would be calm, phlegmatic, used to delay. All the pros I've known have been just the opposite. Nonetheless, strive for patience. There will be setbacks. There will be about three times when you think the whole project is impossible and doomed to failure. It won't be. When you are living in your completed house, you'll look around and say, "Did we really do this? It's great!"

You'll need confidence. Believe me, you can do it. Lots of people dumber and clumsier than you have built decent houses. The best thing you have going for you is the ability to read and understand directions. Study this book and others: books on plumbing, wiring, framing, windows and doors, and so on. (Of course, you don't really *need* any other books, but they'll help.) Read them over and over until you see the paragraphs in your dreams. At first some parts won't make sense. Read them again; compare two descriptions of the same process, if possible. Most of them eventually will make sense before you start. In some cases, you will see the light only when you actually begin the process.

Finally, nothing will happen to you as bad as what happened to us. Before we had the "cap" (the subfloor) finished, I suffered a stupid, careless fall and tore my knee badly, requiring surgery. I was in a cast for six weeks, then on crutches. I was fifty-nine years old and certainly not in better-than-average physical condition. Even so, we were able to move in before snow fell and finished the interior before spring. You still think you can't do it?

WHY YOU SHOULD DO IT YOURSELF

There are some aspects of construction, such as foundation building, that a pro can do better than you can. That's why we recommend that you leave these areas to the professionals. There are other things, like framing, that probably would be about as well done by a professional as by you, although it depends a lot on how conscientious the professional is. Some jobs, though, will never be done by anyone else as well as you will do them.

For example, stuffing fiberglass insulation into walls and the cracks around door and window frames is hot, dusty, painstaking work that sometimes makes the worker cough or break out in a rash. It doesn't require any great degree of skill, just great pains. Insulation must not be too loose, and there shouldn't be gaps between one roll or batt and the next, but it also mustn't be packed too tightly, since the actual insulation value resides more in the air spaces between the fibers than in the fibers themselves.

Other similar jobs include stretching and taping the clear polyethylene vapor barrier around the inside of the house so that there is not a single crack, caulking all external cracks before staining, and organizing your cedar clapboards so that the best-looking ones go on the front and the others on the back. The contractor would solve this problem by buying expensive clapboards that wouldn't require sorting. This would actually save you money, otherwise you would have to pay the high labor cost for his employees to do this fussy work. Your time is worth much less. Do you think anyone not working on his own house would take the time and care that you would on tasks like these?

Another reason you should do most of the work yourself is that passive solar construction, especially the double-wall type that is recommended in this book, is somewhat unconventional. A carpenter or contractor may have built hundreds of houses without ever departing from traditional patterns, and it may be hard for him to see why this house should be different. For you, on the other hand, one way of framing a wall is just as new and different as another.

The final reason for building the house yourself is that you'll "know where all the bodies are buried." You will remember, presumably, that one wall has studs twenty-four inches on center and that another has them sixteen. You'll remember that a particular stud was bowed more than it should have been, so that the Sheetrock isn't well supported, and you won't hang a picture there. You'll have a pretty good idea where the wires and pipes run in the walls, so you won't be so likely to drill through them or drive a nail into them years later. You'll know just how high and wide the headers are, when it comes time to put up drapes and valances. And so on.

Of course, there shouldn't be mistakes, like the bowed stud, but there will be. It's astonishing how much easier it is to live with your own mistakes than with those of a hired hand, especially one that you were paying $37.50 per hour. It is also surprising—and gratifying—how those places you grieved over so much at the time, the places where the corners aren't perfect or the wallpaper doesn't quite match, fade into insignificance with time. After you're living in the house, nobody ever notices them but you.

9

Parts of the Job to Be Contracted Out

IF YOU'RE LIKE MOST PEOPLE, you have probably built a doghouse or chicken coop, or at least a workbench. The prospect of framing a wall with 2x4s or shingling a roof doesn't frighten you, but you don't think you can do plumbing or wiring. Aren't they difficult or dangerous? Not really. On the other hand, you probably ought to leave hanging and taping Sheetrock to an expert. If you do it yourself, you may be looking at lumpy walls for years to come.

Before we began our house, we talked to every expert we could get to stand still long enough to listen to us. The agreement was universal—unless you have special skills, you shouldn't tackle the following: excavation, foundation, stonemasonry, and Sheetrocking. Opinions on the other aspects of construction were summed up by a young contractor in Athens, Georgia. "I'm sure I can handle framing," I told him, "but what about plumbing and wiring?"

"Oh, that's just Mickey Mouse," was his reply. And so it is.

There are people who have successfully done their own excavation, renting a bulldozer and operating it. Many people have laid up their own foundations, usually using cement blocks. That's one of several reasons we recommend hiring a contractor; a poured foundation is much stronger than one built up of cement block.

A close friend of ours built the fieldstone chimney of his own passive solar house, gathering the stones from his own property. Although his chimney is perfectly safe and functional, he says that if he had it to do over he would probably hire a stonemason.

I know people who have hung and taped their own Sheetrock and are satisfied with the results, but we consider the money we spent to hire experts to be the best investment we ever made. You are the only one who can decide whether you have the skills and temperament to do any of the jobs mentioned above.

EXCAVATION AND FOUNDATION

If you take our advice, you'll hire one contractor to do the excavation and foundation. He'll do anything else that involves digging big holes, such as putting in the septic tank and leach field; digging a trench for electric wires, if you want them buried; or erecting a power pole or poles.

If the foundation is weak or not true, the house will never be right. Talk to and get bids from three or four contractors. Ask them to supply you with the names of recent residential customers, and be sure you talk to those customers. You may be surprised; sometimes a customer the contractor thought was satisfied actually wasn't. Ask around in the community as well. Most of the bids will probably be in the same ballpark. If one is much higher, regard it with suspicion. If one is much lower, be sure not to hire that guy.

In our experience, most contractors are honest and competent. Yours will probably bill you, at the end, almost exactly what his estimate was. In most states, he can't exceed it by more than a certain percentage, unless you make changes in the "specs" (specifications). If you do, it is probably best to have a written understanding of what the changes are and how much they will add to (or, conceivably, subtract from) the estimate.

One thing you might try to keep an eye on, without giving offense, is the steel reinforcing bar (rebar) that goes into the concrete. The specs make it quite clear how thick and how many feet apart the rebar should be. It is essential that your foundation be adequately reinforced with steel.

We don't personally know anyone who experienced one of those horror stories you hear about contractors. Ours did beautiful work and, in spite of some small changes we made during the job, sent us a bill for exactly the estimate. He didn't start when he said he would, but we'd still recommend him highly. If any of your contractors start when they said they would, either their work isn't highly regarded or, more likely, your area is in the depths of a recession.

The foundation contractor will work from blueprints you supply him. In order to make sure the house is oriented just the way you want it, you may want to erect rough batter boards to guide him. Batter boards are easier to erect than to describe, but basically you should, using a compass and a 50-foot tape measure, lay out a line on the ground to represent the front of the house, which will face south or slightly east of south. Bear in mind that the compass will point to magnetic north, not true north. Depending on where you live, you may have to make a slight compensation for that.

Drive stakes into the ground roughly where you think the four corners of the house will be, and connect them with twine (mason line or chalk line). Use the square to make sure the corners are square. What you will find, of course, is that the corners aren't square and the lines aren't exactly the right length. To fine-tune your foundation lines, use batter boards.

A couple of feet beyond each stake, drive in three stakes forming an L, and connect them with 1x3s in such a way that, even allowing for considerable error, the eventual corner of the house is certainly going to come within the L. Run four lines from batter board to batter board. Don't tie them to the boards; drape them over them, with fishing weights or small stones holding them in place. Now twiddle the lines slightly east and west, north and south, until the intersections of the strings, out over space, are as near perfect as is humanly possible. To keep them there, mark the boards with pencil, move the strings, and make a small saw cut (kerf) at exactly the right place. Now the string will stay in that place. In doing this job it is useful to know that if the two diagonals of a rectangle are the same length, the corners and sides are right.

You may not have to lay out batter boards, but be sure that the contractor is impressed with the necessity of having the house oriented correctly. Many otherwise experienced contractors have never done the foundation of a solar house.

It may surprise you that the foundation walls will be poured first and the floor last. The contractor may not want to pour the basement floor until after the cap has been constructed above it. Try to persuade him otherwise, since you really want the lolly columns (see chapter 12) on the floor, not in it.

You can probably persuade him to let you do certain parts of the job. These include coating the outside of the walls thoroughly with a black tarry substance that waterproofs them, putting insulation panels

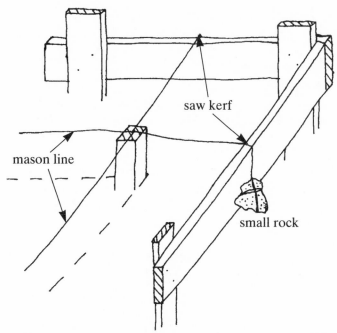

saw kerf

mason line

small rock

Fig. 13. *Batter boards can be used to ensure that the excavation is made and the foundation poured in precisely the correct place. When the lines are adjusted perfectly, a single saw cut is made in the proper place in each board, and a small post is driven in under the intersection of the two lines.*

outside the walls, and laying down similar panels and a vapor barrier over the gravel base before he pours the floor.

Before the walls, footings have to be poured. These are larger and rougher masses of reinforced concrete that support the walls. The contractor will know how deep they have to go (well below the frost line); the specs will tell him how much rebar to put in them. Footings also go under other heavy or weight-bearing structures, like chimneys or lolly columns, which means that the plans have to indicate clearly where these features will go and that later on you will have to put the features exactly there, even though you can't see the footings through the floor.

STONEMASONRY

A person who builds chimneys, fireplaces, and stone walls is a stonemason. Good ones are hard to find and even harder to get to the job. Follow the same procedure suggested for selecting a foundation contractor. In addition, you can get a look at a stonemason's previous work in customers' houses. It should be exactly level, plumb, and true, Stonemasonry is probably the most skilled and artistic of all the building trades.

The stonemason will not build the chimney first and let you hang the house on it; he will expect you to leave holes in floors, ceilings, and roof exactly the right size and shape. This is not quite as hard as it sounds, since code requires that the holes be two inches larger all around than the chimney, the space to be filled with fireproof insulation.

Besides wanting you to have the house all framed, the mason will probably be unable or unwilling to work on a site that does not have electricity and running water. This means that the rough wiring, as well as the well and pump (or city water connection), must be finished before he starts. The plumbing does not have to be beyond the point at which one tap is operative, just as the wiring need only have a working panel box serving one or two circuits.

Anyone you hire to build a chimney will know how to include a fireplace, if that is in the plans. Read chapter 25 so that you can converse knowledgeably with him about all aspects of the fireplace and woodstove, if any, flues, and the like. Like other subcontractors, the stonemason is a good source of information on local building customs or the best ways to do things. You should usually, but not always, go along with his ideas.

The usual material for a chimney is brick; the mason will show you a wide variety of colors and types of brick to choose from. If you want fieldstone (random sizes and shapes of stones that look like they were picked up around your house) or some other material, in most localities it will cost you more. In any case, the chimney is built for the most part of cement block and concrete; the brick or stone is just the outer facing.

SHEETROCK

You may choose to have no walls in your house covered with Sheetrock, just a few, or all of them. Even the most expensive custom-made homes usually have most of the walls made of Sheetrock, with a few special areas of wood paneling; when you price alternatives to Sheetrock, you'll find out why. No matter how rich you are, you *must* use Sheetrock over combustible insulating board. Even if the code doesn't require it, you'd be a fool not to.

There are two parts to the Sheetrock job—hanging and taping—and they aren't always done by the same people. Both jobs are incredibly dusty, dirty, fussy, and irritating, which is why, even though you *could* do them yourself, you'll probably be happier if you let someone else do the work. It is possible that a small local Sheetrock contractor will allow you to assist him, which is a good way to save money if you can stand the strain.

Perhaps because of the nature of the work, Sheetrockers, especially hangers, tend to be rough and ready. They frequently drive long distances to a job, work eighteen hours or more a day on it, and get it all done in a remarkably short time. Their price for this short period may seem high to you, until you try to do it yourself. Like all contractors, they will usually charge you for labor and materials separately, charging retail for materials they get at wholesale. This practice is standard; it does no good to complain about it. Your auto mechanic does the same thing.

Taping (covering the joints between the sheets) takes as much time as and more skill than hanging. Some people do their own hanging, then hire a taper, who will complain bitterly that he is expected to make up for the faults of the hanging. (He would do the same thing no matter who had done it.) If both parts aren't done very skillfully, the imperfections in the finished walls will always show.

If you're not involved at all, you probably don't need to know this, but there are several different types of Sheetrock. Half-inch (thick) is standard, and it is unwise to skimp by using thinner material. Five-eighths-inch fire-resistant is required in danger areas, such as the walls between a built-in garage and the rest of the house, and special material that is more resistant to moisture is used in bathrooms and similar areas. Amateurs buy and install Sheetrock in 4-by-8 sheets; professionals use 4-by-12 or even larger. These large sheets are very hard to handle, since they will break under their own weight, but for one who has the skill and tools, they make the job go much faster and, best of all, leave fewer joints that have to be taped.

No matter who does it, or what they use, you will have an unholy mess to clean up after they leave. There's no use complaining about it; the stock answer of any skilled craftsman is, "Would you rather clean it up yourself or pay me thirty dollars an hour to do it?" I'd love to have the money to take one of them up on that, because I suspect Sheetrockers wouldn't clean up their mess for any price.

The cleanup involves, at a minimum, wiping down the finished and thoroughly dry walls with a damp (not wet) sponge, vacuuming every inch of the subfloor with the fine nozzle of the vacuum, giving special attention to cracks, then wiping the entire floor with a damp sponge. The fine, white dust, which will be everywhere, may injure your lungs if you don't wear a mask and won't be good for the vacuum cleaner; use a heavy-duty shop-type machine or a very old one you don't care about.

OTHER WORK

A house can be built with any combination of contracted-out and owner-done jobs. As mentioned above, local code may require licensed electricians, plumbers, or both. A stonemason building his own house may do excavation, foundation, and stonemasonry, then hire the rest of the work done. For most nonprofessionals, however, the best division of labor is the one suggested above.

One rather popular technique is to have professionals erect the shell of the house and finish the interior yourself. It's popular, that is, with those who haven't tried it. You'd be better off erecting the shell yourself and letting the professionals do the interior finish, because cabinetmaking is a fine art. You should do it yourself only if no one who is to live in the house is a perfectionist. Most people can construct bathroom cabinets and bookcases that will be satisfactory and reasonably good-looking if painted, but they can't build fine furniture. You might want to have a local craftsman build the inside stairs, mantel, and countertops. You could build the structural parts of cabinets and have him hang the doors on them, or you could buy cabinets at a building supply store. They come in a dizzying range of styles, finishes, and prices, but like everything ready-made, they weren't designed to fit perfectly into your house.

Whatever part you do, or anyone else does, of the interior and exterior finish, certain things are true of it. You will be acutely aware of minor imperfections, but other people won't notice them at all, unless they are cabinetmakers, in which case politeness should cause them to refrain from comment. As time goes by, even you will cease to fret about the two doors of the bathroom cabinet that don't match exactly.

Secrets You'll Never Learn Anywhere but Here (and Mistakes We Made That You Can Avoid)

THE TITLE MAY BE a bit overstated; you might learn some of these things from your lumberyard man or electrical inspector, but most of them we learned the hard way.

BUILDING INSPECTORS

Who are building inspectors, and are they as difficult as you may have heard?

In many rural areas there are no building codes, or almost none. Cities have codes, and some are tough. For example, in a city the law may require the hiring of a licensed electrician, even for a minor change.

Some states have statewide codes, often enforced by local officials. These will probably be reasonable people. If your code is like most, you will have to pass at least one inspection by an electrical inspector and several by code enforcement officers. The electrical inspector works for the insurance underwriters rather than the municipality, but that won't matter to you; you will still have to pay a fee for the required inspections.

The person who converts your sketches to blueprints, any professionals you hire, your lumber dealer, and the electric and plumbing suppliers can all inform you about provisions of the code. While there are exceptions, most provisions make sense—you wouldn't want your house to fall down or burn up.

Code enforcement officers will visit a construction site at several stated times. When you apply for your building permit, and on your first visit to the electrical inspector, find out when these visits will come. Generally, inspectors want to see work done by you or by others before it is covered up; for example, they may want to see the septic tank and leach field installation before it is backfilled, or the roughed-in wiring before the wall paneling is put on.

SPECIFIC ASPECTS OF CONSTRUCTION

The way to learn about a particular aspect of construction—for example, how to install a toilet—is to first acquire all the books you can find on the subject. Buy some that look good; check the rest out of the public library. Read them, over and over, until you think you understand. Then ask an expert. The salesman that sells you the toilet ought to be able to tell you a lot about how to install it; if he can't, don't buy it there. It is astonishing how friendly and free with advice professionals are, when you consider that we are taking the bread out of their mouths. You have to catch them at the right place, however, like the counter at the plumbing or electrical supply store. Don't call up an electrician, a total stranger, at his home and ask him for advice. You won't get it.

Your architect and other professionals you employ, like a stonemason, are founts of knowledge. Code enforcement officers are also sources of free information. Often they were master craftsmen, carpenters, electricians, plumbers, before they became inspectors, but now they don't regard you as competition.

On one occasion, the electrical inspector had visited our house in our absence and left notes over the pump and the water heater: "Install service disconnect!" I didn't have the slightest idea what that meant, and the inspector wasn't available, so I went to my electrical supplier. He quickly provided me with two service disconnects and all their appurtenances and started telling me how to install them, when the man standing next to me, a professional electrician, took over and explained slowly and cheerfully all I needed to know. All *you* need to know about service disconnects is in chapter 18.

WHEN EXPERTS DISAGREE

Always get a second opinion. If the first two experts disagree, get a third opinion. If a couple of people who should know (not your cousin

Charlie) both say you ought to do a certain thing a certain way, you probably should. This does not always hold true, however. If you're sure you
understand the problem thoroughly, your own common sense should tell
you what would be unwise.

In many cases, standard construction techniques in a given area are
what are easiest, cheapest, and safest *for a contractor-built house,* which
doesn't always mean that an owner-builder can't take another route. The
building trades are notoriously conservative. As soon as you get into an
unusual technique, like the double 2x4 wall discussed in chapter 13,
experienced people will wag their heads and say, "We've never done it
that way." That doesn't necessarily mean it can't or shouldn't be done
that way.

CAUTION: The above does not mean that you should ever go
below specs with regard to size or strength of materials. If the
rules say you should use 2x8 joists to span a given distance, use
2x8s or 2x10s, but don't ever use 2x6s. They probably would support the load, but why take a chance? The amount saved would
be a very tiny percentage of the total cost of the house.

Here are a few examples of areas where experts disagree:

As you drive around the countryside, you will probably notice
house after house being built with polyisocyanurate sheathing on the
outside (you'll be able to read the advertising for Dow or DuPont from
your car). When vinyl siding is applied, this same sheathing is often
slapped on over the old clapboards before the vinyl is applied. Every
house that you see like this is being built or rebuilt WRONG! The contractor will disagree, of course, but that's not just my opinion—it's the
opinion of a man who sells that material and of construction experts.
Chapter 24 explains why, but it is just as well to mention here that many
experienced builders don't understand the problems of moisture
buildup in a tight house.

As another example, we painted all the interior walls of our house
with a base coat of special expensive alkyd (modern version of oil-based)
primer-sealer to form a moisture barrier. Over this, in some rooms, we
put latex paint. One expert, not a painter, strongly advised against this,
saying that at a minimum we would have to fine-sand every inch of the
wall between coats. We got a second opinion from a professional painter.
He said, "Go ahead," so we did, without sanding and with good results.
(The walls have a very slightly rough texture that can hardly be seen but

can be felt. Some people might not like that. We think it's a cheap price to pay for keeping moisture out of our walls.)

Specs for our lolly columns (see chapter 12) called for concrete-filled steel posts, which proved expensive, impossible to get in exactly the right lengths, and well-nigh impossible to cut to fit. Everyone said we had to have these—nothing else would do—until we asked the inspector if we could use treated wooden 6x6s; he said, "Sure."

THE TWO BIGGEST MISTAKES WE MADE

We've never told anyone else these secrets, so please don't reveal them.

The closest thing to an irreparable mistake we made, or rather, I made, was while installing prebuilt, louvered, folding closet doors. I put the first set on correctly, but the second set I put on upside down: The solid panel is above and the louvers below, slanting the wrong way. The mistake couldn't be corrected because the mounting technique involves driving metal doohickeys into predrilled holes. Like most factory-built items, the doors had holes in both ends, even where they weren't needed, and once the hangers were driven into the bottom holes, I couldn't get them out. No one else has ever noticed.

I made a more serious blunder when mounting fixed-glass windows in the walls. It wasn't until the job was done that I realized I'd made no provision for ever removing the windows if they should break or be defective. So far we have been very fortunate, but someday we may have to tear apart some of the side of the house to take out and replace a window. Be warned: Make sure you install such windows with some kind of wooden frame that can easily be removed.

OTHER SECRETS AND USEFUL TIPS

Amateurs try to do everything from ladders; professionals use scaffolding. It is remarkably cheap to rent, even for a month or more. Although it requires some thought and care to set up, once it is in place a lot can be done from it before it needs to be moved. Don't overlook using it indoors. Scaffolding used outdoors can be moved inside, with the addition of wheels (which can be locked).

Every piece added stiffens the house. The first wall you erect will flex around and wave in the breeze, and you will despair. Adding the rafters makes the walls more rigid; adding the decking makes the roof more rigid.

"Houses are built of duck tape and caulk." There is no overestimating the value of duct tape, which is always pronounced as though it were used to bind mallards. Always have plenty on hand for sealing cracks between insulation panels, binding or repairing shutters, and myriad other uses. In exterior finish, around windows, and everywhere else there is any kind of crack, use caulk. You can't possibly overcaulk a house. Between siding and corner boards that are stained the same color, use colored caulk; use white everywhere else. Always wipe off the excess immediately. Around the openings for fixed windows, it is worth using expensive rubberized caulk; everywhere else, the cheapest seems to work just as well. This is one of the few exceptions to the rule that the most expensive materials are the best. Start with a gun and a putty knife; eventually you'll always resort to your fingers.

Carpenters and other workers love Sheetrock screws and use them everywhere they don't use nails. They are black, cheap, easy to drive (especially with an electric screwdriver), and have many uses.

Although the following idea is mentioned several times elsewhere in this book, it bears repeating: Labor is expensive; materials are cheap. You may want to save money by not buying fancy finishes, but never stint on strength or quality.

Don't save money by always taking the cheapest bid on everything. If three stonemasons all quote around $7,500, and another bids $5,000, never hire that one; he knows what his work is worth. Fortunately you're not a government agency, required by law always to take the lowest bid, which is why so many school and courthouse roofs leak.

Half the labor of construction is moving materials around. The "clerk of the works" on big projects earns his considerable salary by arranging that materials arrive on the job precisely when needed, as well as planning so that the electricians arrive after the carpenters and before the Sheetrockers. You don't have enough clout to accomplish all that he does, but remember that flow control is important. Think, plan, and scheme about what you want delivered when, and where you want it put. You will most assuredly have to move most of the dimension lumber at least once (all the lumber for a moderate-size house can and will be brought to the site in one truckload), but you may be able to avoid moving some of it four or five times.

Take the time and energy to talk to the lumberyard driver himself, not just his boss, to be sure he knows how to get to the site. We had a truckload of lumber dumped in our neighbor's driveway, which didn't please him, us, or the company. A load of Sheetrock was taken back to the yard by a driver who "couldn't find" our house, while the Sheetrockers stood around with nothing to do.

Spend plenty of time and thought with a hand calculator estimating how much of everything you should buy. Count the joists, rafters, and studs necessary, or you'll forget that you need one on each end. If studs are twenty-four inches on center, a ten-foot wall will require not five, but six or maybe seven because at least one will be too knotted and twisty to use. That's why you should probably add 20 percent, not 10 percent, to your estimate. Most building supply houses will take back surplus. Discuss this in advance, but don't worry: There won't be any surplus.

A house is the most expensive object you will ever buy. It's worth taking more than a few minutes, and even asking embarrassing questions, to get the very best materials, craftsmen, and techniques.

11

Labor, Materials, and Tools

IN THE COURSE OF CONSTRUCTION you will discover what every contractor knows: Materials are cheap; labor is expensive. By doing most of the work yourself, you will be saving a great deal of money on labor; put at least some of it into good-quality tools and materials.

LABOR

Most of your labor will be free, performed by you, family members, and friends. When you contract out parts of the work, such as the stonemasonry, you will discover that skilled laborers in house construction today command high wages. Every time you put in an hour on building your house, you can say to yourself, "I just made thirty dollars." Probably, by the time you read this, it will be more.

Should you pay friends who work with you? This book cannot answer that question, except to say that, in most cases, your homeowner's insurance will cover family and friends who are *not* getting paid, if they should get hurt in the course of construction. If they are paid, it will not cover them, and the kind of employee insurance contractors carry is very expensive.

Most fortunately for us, no one was hurt while we were building our house except the author, who was of course not being paid. *Getting injured, slightly or seriously, while building a house is a very real possibility.* Take every safety precaution possible, but also be certain that you won't be on the receiving end of a major lawsuit. Talk this over with a knowledgeable insurance agent before beginning construction.

Subcontractors, like the stonemason and foundation contractor, should have their own insurance. Be sure that they do. Generally, if you use established, reputable firms rather than your friend's cousin Willy, this won't be a problem.

Our Sheetrock hanger let me work as his assistant, which saved us some money. Some small subcontractors will do this. If you assist such a person, for insurance reasons make it crystal clear that *you* are working under *his* direction, rather than the other way around.

VERY IMPORTANT TIP: Have only two types of people employed in building your house: professionals who supervise themselves and their employees, and amateurs who are under your supervision. For example, if you don't feel up to doing the wiring yourself, hire a good licensed electrician. Don't turn the work over to a friend of a friend who's supposed to know how to do wiring and will make all his own decisions without listening to you. There is no reason (except for a local ordinance) that you can't learn to wire your house and do it. If you do it, you'll know it was done the way it should have been done. If a pro does it, you'll know it was done in full compliance with the code. If your brother-in-law does it, you'll regret it.

You may have a friend who is a skilled carpenter and would like to give you a hand. By all means let him, learn from him, and take his advice when it seems sound, but don't let him build an entire wall without your supervision. For one thing, the type of double-wall construction described in chapter 13 is new to most experienced carpenters; some of the techniques they have always practiced won't work with it.

Don't think only grown men can help with house building. More and more construction crews include women swinging hammers or driving bulldozers. Very few house-building tasks require the strength of a Bulgarian weightlifter. If one does, just use more than one person. Let your children, if any, help. There are tasks like sorting nails and inventorying lumber that most kids over six can do and will enjoy. Older children can do more: After a little instruction, our thirteen-year-old daughter shingled an entire roof. Aside from the real help children can give, the memories acquired stay with them forever.

Keeping an eye on the subcontractors you've hired requires the tact and skill of a U.N. negotiator. You have to bug them just enough, but not too much. No good excavator, stonemason, or Sheetrock hanger or taper ever starts a job when he has promised to, unless the economy is totally depressed. Usually you'll have to call them two or three times to remind them, politely, that the day they promised to start has come and gone. Most are conscientious people who honestly believed that they would be able to start then and really want to do a good job for you. In our opinion, it doesn't pay to take too haughty an attitude. The line to take is "I knew you would be busy, but I really wanted you, because everybody says you're the best. But it's kind of hard on us, because we have carpenters waiting to start."

After they start, don't spare the praise. Tell all the workers what a good job they're doing, and ask a few questions about technique. You might as well learn something; you're paying enough. Obviously, if you are constantly looking over their shoulders and asking, "What are you doing now?" or "Why are you doing that?" they're going to get sick of you, and the people you want on your side most are the ordinary workers. If you haven't made them dislike you, they might put in an extra hour Friday afternoon to finish the job.

It pays to try to get some idea of what they're doing and how it is done, and how it relates to your plans. For example, I watched the foundation workers erect the concrete forms for our greenhouse. Finally, reluctantly, I said to the foreman, "Bill told you about the door right there, didn't he?" It turned out Bill hadn't; it was Bill's fault, and the foreman, although not thrilled, was grateful. Of course, it would have been their mistake, rectifiable after the concrete had been poured by a few hours' work with an air hammer, but we were all a lot happier this way.

It's nice to offer workers coffee and doughnuts on a cool morning or cold water on a hot afternoon, but don't ply them with beer. Believe it or not, most of them won't want it, and you won't like the results if they do.

MATERIALS

Buy the best! Ten years later, living in the house, you will never say, "I wish we had put in a cheaper door there," but you may say the opposite. The best will not always be the most expensive, but it often will be.

There is one way you may be able to use less expensive materials than the contractor and be happy with the results. In every fair-sized town, someone makes his living selling secondhand doors, windows, and other building materials. You can use these where the contractor can't, because you can redesign your house as you go along. Windows, of course, would have to meet your thermal specifications, but you may be able to get a buy on something like insulation, and you definitely should be able to find doors, especially interior doors, that are both better for your purposes and cheaper. Be careful, though. Wet insulation is not a bargain, nor is a door that will take you forty hours to strip and refinish.

Devote a lot of hours and brainpower to estimating the job. It is not difficult, just time-consuming, and a hand calculator is a must. You simply have to count every stick. For example, if the house is 24 by 64 and the specs call for 2x10 joists, you have to go through the following process: "The joists will be butted together at the girder, so we need 12-foot 2x10s. They'll be 16 inches on center, so I divide 64 feet by 16 inches, which comes to about 48. I always have to add one more for the open end, then I need twice that amount—one on each side of the girder—which makes one hundred 12-foot 2x10s for that part of the job, plus between 10 and 20 percent extra for wastage, so I'll order 110."

You can probably get away with ordering only 10 percent extra dimension lumber; with plywood and other panels, however, it is best to order 15 to 20 percent too much. With materials like #2 cedar siding (clapboards), wastage may approach 30 percent. A good building materials supplier (lumberyard) will cheerfully take back almost anything, although policies do vary widely.

Materials, particularly wooden ones, are not perfect. You should expect to use a certain amount of mildly defective lumber, as long as it is structurally sound, in places where it doesn't matter. You can return materials that are too bad, especially if the yard picked them out and delivered them. But you will drive yourself and the dealer crazy, and never finish the house, if you refuse to accept a single 2x4 that has even a slight blemish.

Material that shows is quite different, however. A blemish or dirt on top-grade 1x4 pine that you're using for trim around the windows will still show through three coats of white paint. Not only should you insist on near-perfect materials for this, but you also should buy them just before using them. Your window trim may acquire an indelible boot mark if it lies around the construction site too long.

Selecting the dealer you're going to use is about as important as picking the site or the stonemason. The cheapest is not always the best. Some big nationwide chains are satisfactory for your purposes; a great many are not. There are definitely different quality grades in lumber.

Be sure you understand the yard's policies on delivery and returns. How little will they deliver, how far, how often? Most yards will give you a "contractor's discount," although it may not be the same one offered their largest and best customer. Have a clear understanding as to what the discount covers. Is it offered only on a big load of lumber they deliver, or will it also cover a hammer you pick up six months later?

Quality is more important than price, but it is quite possible to find a yard that is consistently cheaper and just as good. Compare sample prices (the actual amount you will be charged) from several lumberyards on a number of items: treated 2x6s, asphalt shingles, Sheetrock, 3/4-inch wafer board (2x4s aren't a good choice for price comparison, as they are often loss leaders). Get a sense of how helpful yard personnel will be. In finally making up your mind, perhaps the best single indicator is your assessment of the customers hanging around in there. Do most of them look and act like contractors who know what they're doing or like home-owners paneling the den for the first time?

TIP: If the place doesn't open at 8 A.M. or earlier, it isn't getting a lot of business from contractors.

No matter what yard you select, you will wind up buying some things at other places. Prices on building materials vary from time to time and place to place. Some other yard may have a carload sale on Sheetrock or factory-made windows, with good quality and prices your yard can't match. In general, try to buy at the right time. Don't buy insulation in the fall when everyone else does, unless your own or some other yard is having a huge carload sale. Above all, don't fret when the price on plywood goes down 10 percent a week after you bought all yours. That goes with the territory. Mostly, prices don't go down—they go up.

TOOLS

By now, you are certainly tired of reading, "Don't skimp on the cost." Sorry, but nowhere is it more true than in this section. You are constructing something that will probably be worth between $100,000 and $200,000, perhaps more. Don't be surprised if you spend 2 or 3 percent of that amount on tools. If you buy the cheapest possible electric drill, you may go through three or four in the course of the job. It's cheaper in the long run to buy one good one.

A journeyman carpenter brings his own set of tools to the job, but you can't expect that of most friends. To have fewer than three hammers available is foolish. If nothing else, the friend who stands around "wishing" he could help may change his tune if you hand him a hammer and put him to work doing something he can't screw up, like nailing down subfloor.

What tools should you buy? It's tempting to suggest that you go to a large hardware store and buy at least one of everything. One of the chief differences between you and a professional is the dazzling array of tools he owns. Here are some lists, necessarily incomplete. Don't rush out and buy everything on these lists; in some cases, it may be better to wait until the need arises. On the other hand, nothing is worse than trying to do the job with the wrong tool because it's Sunday and the hardware store is closed.

Basic tools for framing, rough carpentry, and general use

Claw hammers, *several*	Nail aprons
Half hatchet	3-pound sledge *(1-foot handle)*
10-pound sledge	Crowbar
Compass saw	Keyhole saw
Line level	Levels, *more than one*
Plumb bob and line	Chalk and chalk line
Allen wrenches, *one set*	Assorted standard wrenches
Jack knives, *one per worker*	Draw knife
C clamps	Pipe clamps
Try Square	Combination square

Carpenter's squares, *two or more*
Tape measures, *several, including a 50-footer (Real carpenters use folding 6-foot wood rules; I find tape measures easier to use.)*
Screwdrivers, *regular and Phillips, wide assortment*
Pliers, *several, including a large and a small "vise-grip"*
Pencils, *carpenter's and ordinary*
Rubber hammer *(has myriad uses)*
Wrecking bars, *a small and a large*
Handsaws, *at least two, a crosscut and a rip*
Hacksaw *(when all else fails, saw through driven nails to rectify a mistake)*

Power tools

Table saw and/or radial arm saw   Saber saw
Reciprocating saw
Electric circular saws, portable, *two or three (often called, regardless of make, Skilsaws), with an assortment of blades, including rip, crosscut, and plywood*
Long, heavy duty extension cords, *several*
Good, heavy-duty (at least 3/8-inch) electric drills, *two (these can also be used as power screwdrivers)*
Complete set of drills, bits, and screwdriver heads for same

Additional tools for specific jobs

Roofing: Tin snips, heavy-duty staplers, cheap brush for compound, cheap trowel or putty knife for cement
Wiring: Electrician's small sharp-nosed pliers, wire stripper, wire cutter
Plumbing: Pipe wrench
Insulation: Razor blade knives
Wall or floor tile: Various trowels, rubber gloves, rubber or plastic kitchen spatulas, several good sponges
Wood Trim: Good putty knives, backsaw and mitre box (if you don't have a radial arm saw), coping saw, an assortment of chisels, a block plane and a jack plane, reciprocating power sander, nail sets
Painting and wallpapering: Various paint brushes and rollers, wallpaper brush and roller, scissors, yardstick.

A good hammer and the Skilsaw will be the primary tools, along with a pencil, the square, and the level. Learn how to use the tools properly; take a minute to change to the plywood blade when cutting plywood, or keep one Skilsaw with a plywood blade and another with a crosscut blade handy at all times. If you can't sharpen things yourself, get them sharpened. Skilsaw blades are usually on sale so cheap, however, that you might be better off throwing the dull ones away.

Read and follow safety instructions. Pointing any cutting tool at yourself or anyone else (so that if it slipped it would cut the person) is on a par with pointing a loaded gun at someone.

I know a grizzled old carpenter. The first thing he does with a new table saw is remove the guard. The man is an idiot.

Framing the Floor

ROUGH FRAMING, FOR MOST PEOPLE, is fun. Getting the hang of it is not too difficult, and it goes very fast. It's like building a stage set. Depending on the size of your house, it's not unreasonable to expect to have it all framed in two or three weeks. At that point, you will think you are nearly finished, when in truth you have barely started.

HOME-BUILDING TECHNIQUES
Methods of house construction have changed over the years. Post-and-beam, the way two hundred-year-old barns in your area were probably built, still finds some use. Seventy-five-year-old houses are balloon framed, which means roughly that the walls were built first and the floors added later. The standard type of framing today—the system described here—is platform construction. The floor is built and used as a platform from which to erect the walls; a second floor precedes the second-story walls.

Your house will also be what contractors call "stick-built," since floor and walls are built one stick at a time rather than of prefabricated materials. Today, contractor-built homes use many prefabricated parts that are trucked to the site.

Your task will be made easier by the similar nature of building floors, walls, and roofs. In each case, the sticks—joists, studs, or rafters—are nailed together, have a rough sheathing material applied to them, and then finally a finished floor, siding, or roof. (The big sticks that floors are built on are called joists; in walls, they're called studs; in roofs, rafters.) Holes in the surface, like doors, windows, or the places that stairs or chimneys will go through, are reinforced in quite similar ways.

You won't build your house exactly the way that is described in the following pages, because some local expert will tell you, "They don't do it that way any more; they've got a new material (or technique) that's much easier." After reading this and listening to him, decide for yourself whether the new material is really better, faster, or easier for you to use, or whether it just costs more. For example, gangnails are gadgets that can be nailed simultaneously to two planks, like a joist and a header, at 90-degree angles. You can look at them, try out a few, and decide whether they're really worth it to you. (See chapter 10 about when *not* to take expert advice.)

Don't try to read just a few paragraphs of this section, then start. Read *at least* the entire section on floor framing before beginning that. You've probably seen a movie in which one bomb demolition expert is reading directions to the other: "You can see a red wire and a white wire. Cut the red wire—but only after you have disconnected the white wire." Parts of the following are written like that.

Before you begin framing, insist that the contractor backfill all around the foundation. That may turn someone's long fall into a short one.

FLOOR FRAMING

You start with the concrete box the contractor built. For your convenience, he will have given you something to fasten your floor to, usually large bolts sticking up out of the concrete. You drill holes in your sills at the correct places, then bolt them down. A much easier system (for you) is for the contractor to embed treated planks, perhaps 2x6s, in the top of the concrete walls. You just nail the sills to those. While you should still be as accurate as possible, you won't have to drill all those holes in precisely the right places. If using the bolt method, make the holes 1/4 inch oversize. Don't worry; when the entire weight of the house is on the sills, they won't move around.

If your basement is supposed to contain a heat sink consisting of seventy tons of sand or a lot of three hundred-pound boulders, get it in there now, before you put the "cap" (floor) on.

GIRDER, SILLS, AND JOISTS

You will probably begin by constructing a girder, because you can't span much more than twelve feet with an unsupported joist. The girder will run east-west along the centerline of the house. It will fit snugly into notches in the foundation walls. Whoever built the foundation will have made these notches according to the specifications on the blueprint. The girder will rest on a number of posts or Lally columns, a trade name for commonly used steel columns filled with concrete. Builders call them "lolly" columns. Lally columns are heavy and incredibly hard to cut. The building code (or inspector) may permit the use of treated wooden 6x6s. These are cheaper and easier to cut, and you can nail things to them later, if desired.

In basements you will often see steel posts containing a screw mechanism, like giant jacks. These are easy to use but are prohibited by code

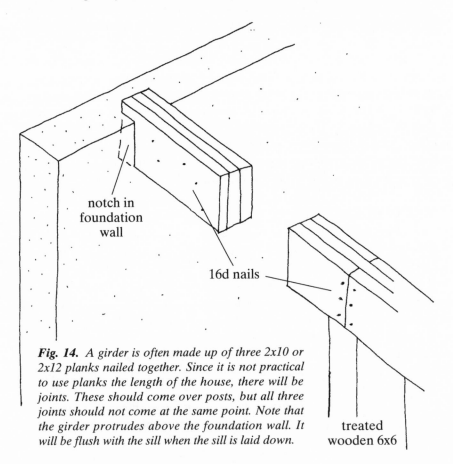

notch in
foundation
wall

16d nails

treated
wooden 6x6

Fig. 14. *A girder is often made up of three 2x10 or 2x12 planks nailed together. Since it is not practical to use planks the length of the house, there will be joints. These should come over posts, but all three joints should not come at the same point. Note that the girder protrudes above the foundation wall. It will be flush with the sill when the sill is laid down.*

in many places. If you use them, be sure that when construction is finished the screw is secured so that it is impossible to turn it accidentally, even if you hit it with a sledgehammer.

The girder can be a steel I beam, but you probably will prefer to make it of three 2x12s nailed together. It must be spliced to make it long enough. Common sense would probably tell you that you shouldn't have the three joints come at the same point and that each joint should come over a post. Unfortunately, you'll find that you can't reasonably achieve both these goals, and you will probably settle for having every joint over a post while never having *all three* joints come at the same point. Each post must go where the blueprint indicates; that's where the footing was poured, which is why you planned all this in advance.

Now is the time to learn about "crown." All planks are bent and twisted. Send the worst ones back to the yard; learn to deal with the others. Sight along the length of each plank and put the crown (convex side) up or, in the case of walls, out. If your 2x12s, in addition to having crown, are wavy, they will pretty much straighten out when you nail them together. You will be dealing mainly with the edge crown—the way a 2x6, for example, is bowed along the 1½-inch edge—but there is also a side crown, the way it is bowed along the 5½-inch side.

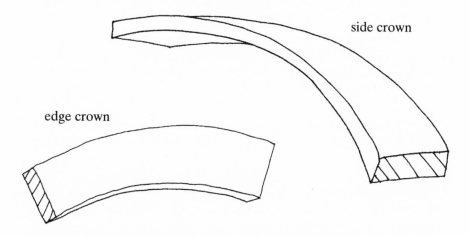

Fig. 15. *Almost every plank is bowed, however slightly, in two dimensions. As carpenters say, the plank has an edge crown and a side crown. The crown is the convex side of the board; sometimes it is pronounced, sometimes almost indiscernible. Side crown is seldom as important to the builder as edge. For example, all joists must be placed (edge) crown up, and all studs with the edge crown facing out.*

This is also a good time to learn about nails. Nails aren't described in centimeters or even in inches but by "penny," according to how much a hundred of them cost long ago. You'll use a 12- or 16-penny common— a good big nail, sometimes called a spike—to nail together the girder. A small *d* is the usual abbreviation for a penny, as "a 12d nail."

Common nails have heads; *finish* nails have only a slight swelling at the end opposite the point. *Galvanized* nails may be finish or common; they are used anywhere dampness might be encountered. *When directions do not specify, common nails are intended.* Buy more of all kinds of nails, especially common, than you can imagine needing. They are cheaper in fifty-pound lots.

No matter how carefully you measure, cut, and level, there will be a place where the post is too short or too long. If it's too long, cut it off (not too much!). If it's too short, shim it. Shimming is how carpenters survive. You'll need a supply of wooden shingles made especially for shimming. Fill a space by driving a shingle wedge into it. After you have toenailed (see below) the girder to the post, the post may be lifted right off the floor. Put the shim under it. Don't assume that the girder will settle. It may, but after seven years, we still have a post that hangs in the air if the shim comes out.

Now, finally, you can actually start the floor. Use treated 2x6s or 2x8s for sills. A sill sealer must go between the sill and the foundation, and an insect bar may. Check with local experts. The modern technique is to use aluminum roll flashing, perhaps six inches wide, under the sill, bending it down over the foundation (and the Styrofoam insulation). This effectively bars insects and acts as a rain shield. The exterior part will always show.

> **TIP:** It's much easier to bend the flashing before it is applied; bend it over a 2x4 with the rubber hammer, the small sledge, and strong fingers.

Putting the sills down is child's play. Make sure the edge crown is out and the side crown is up, since the sills go down flat. The foundation ought to be perfectly level, and the sills should be, too. Use the level; shim if necessary. Cut and fit; make sure your corners are square. Notice that the notch in the concrete wall for the girder was carefully planned so the top of the girder is level with the top of the sill; that means that the girder sticks up above the foundation wall, and you have to cut out the sill to go around it.

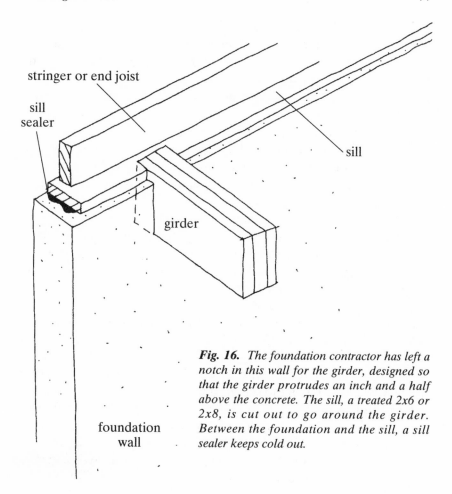

stringer or end joist

sill
sealer

sill

girder

Fig. 16. *The foundation contractor has left a notch in this wall for the girder, designed so that the girder protrudes an inch and a half above the concrete. The sill, a treated 2x6 or 2x8, is cut out to go around the girder.* foundation *Between the foundation and the sill, a sill* wall *sealer keeps cold out.*

Next, mark where each joist is to go on the sills and the girder. Now you learn the basic principle of all framing: Everything is a multiple of, or divides into, 4 feet by 8 feet. Plywood, wafer board, and similar material comes in 4-by-8 sheets, so your joists have to be eight feet "on center" (OC), so that two sheets will meet exactly in the middle of a joist. Since joists must be much closer together than eight feet to support the load, their distance apart OC will be a factor of eight feet. Your joists will probably be 2x8s or 2x10s set 16 inches OC.

If your house is more than twenty or twenty-four feet wide, you will have to use joists that span half the width and meet at the girder. Where they meet, they have to be joined in some way. The usual way is to over-lap them at the girder and nail them together. This is easy; unfortunately, as you will see, it means that the floor panels on the south half of the house will not match those on the north half; they'll be off by 1½ inches, the thickness of a 2x10, and you'll have a crack in the subfloor exactly over the girder running the length of the house.

If you must have joists that meet at the girder, scarf them. "Scarfing" is joining two planks, such as 2x10s, together to make one long piece by nailing a thinner board, like a 1x10 or even a 1x6, to each. Such a joining won't stand a great deal of strain, but it won't have to. It merely holds the planks where you want them until all the other nailing is done.

If the house is twenty feet wide or less, use joists as long as the house is wide; it's easier and won't cost much more. You may elect to use pre-fabricated or "truss" joists, made of lighter lumber and laminated board with diagonal supports. These consume fewer trees than regular dimension lumber, are much straighter, are lighter, and are said to be as strong or stronger. They can be used anywhere large dimension lumber is used—in rafters, for example—and are probably the wave of the future. At present, they are more expensive than ordinary lumber.

All of the joists will be 16 inches OC, which means that the space *between* each pair of joists will be 14½ inches; all, that is, except the first pair. You want the *first* sheet of wafer board to end not in the center of the outermost joist, but flush with the edge. This means that the distance for these two joists (center to center) must be 15¼ inches rather than 16 inches. This may be true at the opposite end (the end where you finish) also, if your overall house length is a multiple of four; otherwise you may have to cut a panel to fit there. Of course, you occasionally will have to cut wafer board, but you should keep it to a minimum, and you certainly don't want to plan so badly that you wind up tacking on a little 1-foot piece at the end. (See figure 17.)

You should thoroughly master the concept that the distance between the first two joists should always be ¾ inch less than the usual distance. You will encounter exactly the same situation with walls and roofs.

Use a carpenter's square to mark the sills where the joists will go. It is a clever device: One leg is 16 inches long and 1½ inches (the thickness of a 2x whatever) wide, the other 24 inches long and 2 inches wide. The usual practice is to measure off 16 inches with the square, draw a line, then put an *X* on the side of the line where the joist will actually go. If you put the line where you want the center of the joist to be, you won't be able to see it when you put the joist down on it. Lay out identical lines on the north sill, the south sill, and the girder. (See figure 18.)

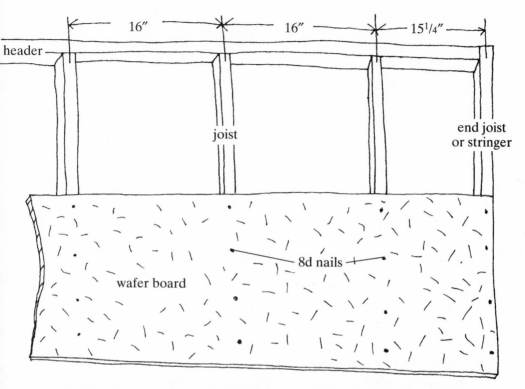

Fig. 17. *An important concept that can be difficult to master deals with the distance between the end plank and the second one in a floor or wall. The joists in this example are 16 inches OC, but in order that the 4x8 sheet of rough flooring extend to the edge of the stringer, not stop at the center, the first distance must be 3/4 inch less than the other distances between joists.*

Wherever there is going to be a partition in the house above, a double joist (two joists nailed together) is run in order to give extra support. With a double joist, of course, the 16-inch center comes between the two joists, giving you more leeway. Lines for double joists must be marked in the correct places on the sills and girder.

It is tempting to think that the positioning of the in-between joists isn't so critical; that is, two sheets of wafer board meet only at 8-foot intervals, so who cares about the joists in between? Avoid this kind of thinking, however. Everything that is done—finish floor, stairs, wiring, plumbing—will be done assuming that the joists, studs, and rafters are exactly where they are supposed to be. It is disconcerting, to say the least, to drill a hole where a joist shouldn't be and find one there.

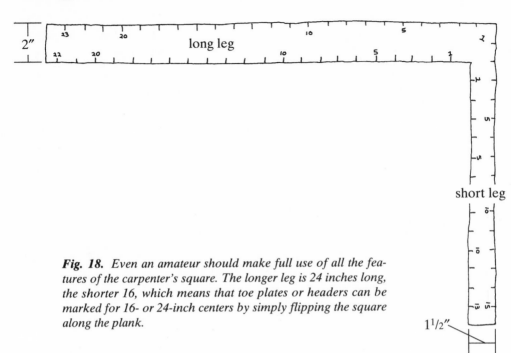

Fig. 18. *Even an amateur should make full use of all the features of the carpenter's square. The longer leg is 24 inches long, the shorter 16, which means that toe plates or headers can be marked for 16- or 24-inch centers by simply flipping the square along the plank.*

FRAMING OPENINGS

Where there will be an opening in the floor larger than 14½ inches wide, as for the basement stairs, the chimney and hearth, or something like a dumbwaiter, you will have to frame it. On each side of the opening is a double joist, which need not run double beyond the girder. Mark the sill and girder for these. The two joists are called *trimmers.* At the back and front of the opening are *headers,* planks that are nailed to the joists at right angles to frame the opening. The headers are double, like the trimmers. The *tail joists,* or *cripples,* which run to the opening and stop, are nailed to these. (Tail joists in floor construction are precisely the same as cripples in wall construction.)

The hole to accommodate the basement stairs will be adequate if it is 3 feet by 10 feet; read the part of chapter 23 about stairs to understand why.

> **IMPORTANT:** It is difficult to drive nails through two joists and into the end of a header, and this doesn't leave much nail to support the header. Exactly the same is true of headers nailed to cripples. Therefore, you must follow a precise sequence. First, nail the *outer* headers to the tail joists and the *inner* trimmers.

Next, nail the *inner* headers to the *outer* headers and the *inner* trimmers. Finally, nail the *outer* trimmers to the *inner* trimmers. It may seem obvious, but it is very easy to wind up with a hole that is 1¹/2 inches too small on each end because you didn't leave room for the inner headers. Try it out and you'll see how it works.

ALSO IMPORTANT: Frame the openings *before* you have the joists next to them in place, or you won't have room to swing a hammer between joists to nail the trimmers together.

You will probably need to put out temporary sheets of plywood or wafer board to have a surface to work from in framing an opening. You could, of course, begin laying the sheets down permanently before you

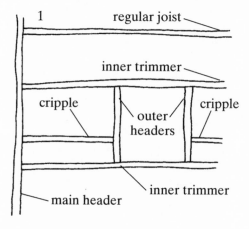

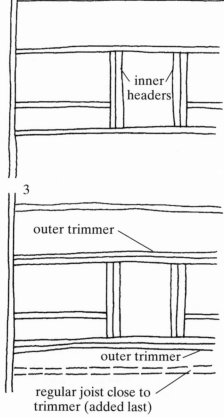

Fig. 19. *An opening in a floor should be framed in a precise sequence. In step 1, the inner trimmers and cripples are nailed to the outer headers. In step 2, the inner headers are nailed to the outer headers. Step 3 shows the outer trimmers added, as well as regular joists that would have impeded a hammer swing if added earlier. The amateur carpenter who tries to do this nailing in some other sequence soon discovers that nailing is difficult if not impossible.*

finish all the joists, but the disadvantages to this procedure far outweigh the advantages.

The plank that is nailed all along the outer ends of the joists is also called a header. The north and south headers and the easternmost and westernmost joists mark the outer extremities of your house. Sometimes these latter two are called "stringers" and are nailed to the ends of the headers rather than inside them.

Snap a chalk line along the sill 1½ inches from its edge, where you want the outer ends of the joists to come. The sill is probably not perfectly straight, and your headers and joists won't be, either, but you might as well start with a straight line.

Most mistakes you make in house construction won't matter as much as you think, but *it is extremely important to have all openings in the floor and all double joists for extra support exactly where they should be.* Even a mistake here is not fatal—very few are—but you'll sure wish you hadn't made it.

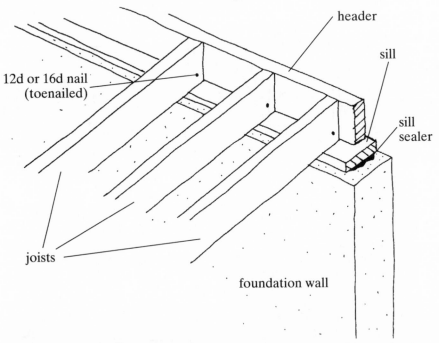

Fig. 20. *The north and south extremities of the solar house are defined by headers, which run along the outsides of the sills. This sill was marked for 16-inch centers with a carpenter's square; then the joists were toenailed to the sill and the header direct-nailed to the joists.*

Now that all the marking is done, you can go ahead and toenail the joists to the sills and girder, frame the holes in the floor, and nail on headers. You will probably use 12d common nails for toenailing and 12d or 16d for direct nailing. *Toenailing* is the term used for fastening two planks together by driving a nail at an angle through both. The technique is used on those many occasions when it is impossible to nail directly. With experience, you'll learn to start the nail at just the right spot and just the correct angle.

ROUGH FLOOR PANELS

Now you're really making progress, and you're ready to put down the rough floor. This will consist of 4-by-8 panels of 3/4-inch wafer board or CD plywood. Wafer board is slightly cheaper and has the added merit of

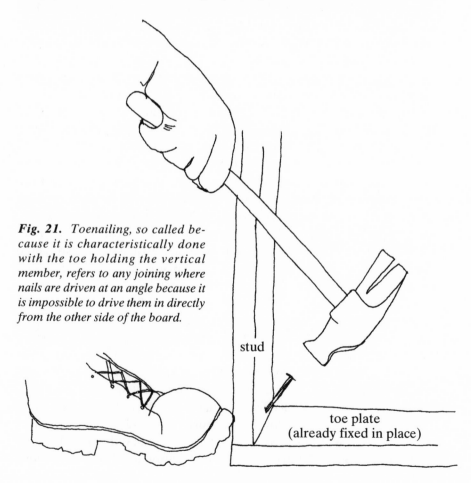

Fig. 21. *Toenailing, so called because it is characteristically done with the toe holding the vertical member, refers to any joining where nails are driven at an angle because it is impossible to drive them in directly from the other side of the board.*

stud

toe plate
(already fixed in place)

being tongue-and-groove. Don't skimp on the thickness; you're going to be walking around on this for quite a while.

Although we recommend wafer board (sometimes called "chip board") for rough flooring, plywood is often used. It comes in many grades. Ordinary plywood is made of thin veneers of pine, fir, or other softwood, glued together. AA would have both sides grade A, the very best. AB is usually the best grade available for construction work. AC or AD is commonly used where one side won't show; it is often referred to as G1S (good one side). CD is often used for rough flooring, wall sheathing, or roof decking, where neither side will show. For extremely wet situations, marine grade is available, but it's expensive; for cabinet-making, birch or other hardwood plywood is vastly better (and a lot more expensive).

Slate or tile can't be underlaid with wafer board. If the finished floor will have such areas, leave holes there, covered temporarily but sturdily, or figure out exactly what thickness of plywood you want (see chapter 23) and put it down. It should be G1S.

When you start putting the rough floor down, you'll discover something horrible: Your studs are exactly 16 inches OC at the sills and the girder, but in between they are sometimes as much as an inch off that standard, because they are wavy. To solve this problem, you may need blocking or bridging, and a pipe clamp is indispensable.

Blocks are pieces of the joist lumber, 14$^{1}/_{2}$ inches long, that you nail between the joists at 4-foot intervals. They give you something to nail the sides of the 4-by-8 panels to and keep the joists a constant distance apart. Bridging is X-shaped reinforcement set between the joists; this keeps them apart but doesn't solve any other problems. Most people buy it ready-made of metal or plastic, but it is still fussy to nail on. Construction experts have demonstrated that bridging is not necessary, but some building codes still require it.

You may be able to skip both blocking and bridging if you use tongue-and-groove panels and glue them. This will save a lot of time, money, and aggravation; make the floor more secure; and prevent squeaking.

To use tongue-and-groove panels, start at one corner of the house. Put a panel down dry, to test. The tongue should extend exactly beyond the header. If the joists run north-south, the panels should run east-west. Panels have an up and a down side, indicated by advertising printing, although with wafer board there isn't a great deal of difference. Lay the panel down and move it to exactly where you want it. Of course, the corner of the panel and the corner of the house should each be a perfect right angle, but. . .

You can always cut off (later) a small, skinny triangle of panel that extends beyond the house, but any error will be multiplied as you progress. In any case, you will cut off the tongue where it extends over the header; do that with a Skilsaw after the glue dries. Draw a line on the joists at the groove side of the panel to show you where to stop applying glue.

Measure the distance between the first pair of joists at the line. If it's not right, squeeze the two together with the clamp or spread them with a temporary piece of 2x4 blocking, but keep the clamp or the block sufficiently clear of your field of operations. Apply the panel adhesive to all the joists and header where the panel is to go. You now have about ten minutes before it dries.

Put the sheet in place and nail it to the first two joists and the header. Use 8d common nails about four inches apart. Now remove the clamp or block, and repeat with joists two and three, and so on. Ten minutes should be plenty of time; you won't always have to use the clamp or block.

Repeat the operation all over the floor. Work diagonally—that is, don't go all across the bottom row, then the next; rather, put down another 4-by-8 sheet beside the first, then one above it, and so on. Stagger the joints: Next to the first piece put a half piece you cut, so that no crack will extend all the way across.

You will probably need a sledgehammer to make the tongues go into the grooves. To avoid damaging the sheets, cut a strip of wafer board about 1 by 8 feet with a tongue on it. Use that to drive the second sheet into the first. It will slide more easily with the glue on it (for the first ten minutes). It also helps to cheat by not nailing the first sheet all the way across to the groove side; instead, leave a foot or so not nailed down until the second sheet is banged into place. Continue in this fashion until the entire floor is covered.

What do you do about the holes in the floor? If they're small, just sheet them right over. You'll cut them out later—perhaps much later—with a reciprocating saw, one of your handiest and most basic tools. If they're big, like the hole where the basement stairs will go through, you'll have to cut sheets to fit. It's usually easier to cut them after they are fastened down. Every piece of joist and header, even a narrow place beside a hole, has to be surfaced with paneling, because something else will go on top of it.

Holes in the floor are no joke. During the rest of the construction, if people can fall through them, they will. Cover them temporarily with tacked-down panels that will easily support the weight of the heaviest member of the crew, build temporary but sturdy barricades around them, or both.

It will rain on your subfloor, and even if you cover it laboriously with plastic every night, some of it will get wet and probably warp slightly. It is unlikely, however, that this will be noticeable or create a problem when the house is finished and the final floor applied.

Even if you have a crawl space, a partial basement, or both, you will need all the above—girder, posts, joists, and so on. If you are building on a poured slab, you will probably use this as the ground floor of your house and begin the walls from there.

Now you've got the whole floor done and you're feeling great. What a fantastic site for a party, with dancing! You'll never have this vast a dance floor in your house again. But it's time to stop partying and get going on the walls.

Framing the Walls

NOW YOU HAVE A PLATFORM for the rest of the framing. Sections of wall will be laid out and nailed together on the floor, then raised into place, much as in an old-fashioned barn raising.

BUILDING A SAMPLE SECTION

The bottom piece of the wall is called the *sole,* or *toe plate;* the top is the *top plate.* The sticks that hold them apart are studs. Let's build an 8-by-10-foot piece of wall out of 2x4s. It will actually be 8 feet, 3 inches high if you use standard 8-foot studs.

Pick a couple of straight 10-foot 2x4s and place them together on the floor with the 1½-inch edges touching. These will be the toe plate and top plate. Have both crowns down. Use the carpenter square to mark off, as you did on sill and girder, 16- or 24-inch centers (let's do 24) on *both* of them at once. Remember that the first space, from the end to the first stud, is ¾ inch less, so that the sheathing will extend to the edge of the plank, not end at its center.

When the toe plate and top plate are marked, move them eight feet apart and put them on edge, with the edge crowns facing up and the side crowns (on the 3½-inch sides) facing away from each other. Pick out six straight 8-foot studs and place them where they will go, with edge crowns up. Starting at one end, nail the first stud into place, keeping exactly a 90-degree angle. Repeat all the way down to the last stud.

As you nail, the wall will "rack" out of true: The corner that was a right angle as you started will be a few degrees off when you finish. Furthermore, as you nail one end, the other end may tend to loosen. There are several tricks to counteract these problems. One is to have two carpenters at opposite ends of the stud, each using a square *(inside* of the angle), nailing simultaneously.

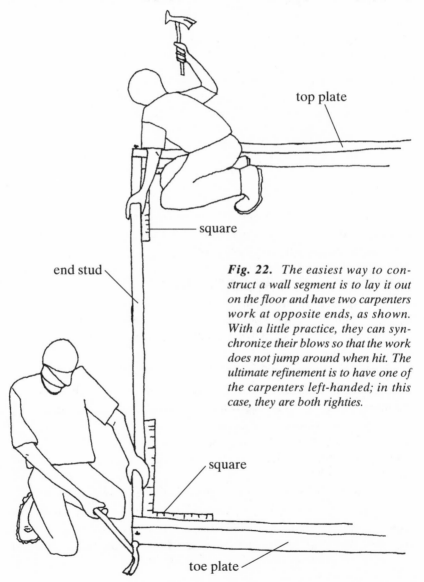

top plate

square

end stud

square

toe plate

Fig. 22. The easiest way to construct a wall segment is to lay it out on the floor and have two carpenters work at opposite ends, as shown. With a little practice, they can synchronize their blows so that the work does not jump around when hit. The ultimate refinement is to have one of the carpenters left-handed; in this case, they are both righties.

If you're working alone, you'll need a jig. Nail two boards to the floor exactly at right angles. Then put the southeast corner of the wall against the jig, which will hold it in place, as you nail the northeast corner. It's nearly impossible to build an entire house all by yourself, but you may, on a given day, find yourself the only one on the job. You will find that you can design and make a number of different jigs for different purposes.

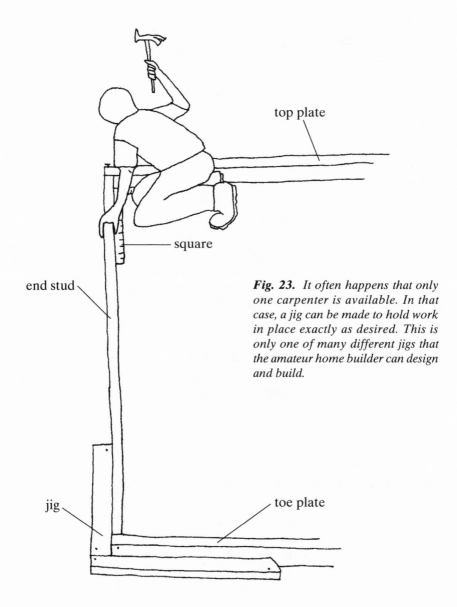

top plate

square

end stud

Fig. 23. *It often happens that only one carpenter is available. In that case, a jig can be made to hold work in place exactly as desired. This is only one of many different jigs that the amateur home builder can design and build.*

jig

toe plate

BRACING AND ERECTING A WALL

Once you have the wall finished, with all the studs correctly in place, nail a diagonal brace or two across it. The diagonal brace should be made of "strapping," lengths of low-quality 1x3s you buy by the bundle. If necessary, you can pull a nail or two out of the brace and adjust the wall to make it more true, then renail the brace. Use double-headed nails for any temporary nailing such as this. Make sure the diagonal doesn't protrude beyond the top, bottom, or end of the wall.

Next push the wall upright and position it exactly where you want it on the edge of the platform (crowns out). If you nail temporary stops to the side of the floor platform, protruding above it, it is easier to slide the wall exactly to the edge. Nail the wall down through the subfloor to the header and joists, using the biggest nails that won't split the wood, probably 16d. You can nail it just into subfloor with 10d nails, but that alone is not enough to hold it. Use a level to be sure that the wall is exactly plumb (vertical) in both dimensions, or as near as humanly possible. Keep checking the verticality as you go along, and make adjustments if necessary.

The first wall will be loose and flexible, but each additional step in construction will make it more rigid. For now, nail blocks to the floor some distance in front of the wall and diagonal braces from the blocks to the studs, or brace it to stakes driven into the ground outside the house, or both. Whichever you choose, you will soon have a forest of temporary diagonal braces that you will constantly be tripping over.

Carpenters often put the rough sheathing on before standing the wall upright. This has many advantages; in particular, it stiffens the wall. I prefer to have the sheathing extend down below the wall to the top of the foundation. This covers cracks between the toe plate and the floor and the header and the sill, making a tighter seal. You want your solar house as tight as you can get it. It also strengthens the connection between the wall and the floor. If you do this, however, you won't be able to nail on the sheathing until the wall is completed, and then you'll probably wait until the roof is on.

LONGER AND HIGHER WALLS

You will want walls longer than ten feet and higher than eight. It isn't practical to build them out of, for example, 20-foot 2x4s, because the wood will be too twisty. You can nail together several 10-foot segments of wall, but you'll have to be sure all the studs are sixteen or twenty-four inches OC the whole length of the wall.

To put together a 30- or 40-foot wall, scarf together several pieces of toe plate and top plate. Use different lengths to be sure that the crack at the top is not at the same place as the crack at the bottom. The scarfs at the toe plate joint can't protrude beyond the bottom, or you won't be able to raise the wall. Such a long wall will, of course, wave around even more than a short one, but with various diagonal braces you'll get it where you want it.

To build a higher wall, for example a 16-footer, build two separate 8-foot walls and nail them together. Use all your wiles to join them securely—scarfs, diagonal braces, strong nails, anything else you can think of. To erect such a wall, you'll need a large, well-coordinated crew. Some will push with long poles attached near the top of the wall, others will push by hand lower down, and still others will stand by to nail the toe plate down and securely brace the wall diagonally as soon as it is in place. Fortunately, most of your walls will not be this high.

FIRESTOPS

The building code may call for firestops every eight feet or less. Firestops are lengths of 2x4 nailed across horizontally between the studs. A heavily insulated house doesn't really need them, since they were designed to fill the hollow wall spaces between studs to prevent those areas from acting as chimneys in a fire. Unfortunately, not all building codes have caught up.

CORNERS

Corners require extra thought, time, skill, and lumber. At any point where two walls join at right angles, whether it be the intersection of two exterior walls or a point at which an interior partition joins a wall, place a stud turned sideways, so that you will have a sturdier nailed connection between the two walls. (See figure 24.)

Remember that sheathing will have to be applied to both the inside and the outside of the wall. At an interior corner, be sure there is a surface for the Sheetrock to be nailed to. If you use the double-wall system described below, you will only have to worry about the exterior corners of the outer walls and the interior corners of the inner walls.

> **NOTE:** You are used to placing the first stud a little closer to the end, so that the 4x8 exterior sheathing will be flush with the end of the wall. Where two exterior walls meet at a corner, however, the sheathing itself will form a corner. The end of one piece of

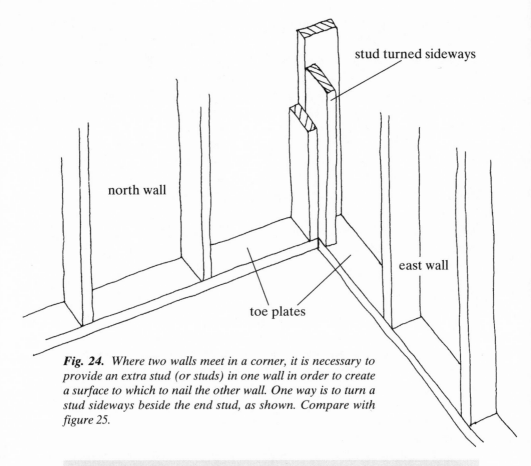

stud turned sideways

north wall

east wall

toe plates

Fig. 24. *Where two walls meet in a corner, it is necessary to provide an extra stud (or studs) in one wall in order to create a surface to which to nail the other wall. One way is to turn a stud sideways beside the end stud, as shown. Compare with figure 25.*

sheathing will overlap the end of the other, so the sheathing on one of the two walls will have to extend *beyond* the corner stud. In other words, if studs are 24 inches OC, the distance between studs will normally be 22½ inches. For the distance between the end stud and the first stud, however, you subtract an additional 3/4 inch to make the sheathing reach the end of the wall. And for one of the two walls that meet at the corner, you subtract ½ inch more, so that the half-inch sheathing on one wall will overlap that on the other.

FRAMING WINDOW OPENINGS

So far you have built a blank wall; now you are ready to frame windows and doors. Be sure to read chapter 16 before continuing construction. Study the blueprints carefully to get the openings exactly where they should go, in

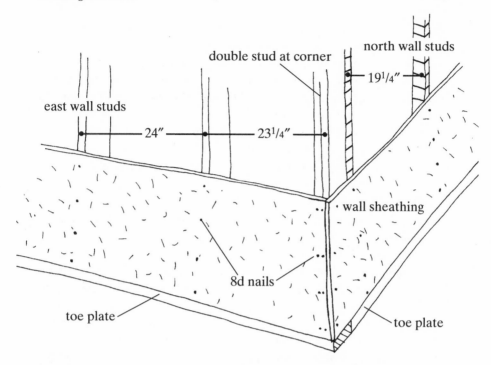

east wall studs

double stud at corner

north wall studs

19¹/₄″

24″

23¹/₄″

wall sheathing

8d nails

toe plate

toe plate

Fig. 25. *Since one 4-by-8 sheet of sheathing must overlap the other when they meet at a corner, end studs must be even closer together than is the case with joists. (See figure 17.) If these walls are built with studs 24 inches OC, the distance (OC) from the end stud to the second stud in the east wall must be 23¹/₄ inches. For the north wall, the discrepancy is much greater. The similar distance must be 19¹/₄ (24–³/₄–3¹/₂–¹/₂). A frequently used alternative is to cut all the end pieces of sheathing on the north wall to fit. (For clarity, north wall studs are cross-hatched in the diagram.)*

both dimensions. You will be creating rough openings (ROs) that should be at least ¹/₄ inch larger all around than the windows and doors that will go in them. Although they shouldn't be too sloppy, it obviously is much easier to work with openings that are too large than ones that are too small. Some of the windows and nearly all of the doors will be ready-made; get the exact ROs from the yard. The fixed windows (those that don't open) you'll buy and frame; figure out those ROs yourself. It's a good idea to have the future doors and windows on hand now; nothing is more accurate than your own measurement of the actual window.

Framing a window is much like framing a floor opening. The bottom of the rough opening, called a "rough sill," is like a header. It is supported by cripples of the requisite length. The sides of the rough opening are trimmers, doubled studs. The inner trimmers, however, only go up to the header at the top of the RO, which they support. The outer trimmers are full-length.

The top header is different from those you have dealt with previously. Because walls support a lot of weight, it functions as a bridge and has to be much sturdier than a 2x4. For a window two feet wide it might be made of two 2x6s turned sideways, while for a double glass door opening it might be made of 2x12s, depending on how high the building will be above the door and, therefore, how much weight the header has to support. Since 2-inch dimension lumber is 1½ inches thick, two pieces nailed together are 3 inches thick. But a 2x4 stud is 3½ inches wide, so you have to make a sandwich of two 2x6s (or whatever) with a piece of ½-inch plywood between them. Or you can buy special header material, similar to truss joists, at your lumberyard. Your dealer, the building inspector, or another expert can tell you how strong a given header will have to be. Don't skimp. If you do, the house probably won't collapse, but it may settle enough to create a big crack in your picture window or make your door inoperable.

Whatever header material you select, the header will go *on top of* the inner trimmers and be toenailed to them. It will go *between* the outer trimmers, which will be nailed to it and to the inner trimmers in the usual manner. You will soon learn the pattern of which nailing to do first and which last, just as you did in framing openings in floors. If there is considerable space above the header, short cripples will go there, just as they do below the rough sill. If these cripples would be about six inches long or less, it is usually easier to make an oversize header to fill up this entire space.

> **NOTE:** If you nail two studs together with 12d nails, the nails will stick out the other side. Shorter nails are not strong enough, however, so use 12d nails and bend the sharp ends down thoroughly or master the elegant technique of driving them in at an angle so that they don't protrude.

FRAMING DOOR OPENINGS

Doors are framed exactly like windows with one exception: There is no rough sill. In planning the rough opening, include the toe plate as part of the opening, because you will saw that away (much later, not now) when you come to installing the door. It helps if you can remember, when placing the wall upright, not to drive too many nails too firmly into the part

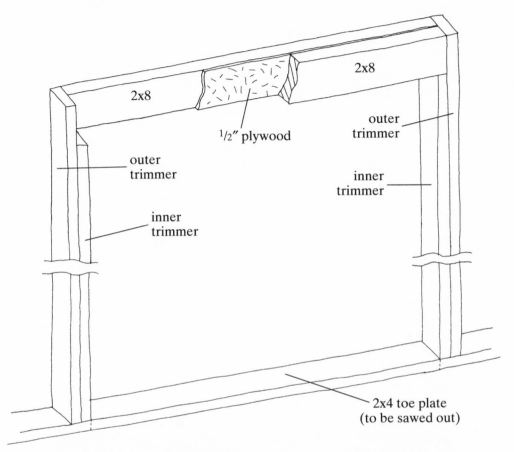

Fig. 26. *This header is cut away to show its construction. Since a 2x4 is 3¹/₂ inches wide, a header for a window or door opening in a 2x4 wall must be made as a sandwich of two lengths of 2x whatever with a piece of half-inch plywood between. (1¹/₂ + 1¹/₂ + ¹/₂ = 3¹/₂.) The rough opening for a door is constructed so that, after the toe plate has been sawed out, the opening is the correct size.*

that is going to be cut away eventually, but you will need a few. Use double-headed nails here.

You will often have a regular stud, one that is twenty-four inches OC, a few inches away from the stud that frames a door or window. Don't omit it to save money. The person who puts on the sheathing, the Sheetrock man, the plumber, the electrician, and the guy who eventually hangs pictures—most of whom will be you—will depend absolutely on finding that stud there.

DOUBLE 2X4 WALLS

Why have we been talking about 2x4 walls with studs twenty-four inches on center? Don't modern houses have thicker and sturdier walls than that? Yes, they do, and we're going to show you the easiest way to build the thickest, sturdiest, and most energy-efficient walls of all.

Early American houses had huge beams: 12x12s, 8x10s, and the like. Then wood (and labor) became more expensive, and houses were built of the smallest sticks possible. In the 1940s most houses had walls made of 2x4s, twenty-four inches OC. Then sixteen inches OC, for more strength, became more common. As energy-efficient homes increased in popularity, walls grew thicker to accommodate more insulation. Today most houses are built of 2x6s, sixteen inches OC, and some builders are going to 2x8s.

A simple technique for achieving maximum insulation value with minimum expense is the double 2x4 wall. In this technique, the builder simply frames the house with a regular 2x4 wall with studs twenty-four inches OC. He then moves in (toward the center of the house) one inch, and erects a second wall identical to the first, except that the studs are staggered—that is, each stud in the inner wall is opposite a point midway between two studs in the outer wall.

By far the easiest way to erect one wall exactly one inch from another is to make spacers exactly one inch wide. Before you erect the inner wall, put spacers on the floor between the two about every three feet. Try to remember to remove the spacers after tacking the wall down with a few nails but before the final nailing. They will be difficult to remove at best and impossible at worst. Don't worry if you can't get them out; they won't reduce the R-value much.

It is a good idea to connect the two walls at the top every three feet or so. If each wall is perfectly plumb, they will automatically be exactly one inch apart at the top. If they're not, use spacers to make them so, connect them, then remove the spacers. These temporary connections will be removed when rafters or ceiling joists are added.

NOTE: Because of roof slope, one of the two walls in the pair should be a bit higher than the other. An easy way to achieve this is to add one more top plate, now or later. This will work unless your roof is going to be exceptionally flat or steep. (See chapter 14.)

The double-wall technique is by far the best and cheapest way to achieve maximum heat retention for the thickness of the wall. Compare it with the nearest thing to it, a wall built of 2x8s. One 2x8 costs more than two 2x4s. A 2x8 wall is actually only 7$^{1}/_{2}$, not 8 inches thick. A 2x8 wall twenty feet long and ten feet high is a massive structure to pick up and move into position, while two 2x4 walls can be moved one at a time.

The greatest single advantage, however, is that there is a minimum of connection between the inside of the house and the outside. Studs conduct heat far better than insulating material does. In a 2x6 or 2x8 wall, the insulation is only between the studs; every sixteen or, at best, twenty-four inches there is a piece of wood. Nailed to it on the outside is sheathing, surmounted by finish siding of some sort. Fastened to it on the inside is Sheetrock or other finish material. Heat travels through each nail, through the stud, and out of the house.

With the type of wall we favor, there are few connections between the two walls. The insulation is not applied upright between two studs but is woven horizontally between the staggered studs. The insulation-filled space varies from 5$^{1}/_{2}$ inches behind or in front of a stud to 8 inches between studs. With exceptions to be noted, it is never zero, as it is every 16 inches in conventional walls.

There aren't many disadvantages to this system, but you'll have to do a lot more planning and calculating. Each inner wall is shorter (in length) than the corresponding outer wall—9 inches shorter (3$^{1}/_{2}$ + 1 on each end). Much more difficult is the fact that if you have the shed roof common in solar houses, inner walls must be taller or shorter by about an inch, depending on roof type and pitch. (See chapter 14.)

This system is unusual. It uses cheaper material and more labor, and it is "fussy"; it requires a smart carpenter who pays constant attention to detail. For all these reasons, it is not popular with contractors but is ideal for people like you.

NOTE: Don't confuse the double-wall system described above with "envelope" construction. The envelope house, which is a type of energy-efficient construction, has an air space between the inside and outside walls, all around the house. This type of construction is still illegal in many places, because the air space forms a natural chimney that facilitates a house fire, should one occur. All the spaces in all of your walls will be filled with insulation.

Wherever there is a window or a door opening, studs will not be staggered, since the trimmers, headers, and so on in the outer wall must be at exactly the same place as those in the inner wall. There will be only

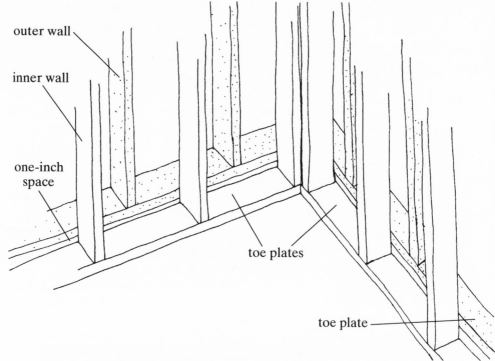

outer wall

inner wall

one-inch
space

toe plates

toe plate

Fig. 27. *Each wall in this example of the double-wall construction is a simple, conventional 2x4 wall; there is a 1-inch space throughout between the two. Studs are 24 inches OC and staggered; that is, a stud in the inner wall occurs midway between two studs in the outer wall. Standard 5¹/₂-inch insulation, which normally would be placed vertically between 2x6 studs, is instead woven horizontally in this wall between inner and outer studs. Note that, except at windows and doors, there is no heat-transmitting material like wood or nails connecting the two walls.*

an inch of insulated space between, for example, inner trimmers and outer ones, but even an inch is better than nothing.

Since a passive solar house usually has almost no windows or doors on the north side, few to the east and west, and many on the south, double-wall construction is ideal for the north wall and suitable for the east and west. The south wall will have so many windows and doors that there you might choose to use conventional construction, perhaps based on 2x6s.

If you live where it seldom snows or goes below freezing, you may not think it worthwhile to build 8-inch walls, although they also make air conditioning much more efficient. Consult local contractors (and your lumber dealer) to find out how most new houses are built in your area. *Then go up at least one grade from that!*

SECOND FLOORS

In two-story construction, a ceiling goes on top of the ground-floor walls. The procedure is similar to the framing of the original floor, except that lighter joists, like 2x6s, may be used, unless additional depth is needed to hide eventual plumbing pipes. Load-bearing partitions must be erected before ceilings are put on, but it is customary to wait until the house is closed in to erect non-load-bearing partitions.

Partitions are often made of 2x4s twenty-four inches OC, although they may be sixteen inches OC if they bear much load. The lighter construction is sufficient for a partition that partially supports an upstairs bedroom; one that assists in supporting the roof needs heavier construction. If pipes will be hidden in the partition, it must be built of 2x6 or wider stock.

All walls have double top plates. The upper one, however, is not added until after the wall is erected, because added strength is attained at a corner, where a wall joins a partition or another wall, by overlapping one upper top plate onto the other wall. In double-wall construction, partitions intersect only the inner walls but ceiling joists rest on both sets of walls.

Construction of an upper floor is identical to that of the first floor, except that a girder is seldom used. Joists are laid across the top plates of

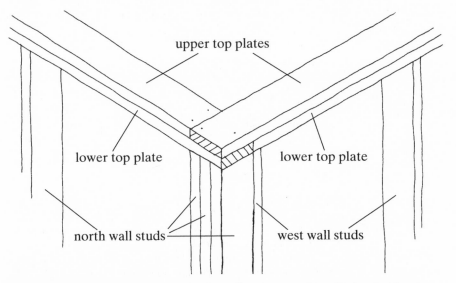

Fig. 28. *Walls always have two top plates, but the second is added only after the wall is in place. At a corner, the top plates are overlapped as shown, to add strength and rigidity to the structure. The corner treatment here is different from that shown in figure 24; instead of one stud turned sideways, the north wall ends with a triple stud.*

the walls, which now function as sills. Since the joists are laid whichever is the short way, they will often run crosswise to the basement joists. Holes for stairs or chimneys are framed the same way, headers are applied the same way, and floor panels are applied the same way, although the floor panels may be 1/2 inch instead of 3/4 inch and may not need to be glued.

BALCONIES

If you want a second-floor balcony, one easy way to do this is to extend a few joists outward a few feet. Such joists must be made of treated lumber. In order not to have large holes in the exterior wall, fill the spaces between these extended joists with blocking where the header would go.

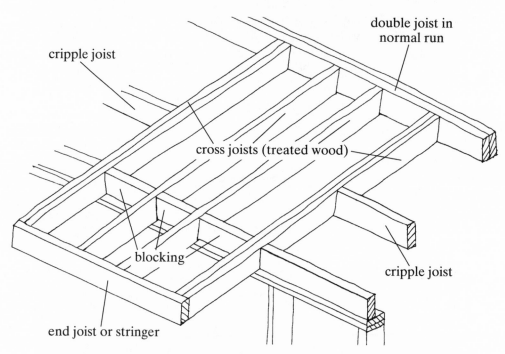

Fig. 29. *The construction of a balcony can be described as framing an opening, then filling it in. Here headers, trimmers, and cripples are used as in the normal framing of an opening, but joists are set in the opening and protrude beyond the house wall. The openings between these joists are filled with blocking. If the balcony had come at the end of the regular run of joists rather than crosswise to it, the construction would have been even easier; the pertinent joists, which would have to be treated wood, would simply be three feet (or the desired distance) longer than the rest.*

If you want the balcony on a wall that is at right angles to the run of the joists, the construction is a little more complicated, but not much. It might be described as framing an opening, then filling the opening with treated joists, at right angles to the others, that extend outside the wall the desired distance. The important thing to remember is that the cantilevered balcony supports must extend into the house twice as far as they extend outside.

After you have built a second floor, you erect walls on it in precisely the same manner that you built walls on the first floor. Now you are ready for the roof.

Framing the Roof

LOUIS SULLIVAN, the great nineteenth-century American architect, said it: "Form follows function." For this reason, all passive solar houses look somewhat alike. Most have a shed roof. Yours may possibly have a modified saltbox roof, with a short, steep pitch in the front and a long, shallow pitch in the back, but it is unlikely to have a conventional gable roof with two equal slopes and the ridge along the centerline of the house.

Many solar houses have two shed roofs. The front one, smaller, lower, and sloping south, covers a sunspace addition. The main roof slopes north. Common in solar construction, the shed roof is the easiest kind to build, but it has one drawback: The rafters will have to be larger than those in a conventional roof. You may need 2x12s twenty-four feet long or longer, which will have to be specially ordered. Rafters this large are needed to span twenty feet or more. Fortunately, they have another advantage: Only rafters that are 2x12 or larger will provide enough space to accommodate the amount of insulation necessary.

Roofs are framed like floors and walls, with one infuriating exception: They slope. The slope of a shed roof is determined by the height of the front (south) wall compared with the height of the back wall, and by the distance between them. For example, a house twenty feet wide with a front wall fifteen feet high and a rear wall ten feet high will have a shed roof with a rise of three feet for every twelve feet of run.

labels on figure: balcony; 3x6 thermal window; 4x6 thermal windows; storm door; steps; deck; concrete knee wall (insulated on exterior)

Fig. 30. *This view from the southwest of the greenhouse shown in figure 12 also shows the house. All of the clerestory windows in this house can be reached from the balcony or the greenhouse roof, which facilitates cleaning them or covering them with shutters. The greenhouse door and storm door are partly glass. The deck is at exactly the same level as the greenhouse floor, so that heavy plants can be rolled in and out easily.*

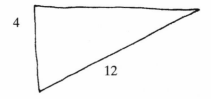

Fig. 31. *An architect's drawing or a blueprint will display a triangle like this just above the roof line. In the example, the roof has a* rise *of four feet for every twelve feet of* run. *Construction people describe roof pitch in this fashion, rather than as an angle of a certain number of degrees.*

CUTTING AND FITTING RAFTERS

Where a rafter at a slant intersects the top plate of a wall, which is horizontal, a cut, called a "birdsmouth" must be made in the rafter so that it will fit snugly and lie at the correct angle. This is the part of construction that gives most novices, and many professionals, fits because it involves trigonometry. Carpentry books are full of complicated techniques for doing this. Here is an easy way.

Lay out an actual rafter, one of your straightest and best, on the large surface of your rough floor. Using a tape measure, a square, and great care, draw on the floor a full-size diagram of your walls. Have the two walls in the diagram precisely the right thickness and precisely the right distance apart, and the front wall exactly as much higher than the rear wall as it is in reality. Lay the rafter to span the diagram exactly as it will the walls, check it carefully several times, then cut the indicated birdsmouths.

> **NOTE:** If you have followed our advice, one or both of these walls will be double, and the north wall of the pair will be about an inch lower. It makes no difference; the diagram will reflect the actual walls, and instead of cutting one large birdsmouth, you will cut two small ones. Surprisingly, the precise amount by which the north unit of a double wall is higher than the south one is not crucial, because you can cut the birdsmouths slightly differently for each wall.

Try the sample rafter in place. It should fit perfectly. If it's an inch or two off, you probably made the cuts correctly, but the walls, which should be exactly the correct distance apart, aren't. Use a tape measure and a level (to test plumb) and push them out or in (carefully, removing a few braces at a time) to make them so. Now the rafter falls perfectly into place and immediately stiffens the walls and holds them exactly the correct distance apart. Don't nail it into place; take it down and use it as a template for cutting the other rafters. It will be the very last rafter nailed down.

> **NOTE:** Anytime you use a piece as a template or model, don't mark Rafter 2 from Rafter 1, Rafter 3 from Rafter 2, and so on. If you do, any slightest error will be multiplied as you go along. Use Rafter 1 as the template throughout.

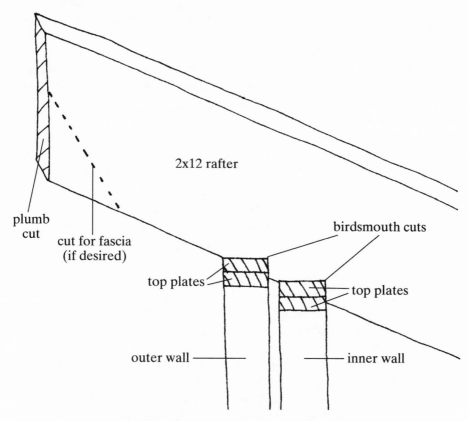

plumb cut

cut for fascia (if desired)

2x12 rafter

birdsmouth cuts

top plates

top plates

outer wall

inner wall

Fig. 32. *Where a rafter intersects a wall, a cut called a* birdsmouth *is made into the rafter. In this illustration, the rafter intersects a double 2x4 wall, necessitating two cuts, but the two small cuts leave the rafter stronger than one large cut would. The rafter shown has a plumb cut, parallel to the wall, at the end. If a 1x6 fascia board is to be added, the rafter must be cut back toward the wall at a point five inches from the top of the plumb cut; otherwise the fascia would have to be more than twelve inches wide. (See figure 46.)*

If the walls are exactly the right distance apart but the rafter cuts are more than an inch off, you made a mistake. Check everything carefully over again. You'll probably get it right the first time, however. Plan so that you have a considerable rafter overhang at the south side of the house and a lesser overhang at the north side. Make plumb cuts at each end of the rafter by cutting a triangle off each end, in such a manner that when the rafter is in place the end will be exactly vertical. These cuts will be parallel to the vertical cuts in the birdsmouths.

At this point, read the part of chapter 22 that deals with fascia boards and soffits, since it is easier to cut the ends now than after the rafters are in place.

Putting on rafters is the scariest part of building a house. People are sitting way up high on walls that shake under them, handling very heavy timbers. It may not be the most dangerous part, because most people are so frightened that they hang on tight and take extreme care. Be sure that the walls are carefully and thoroughly braced in every conceivable way, that nobody has driven a truck into one of the outside braces or removed one of the inside ones because he or she kept tripping over it. Use good ladders according to the directions on them. Rent scaffolding, if necessary; you'll be using it later. Most important, don't let anyone stand under anyone working; the most common accident occurs when a carpenter drops a hammer (or a rafter) on a worker immediately below. Wear hard hats.

BLOCKING

After the rafters are cut, install them 16 inches OC. The easiest way to get them the right distance apart while hanging on by your teeth is to install blocking at this time. There will be large holes on the front and back of the house, between the rafters, if you don't do something about it. These spaces must be filled with blocking.

If the rafters are 2x12s sixteen inches OC, the spaces are 14$\frac{1}{2}$ inches by somewhat less than 11$\frac{1}{4}$ inches, the somewhat less being caused by the birdsmouth cut and the slant of the rafter. If you're a perfectionist, you'll make the blocks with slanting tops to match the rafters, but it really isn't necessary; all the cracks will eventually be caulked.

The easiest way to make blocking is to measure the hole, then have someone at the table saw cut 14$\frac{1}{2}$-inch blocks just that size out of 2x12 (or whatever the rafter size is) stock and toss them up to the workers on the rafters as requested. There will probably be some openings that will be narrower, around the chimney opening or at the edge of the roof. Cut blocking to fit them.

Ventilation must be provided. Having just closed off these holes, you must now partially open them again to allow air to circulate just under the roof. (See chapter 24.) Cut a hole in each block, at the top, about 6$\frac{1}{2}$ inches wide and 3 inches deep. If the block is smaller than normal, cut a correspondingly smaller hole. At some point, these holes must be covered with screening to keep insects out, but it is probably better to do that later (from a ladder), extending the screening an inch or so up onto the underside of the roof decking. There must be ventilation holes in the blocks on the lower (north) side as well as on the upper.

Rafters are toenailed to the top plates at the birdsmouths. The wood will split maddeningly just where you don't want it to; you may have to use 10d nails instead of 12d, or you may want to use special gangnails or brackets designed for the purpose. Until intermediate blocking and decking are nailed on, the rafters, which are only toenailed at the base, will have a maddening tendency to twist; they will be the requisite 14½ inches apart at the base but more or less than that at the top. Walk on them as little as possible until decking is nailed on. You may want to begin adding the decking before you finish putting on all the rafters.

OVERHANGS

In addition to overhangs at front and back, you will want overhangs at the east and west ends. Considerable overhang on all sides helps a lot to keep rain off the walls, as well as to make the house look more attractive. Front and back overhangs are easy: Just order the rafters that much longer than you need them.

End overhangs are more difficult. The traditional way to construct them is with "lookouts" and "fly rafters," essentially cantilevered construction. As you will discover, however, since your 2x12 rafters are much heavier than traditional rafters (which span a shorter distance at a steeper angle), lookouts and fly rafters are impractical.

An alternative is this: As you lay decking, extend it about 1 foot out into space at the end. You will not have to change the spacing of the rafters; in fact, unlike joists and studs, even the end rafters can be 16 inches OC, but you will have to cut each 4-by-8 decking panel that goes on the end. The first one will span six rafters and overhang a foot, so it will be 92¾ inches long (5 x 16 + ¾ + 12). In order to stagger the cracks, the next one will be 76¾ inches long. You will alternate these as you go up the roof.

When you have one end of the roof all decked, nail a 2x4 or 2x6 all along the house wall snug under the decking, and nail the decking to it as well. Nail a similar piece to the outer edge of the decking, and join the two with short pieces nailed crosswise at 4-foot intervals. Do this from ladders or scaffolding, *not* by leaning over the edge. It is easier to describe than to do, but it can be done. At some point in construction, you will box in this structure with plywood applied underneath; this is a "soffit."

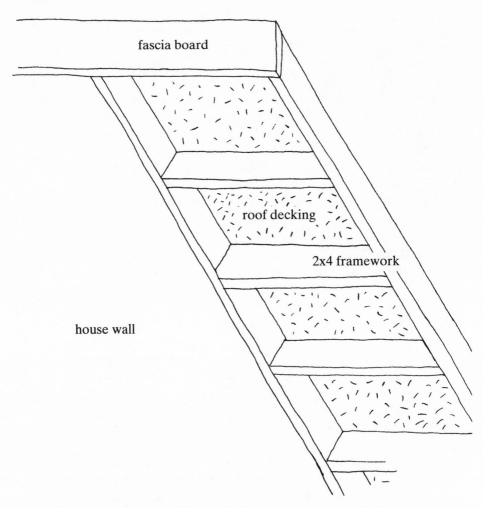

Fig. 33. *In this view of the underside of a side roof overhang support, a sort of "ladder" has been built of 2x4s, then nailed into place against the house wall, with the plywood roof decking nailed to it from above. The openings will be covered with a soffit.*

CAUTION: Obviously, if you do this, *no one* should *ever* step on the edge of the roof, although it would probably stand the weight. Of course, no one who is not a circus performer would stand up and walk within one foot of the roof's edge. If you have to work at or near the edge, do it lying on your stomach or on hands and knees.

If you start at the west end, when you reach the east end in the decking process, you will have to do some juggling and cutting to have the decking extend out over space the same amount. How the 4-by-8 sheets will come out depends on the length of the house. Don't patch with small pieces at the edge; any plywood sheet that extends out a foot should be at least 60 inches long. If you follow this procedure for overhangs, you should also use decking that is plywood, not wafer board, and is at least 1/2 inch thick; although 5/8 inch would be better.

FRAMING ROOF OPENINGS

Frame holes in the roof just as you did holes in the floor. There will probably be just one, for the chimney. Use a plumb line to get the hole exactly over the hole in the floor below. As soon as you deck, cover this hole very securely. It's even worse to fall through the roof than through the floor.

DECKING AND INTERMEDIATE BLOCKING

Once all the rafters are in place, or as you go along, nail the decking to the rafters. Stagger the sheets, and nail them with 10d nails about four inches apart. This time you'll definitely need blocking, to which you'll nail the sides of the 4-by-8 sheets; the blocking will also keep the rafters the right distance apart. They have a longer unsupported run than the joists and will be much too far apart or too close together at some places in the middle of the run. Use the pipe clamp as you did with the joists.

In this case, the blocking should not be 2x12 pieces inserted vertically; if you used that, there would be no free passage of air for ventilation under the roof. The blocking should be 14 1/2-inch lengths of 2x4 put in flat side up; this is easier and cheaper, and provides a wider surface to nail to. If you have odd hunks of 2x6 lying around, you can use those as well. As you will discover, blocking can only be nailed directly to the rafter at one end; at the other end it must be toenailed.

Begin decking at the lower edge of the roof and work up and across. Once you have the lowest course started, it is relatively easy to put the next sheet on and let gravity bring it down to where you want it. The more decking you get on, the more stable the roof becomes and the easier your task is.

> **TIP:** It's really easier to nail the blocking in as you go along with the decking rather than to scramble all over the open rafters, measuring, marking, and nailing.

Now it's done. You have a house. Not only that, you won't have to work high up on a shaky roof anymore. You still have to apply the wall sheathing, but you will probably add the roofing before doing that. If you have several different roofs, finish one completely first. Now, at last, you have a waterproof roof under which the radial arm saw can be stored or the crew can eat lunch on a rainy day.

Finish Roofing

You BEGAN BY FRAMING the rough floor, then the rough walls, and then the rough roof. Now you reverse the procedure, completely finishing the roof, then the walls. The finish floor will come last; you may even have been living in the house for some time when it is done.

The reason is obvious: The sooner you can get a waterproof top on the house, the better. After that, it's nice to have waterproof sides. A beautiful parquet floor, however, will not look so nice after the Sheetrockers have ground plaster dust into it, so you'll build that only after everything else is done.

PROBLEM AREAS

Roofing is not very difficult, *except* where two surfaces come together at an angle, at peaks (ridges) or valleys. Even peaks aren't much of a problem, but valleys are, which is why a shed roof, which has none, is easier to do. You can build a roof that doesn't leak a drop, even if it has several peaks and valleys.

Holes in the roof are also problems. If you have taken our advice, your roof should have only one hole: where the chimney comes through. You can wait until the stonemason is through to shingle the roof, but a better arrangement is to leave a foot or so unfinished around the chimney hole. He will incorporate "flashing," probably copper, into your shingling. Then he'll build a second layer of it, called "cap flashing," into the masonry. This will overlap the lower layer but not be fastened to it, because the chimney and the house may expand and contract in minutely different ways. If you hired a good stonemason, you won't have to worry about chimney flashing or leaks around the chimney.

If you have to cut holes in the roof for plumbing vents, buy rubber flashing, which fits very tightly around pipes and spreads out in a mat. You won't make those holes in the roof now, however, but much later. You may shed a tear or two when you cut through the plywood, tar paper, and shingle in your beautiful leakproof roof. You should have used those tears on the building inspector to persuade him to let those vents come out the side walls instead.

BASIC PRINCIPLES
The basic principle of constructing a roof that will shed rain has been the same since the first houses were built in Asia Minor thousands of years ago. Perhaps some ancient man looked at a duck's back and got the idea from that. All roofing, except for some high-tech materials only professionals use, is based on the simple principle of overlapping layers. The layers are made of the most waterproof material available: straw, baked clay tile, split wooden shingles, large flat sheets of metal, or modern asphalt shingles. Whatever the material, the job always begins at the bottom, and each successive row overlaps the one below it.

Most people consider various materials and wind up with asphalt shingles. They are easy to use, cheap, fairly good-looking, and most important, fireproof. You will probably start by thinking how lovely old-fashioned wood shingles would look. Then you'll price them, then find out how much harder they are to install, then learn about the increase in your insurance rates involved. At this point, asphalt shingles will have become extremely beautiful.

UNDERLAYMENT
An underlayment is necessary. It will probably be what everyone calls "tar paper," even though the manufacturer says it's "asphalt-impregnated felt building paper." The first item to go on, before the tar paper, is a long, narrow metal *dripedge,* or *drip strip,* which is nailed to the lower edge of the roof. It is applied with galvanized roofing nails according to the directions that came with it. Next comes the lowest course of tar paper.

NOTE: Where winter weather is alternately snowy and mild, ice buildup on the lower edge of roofs can be a major problem. The buildup forms a "dam," which can back up water under the shingles and cause leakage into the house. There are various solutions to this problem. One is to purchase a special and expensive thin, rubber flashing to go under the tar paper at the edge. Another, much cheaper, solution is to put down a double layer of tar paper as the first course, with the two layers glued together with roofing compound. We find this works perfectly.

Tar paper is applied to protect the roof decking until the shingles can be put on, to add another layer of protection from water, and to keep asphalt shingles from coming in contact with resinous places in the decking. It comes in three-foot rolls sold by weight. Fifteen-pound is common and is sufficient. It should not be confused with roll roofing, which is a cheaper form of asphalt shingling material in a roll weighing sixty-five pounds or more. This is satisfactory for sheds but will not last long enough to be used on a house. Good asphalt shingles are guaranteed for periods ranging up to fifty years.

Any roofing should be applied only when the surface beneath it is completely dry and the air temperature is not above 75 degrees nor below 50 degrees. If the sun shines directly on the roof, you may have to wait until a cloudy day.

After the drip strip is on, roll out a sufficient length of tar paper and cut it with tin snips or a linoleum knife. Leave about six inches extra on each end. Fasten it to the roof with heavy staples from a staple gun, every foot or so in all directions. It is irritating material to work with, since it tears and sags, especially in heat. Start stapling in the middle at the top and work toward both ends. This is a two-person job. As much as possible, try to avoid creasing or wrinkling the paper, although a few small wrinkles are inevitable.

Fortunately, this is a job that gets easier as you go along. After the first course is on, doubled if desired as described above, overlap the second course at least two inches and continue up the roof, keeping courses as straight as possible. The material has lines on it to help, but use a tape measure and snap an occasional chalk line. Straightness matters more when the shingles are applied, but it's harder to put shingles on straight if the tar paper is crooked.

Eventually you reach the top. If you have a shed roof, you don't need to do anything further; if it is a peaked roof, repeat the process on the other side, again starting at the bottom. When you reach the peak, bring the sheet over and staple it on top of the sheet on the other side, covering the peak. Be sure not to crease or crack it.

Sooner or later you come to the end of a roll. Start another, using a four- to six-inch overlap. Try to plan so you'll have as few of these as possible. It is probably better to throw away ten feet or so of material than to have an end overlap.

You haven't yet cut off the ends where they overhang the sides of the roof. Do it now, then nail drip strip on top of the tar paper on the roof sides. (At the bottom edge of the roof, the drip strip goes on first; at the sides, it goes over the tar paper and under the shingles.)

If one or both roof sides end in a valley or at a vertical house wall, use flashing. The lowest level of flashing, which is done now, is made of tar paper. For a valley, simply carry the end of the sheet across the valley onto the next roof. It will of course go up that roof at an angle. Then, before doing any shingling, tar paper the other roof, carrying the end through the valley and well onto the first roof at an angle. The whole idea is to present an unbroken surface to water at the bottom of the valley and well up the sides. Intersections of roofs and walls are even easier: Just carry the tar paper well up the wall. Don't worry about how it looks; it will all be covered by exterior siding.

APPLYING SHINGLES

Now you have a waterproof roof. If necessary, you can wait a few days before putting on the shingles, but if you wait too long, eventually a strong wind will tear the paper off and you'll have to do it all again. Applying asphalt shingles is easy; just follow the directions on the package. Getting the heavy bundles up on the roof is the hardest part. Professionals use some kind of machinery for this; you may want to improvise a block and tackle. Before you start the job, there should be bundles of shingles scattered about the roof so that there will always be some available when needed.

Asphalt shingles usually have three "tabs," so that when the roof is finished, it appears to be made up of individual small shingles, when in fact it is made up of units of three of these. To begin with, lay a course of shingles along the bottom of the roof facing the wrong way—that is, with the tabs up. Nail them in place with galvanized roofing nails that are just long enough to penetrate two layers of shingle, the tar paper, and the roof decking. You can rent a power stapler for this, but a hammer and nails work about as well.

Apply a second course directly over the first course, but with the tabs facing down, then keep moving up the roof. The third course overlaps the second just enough to reach the slots between tabs and cover the nails, which are put in about 1/2 inch directly above each slot. Each course also is staggered with regard to the course below so that the slots don't line up.

At the sides of the roof, shingles will have to be cut to fit. Large tinsnips or a utility knife will do this; either will get gummed up with asphalt and have to be cleaned from time to time. It may be necessary to cover nailheads with roofing cement where cut pieces of shingle are used, but in general you won't need quite as much as you may have feared to hold down the shingles themselves, because they are self-sticking: They have a built-in strip of tar, and after the first hot or sunny day, they will be well stuck down.

Roofing compound and roofing cement are black, tarry substances that are an important part of this job. These substances are used to glue layers together and to cover any exposed nailheads to make them completely waterproof. Compound is thinner and is usually applied with a cheap brush; cement is supposed to be applied with a trowel, but many roofers use any old stick, like a piece of wooden shingle, since the mate-

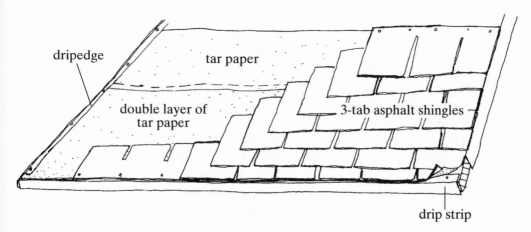

Fig. 34. *Roofing begins with the application of plastic or metal drip strip to the lowest edge of the roof. Over this is applied tar paper. Dripedge along the side of the roof goes over the tar paper. Finally, asphalt shingling is applied. The first row is upside down, as shown, and the second row is directly over this, so that there is always a layer of asphalt under the grooves in the shingles. Extra protection against leaking caused by an ice dam can be obtained by doubling the first layer of tar paper.*

rial is very difficult to clean off a trowel. Whatever cleanup can be done is done with gasoline, kerosene, or a similar substance.

Wear absolutely the oldest, rattiest clothes for roofing; when you are sure you'll never do any more roofing, burn them. Shingling is designed so that most nailheads are hidden. This keeps the use of the tar to a minimum, but you'll still get it all over you. If the day is not warm, the tar will need to be kept warm somewhere so that it will flow.

About halfway up the slope, start laying out courses by measuring down from the top rather than up from the bottom. The top and the bottom may not be perfectly parallel. If you are way off, don't correct the problem all in one course; adjust several courses, 1/4-inch at a time.

To make a double layer at the top of a shed roof, cut off individual tabs and apply them over the top half of the last course. It should be possible to plan ahead and adjust the courses so that you'll come out even. Nailheads will show here and have to be tarred.

If the roof has a peak, shingle up both sides to it. To cover the peak, cut the three-tab shingles in thirds. Apply these pieces over the ridge so that they lap the underlying shingles on both sides; make sure they also overlap each other about an inch. The nailheads will show here and will have to be covered with cement. The shingles must be warm enough that they will not crack when bent; don't crease them. At valleys, carry alternating courses of shingles (first from the section of roof on one side of the valley, then the other) well across the valleys and up the other side.

If part of your house is one-story and part two, at some point a roof intersects a vertical house wall. You have already flashed this with tar paper. Now add metal flashing, which can be bought in rolls of various widths at a building supply store. Aluminum is cheaper than copper and just as effective. Cut pieces half the width of a shingle. As each course of shingle reaches the wall, apply an aluminum "shingle" that is bent to reach well up the wall. The lower half of the asphalt shingle, the part that shows, goes over the aluminum "shingle," which in turn goes over the upper half of the shingle below. Eventually the aluminum that shows will be covered with the finish siding applied to the wall.

SAFETY PRECAUTIONS

You're working on a high roof. A fall could be crippling if not fatal. Don't take any chances, and don't ever get inured to the danger. Whether it's applying tar paper or shingles, the job gets easier and safer as it goes along. The first few courses are the most dangerous. You may do them from below, using ladders or scaffolding, or if the pitch is not

aluminum flashing
"shingles"

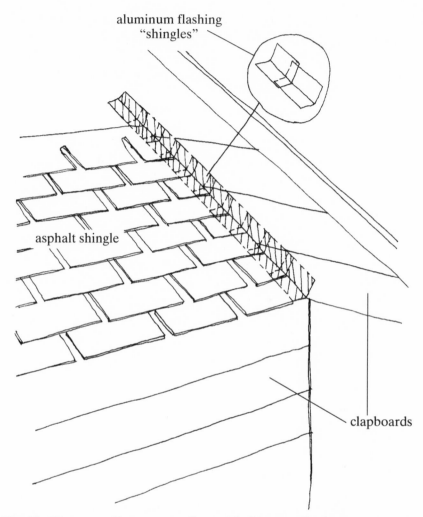

asphalt shingle

clapboards

Fig. 35. *Where a roof intersects a wall, metal flashing, usually aluminum, is used.*
"Shingles" of aluminum, half the width of the 3-tab asphalt shingles, are cut and
folded so that half the length of the aluminum goes up the wall. The other half goes
on the roof, over one shingle and under the next. When the job is finished, the wall
siding and the shingles cover the metal flashing.

steep, from above, lying on your stomach facing down. If the latter, don't
be too macho to use some kind of rope harness for security, but be sure
you know how to tie knots, or you may wind up strangling yourself.

Put all tools and materials not in use well above the work zone, and
keep moving them up. Fire anybody who leaves things around for some-

one to trip over or step on. It's not a good idea for one worker to lay out the shingles and another to nail them down. Stepping on a shingle you thought was nailed down can lead to a wild ride. Use a broom to sweep off loose crumbs from the shingles from time to time, but keep the broom well above when not in use.

When you have finished, you will have a totally leakproof roof, and you will have added several tons of weight to the load carried by the rafters. This weight, spread over the entire area of the roof, will be easily supported and will help to hold the roof down.

If you haven't already put rough sheathing on the exterior walls, read chapter 22 and do so now.

16

Windows and Exterior Doors

WINDOWS AND GLASS DOORS are the heating engine of a passive solar house; it is worth giving considerable thought and care to their design and installation. Your house will have two kinds of windows: a number of large areas of fixed glass, mostly on the south side, and a few openable windows, mostly on the east and west. It will have several doors—some glass, some opaque.

Windows and glass doors are large holes in the house. They let in sunlight, which is converted to heat energy, during the day, and let out heat at night. You want to maximize the first part and minimize the second. Passive solar construction does this primarily by placing almost all of the windows where they face the sun as much as possible. Techniques to cover the windows at night may also be employed, but they are secondary.

Various high-tech devices have been invented to make windows more efficient solar collectors. Presuming you have read this far, you know that this book is generally unenthusiastic about high technology in a dwelling. Too many things can go wrong. We heard about one high-tech house that had, as many do, wide sweeps of drapes, activated by an "electric eye," across huge windows. When the sun shone on the photo-electric cell, the drapes opened. When it was dark, they closed. One night, the lady of the house emerged from her bath and stood, stark naked, securely behind her drapes. Unfortunately, a passing driver chose this time to make a U-turn in the road in front of her house. As the head-lights swept across the electric eye . . . guess what.

Skylights, like fireplaces, are charming but impractical. You may want them anyway. They let more light (and therefore heat) into your house in summer and less in winter, which is just the opposite of what you want. They let much more energy out of your house at night than vertical windows, and it's usually not practical to crawl onto the roof every night to cover them.

THERMAL WINDOW MATERIALS

The standard thermal window used to be double glass with a vacuum between, sometimes referred to by the trade name Thermopane. Now triple panes are commonplace, and there are windows with inert gases, such as argon, between the panes. Generally speaking, having more panes lets out less heat but lets in less light, and the newer, fancier models are considerably more expensive than older versions.

If you are thinking of using extremely high-tech windows, be sure you understand what they can and cannot do. Don't just rely on the sales-man. At best, he may be not as well informed as you. At worst, his liveli-hood depends on selling the windows. Before you make a final decision, read chapters 24 and 26.

In most cases, the easiest and cheapest fixed glass to buy is the stan-dardized, factory-made material designed for glass doors. It comes in two sizes, roughly 4 by 6 and 3 by 6, and can be bought at glass specialty stores. You should get a substantial discount if you buy a large number (more than five) of these. In nonstandard sizes, such glass is vastly more expensive; a piece half the size may be twice the cost.

All thermal glass is extremely difficult to handle, being one of those annoying materials that combine considerable weight with great fragility. It will of course break if dropped, but it may also bend and destroy the vacuum seal if it is not supported equally at both ends, and for the larger pieces, in the middle as well.

This type of glass is usually guaranteed for five years. The guarantee is void if you install it out of plumb, for example in slanted windows in your sunspace. In any type of installation, pinholes can develop; these allow air to leak into the area between the two panes. This is likely to happen if the glass is not handled carefully, but it may happen in any case. If pinholes develop, condensation occurs within the window, which

will considerably lower its R-value, impede the passage of light somewhat, and make the window look slightly dirty all the time. After six
years, this happened to one of our twenty-four such windows; it is not yet
sufficiently troublesome that we have replaced it.

In spite of these drawbacks, there is nothing you can buy that is
more practical. With reasonable care, such windows will last many
years.

INSTALLING WINDOWS

The store where you buy the windows will give you small hard rubber
pads. These are used to support the windows while they are being stored
(as nearly upright as possible) and are placed under them as a permanent
part of their installation. This store will also sell you a rubberized caulk,
smelling strongly of ammonia, which is the best material for embedding
the windows and sealing any cracks.

Aside from the cautions above, putting in fixed windows is not very
difficult. As advised earlier, you've made the ROs 1/4 inch larger all
around than the windows. Decide whether it will be easier to install each
window from inside or outside the house. In most cases, it will be inside.
In either case the procedure is the same.

Nail a frame of 3/4-by-1/2-inch stock ("parting bead") around the RO
where you want the window to go. Sometimes, for a large window, 1-by-
2-inch stock is used. Insert the rubber "bumpers," and caulk all around
the opening. Put the bottom of the window in place, and tilt the top in.
You may have to slide the window around slightly, but it should fit if the
RO is large enough and the corners are all 90 degrees.

The walls of your house are thicker than normal. Put the window
closer to the outside, three-quarters or more of the distance. This is better for solar heating; it will also give you attractive, deep windowsills that
are handy places to display plants or gewgaws.

Cut off the excess rubber stop with a razor blade and save it for the
next window. Make sure there is enough caulk all around, then nail a
frame similar to the outside frame flush against the window.

> **TIP:** Glass does not respond well to a wimpy, tentative
> approach. Even large panes will stand a lot of hammer vibration
> and an occasional glancing blow. (If you're by nature aggressive,
> ignore this advice.) With large panes, light pressure on the cen-
> ter by the assistant's hand while the master does the hammering
> will reduce the effect of vibration.

Nail with finish nails, countersink, and putty the holes. Use galvanized nails indoors and out; there will be moisture on the glass indoors at times. At some point in the finishing process, make exterior sills that match the parting bead and slant slightly downward for water runoff. The rest of the interior and exterior finish can be done to your own taste. Sills must be wood, but side and top interior frames may be Sheetrock that is eventually painted or papered. Be sure to plan your final framing of fixed windows so that you can remove broken ones without tearing the whole house apart.

CONVENTIONAL WINDOWS

Compared to the above process, installing a conventional window is child's play. All you have to do is boost the window into the rough opening from the outside, shim it up so that it is level and plumb, fill all the cracks with odd bits of insulation, and nail it into place. It doesn't require lots of nails to hold it forever. Don't drive nails through anywhere that says, "Don't nail here," or where common sense tells you nails shouldn't go. Double-hung windows work with sash cord and pulleys, all of which are hidden inside the side members. If you drive a nail through there, the window won't open and shut.

Conventional windows are still built mostly for conventional walls. You can buy them with special extensions for thicker walls. Don't bother. Finish the inside approximately the same way you did with the fixed windows.

Windows may be double-hung (the ordinary slide-up-and-down kind), casements, awnings, or many other types. For the most part, double-hung are fine, but it's nice in summer to have at least one large awning window under the roof overhang, which can be open even during a pouring rain.

It's no fun to install large windows from ladders or scaffolding, but it can be done. Keep this in mind when designing the whole house. The roof of an attached greenhouse or sunroom on the south side can be a very handy place from which to install or clean windows or put on shutters.

DOORS

Exterior doors can be glass or conventional wood or steel. Most glass doors slide open, but some companies have come out with double glass doors, one panel of which swings open like a conventional door. These cost more and, in our opinion, aren't as good. One drawback is that guests will invariably grab the handle and nearly tear it off in their

awning window

sliding door

main entrance
patio door (swings open)

Fig. 36. *In this view of the south side of the passive solar house shown in figure 30, the glass doors are all standard 6-by-6 double-pane, wood-framed. Except for the awning window and the three 4-by-6 windows in the greenhouse, all windows shown are standard 3-by-6 double panes manufactured in quantity to be used in doors, and consequently relatively cheap. This house has four windows on the west side, one large one to the east, and no door or window to the north. The percentage of wall area devoted to glass is not greater than that in a conventional modern house. All windows on the east and west are openable, as is the awning window; the others are fixed.*

attempts to slide, rather than swing, the door open, and there are other, more serious drawbacks as well.

A door on the north side of the house should have no glass in it. On the east or west side, it is a toss-up. Doors on the south should be glass. There are drawbacks; glass doors don't keep out burglars much. But neither do windows. As a matter of fact, men doing time for burglary all agree that no door short of a very special one, regardless of bolts and deadlocks, will keep them out for more than fifteen seconds.

People can see in, as well as out of, glass doors and windows, which is why drapes are a good idea. Birds may fly into glass areas. Most of the time this will not break the glass, but if this is a problem in your area, you may want to put a masking tape pattern on the windows and doors during the "silly season" for grouse.

For non-glass doors, use wood, not steel. I know what the salesman says; I also have firsthand experience. A wooden exterior door is fairly similar to an interior door; read chapter 23.

Sliding glass doors, like all other construction units, come in a dizzying variety of makes, models, and prices. Do buy wood-framed ones; it is disconcerting to have a fuzz of frost on the inside door frame all winter. See chapter 7 about using metal-framed ones between house and sun-space.

Installing doors is much like installing preconstructed windows, except that they come knocked down and you have to put them together. Assemble all the right tools and a choice collection of swear words, read the directions several times, and follow them carefully, even when they sound ridiculous.

> **TIP:** When all else fails, in this and similar areas, don't reject entirely the possibility that they made a mistake at the factory, like drilling the hole in the wrong place. It happens more often than you would suppose, usually on a Monday. Unfortunately, lumberyards can't guarantee that items were made Tuesday through Thursday.

After the doors are assembled, install them exactly as you did the prefab windows: from the outside, shimmed, insulated, with your own desired trim (which can wait until much later) inside. One big difference: The toe plate must now be sawed out of the rough opening. You can't do this with a conventional power saw, because you won't be able to get the blade flush to the trimmer. A sabre saw or reciprocating saw will probably work, but it's not too tough a job by hand.

Now your house is, essentially, closed in. It looks and feels like a house and may even be a trifle warmer inside than out. That's good, because it's probably October by now.

> **OOPS! IMPORTANT TIP:** Certain things you might want inside the house, like some bathtubs, fancy all-in-one shower stalls, preconstructed saunas, hot tubs, and the like, won't come through the door. Get them in before you put the last door on. Not only that, get them in their approximate locations before you build the partitions. Fortunately, most ranges, refrigerators, and other appliances will come through standard exterior doors.

17

Roughing-in Wiring

WIRING AND PLUMBING are not too difficult for the amateur, but one circumstance could prevent your doing either yourself: Local building code may require that you hire a licensed electrician, plumber, or both. This is more common in the city than in the country, but if it is the rule where you want to build, you'll just have to grin and bear it. It is possible but unlikely that you can find a licensed plumber or electrician who will let you work as his assistant. Read chapters 17 through 20 in order to understand what the pros are doing, if you can't do it yourself.

Electrical work and plumbing are done in two parts: roughing-in before the Sheetrock or paneling, and finish wiring or plumbing later. Bringing water and electricity into the house to start with must be done very early, even before roughing-in.

HOW ELECTRICITY WORKS, SORT OF

Many books of this type explain how electricity works. This one does not, because a) the author doesn't understand how electricity works; b) you don't have to know how electricity works to wire your house; and c) nobody, not even a physicist, truly understands *why* electricity works, although a physicist can describe *how* it works. You can skip the next few paragraphs, but you might feel better if you know why to use a 200-amp service entrance (called in the trade a panel box) or a 20-amp circuit breaker.

Take as an example a 100-watt bulb. To make it light up, current has to flow to it and also away from it. Electricians say that current flows to it through a "hot" wire, usually black but sometimes red, and back to the source through a "cold" (neutral) wire, usually white. In earlier days, that was all you needed to know. Now all systems involve a third wire, a ground. In most cable this wire is bare, wrapped only in paper, but it can be green.

NOTE: "Cold" is only a term of convenience; either wire can, under optimum circumstances, kill you.

In earlier times the standard alternating current was 110 volts. Voltage went up gradually, until today the standard is about 125 volts. It doesn't make much difference to you, as long as you know that most items, like light bulbs or TVs, require standard voltage, but heavy appliances like ranges or water heaters take double that, 250 or thereabouts. As a matter of fact, the power coming into your house is not exactly 125 volts at all times, but only approximately that. In any case, two "125 volt" lines enter your house; you can use either one for a lighting circuit or combine them for the kitchen range.

NOTE: Certain appliances, like a computer, can be injured by a surge, or sudden change in voltage. Such items should be plugged into a surge suppressor.

You need to know how much amperage each circuit in your house will need and how much all of them together will require. Never mind those explanations of which is current flow and which is "pressure." Amperes (amps) equals watts divided by volts, which means that a 100-watt bulb takes less than 1 amp, since $100 \div 125 = 0.8$. Not much, is it? Most of your circuits will not need more than 10 amps, but you'll use 15-amp circuit breakers for lighting circuits and 20-amp for heavier-use circuits, like those in the kitchen. A water heater usually requires 30 amps and a range 50.

Radios, TVs, computers, and other similar items don't require much more power than light bulbs. Household items with heating units, like a 1000-watt toaster or a 1500-watt portable heater, require a lot. That's why if you're going to have electric heat as your backup, you may have to beef up the suggested maximums in this chapter. If a toaster draws 8 amps and a heater 12, if you added a light bulb, you'd need more than a

20-amp breaker, so you plan to have the two appliances on different circuits. Even if someone plugged the heater, the toaster, and something
else into the same circuit and turned them all on, all that would happen
is that the lights on that circuit would dim, the circuit breaker would kick
out, or both. (In earlier times, a fuse would have blown.)

If the average circuit in your house is 20 amps and you have twelve
such circuits, do you need a 240-amp service entrance? No, for the same
reason as in the last paragraph: You'll never have all twelve circuits fully
loaded and blazing away at the same time. Even the very conservative
underwriters suggest that you estimate only a 40 percent demand on
your circuits after the first 10,000 watts. Take our word for it: Unless you
are designing a mansion, a 200-amp service entrance will be big enough,
and you might as well install one; it won't cost all that much more than a
smaller one.

PLANNING THE WIRING

In the design stages, you should think about where you'll want which
kinds of electrical outlets. At some point, sketch out a rough wiring diagram. It doesn't have to be fancy, and it will change as you go along.
Much of it will be determined by the local electrical code. You may feel
that six "duplex receptacles" (double outlets that receive plugs) in the
living room are enough; the code may require one every eight feet, a certain distance above the floor. It may require at least one outlet in any
bathroom and that these outlets be "GFI" (ground fault interrupters, see
below). In most cases the inspector will be reasonable: If a wall has two
8-foot glass doors on each side of a 12-foot-wide chimney, he'll agree that
it can't have an outlet in the middle.

Your wiring diagram will be determined by the code plus common
sense. For example, it's better to have two circuits each serving half of
one bedroom and half of another than one circuit for each bedroom. It's
better not to have all the cellar lights on one circuit; that way, they won't
all go out at once. Don't forget anything: outdoor lights, outdoor outlets,
smoke alarms, duct fans, water softener if needed, all those things only
you know about. As in all other elements of house design, you will find
yourself driving your friends crazy studying their service entrances, lighting systems, and appliances.

You shouldn't plan to have more than seven or eight outlets on the
same circuit, even if all of them are lights. (Switches, which don't use any
electricity in and of themselves, don't count.) In kitchens, baths, laundries, workrooms, and other places where appliances will be in use, three
or four outlets to a circuit is plenty, and the outlets should be staggered—

that is, two adjoining outlets should not be on the same circuit. Any 250-volt item, like the kitchen range, water heater, or well pump, will have a circuit to itself. Some codes require that a refrigerator, although it takes only 125 volts, be on a circuit by itself.

Even with all these requirements, it is unlikely that you will wind up with more than fifteen or twenty circuits. A 200-amp service entrance has room for 40 circuits, so it's big enough, even though 250-volt appliances take up two slots.

The knottiest problem in planning wiring is the location of switches. You'll want switches for overhead or wall lights, and you may also want some switch-controlled duplex receptacles. You may have to think long and hard and study some friends' homes again before you're really sure whether you want the bathroom light switch inside or outside the door, or where you want the three-way switches at either entrance to the living room. Don't locate a switch behind an opened door unless you absolutely have to.

BRINGING THE POWER IN

Occasionally it is necessary to bring in a gasoline-powered generator, but most house sites have service from the power company from day one, for the convenience of the contractors as much as that of the owner-builder. You may have to have a temporary entrance—a panel box on a pole or tree, with a makeshift rain shield over it—but if you're fortunate, you can install your panel box in its permanent location and work from there. The inspector will probably permit the permanent installation, in the basement for example, from the beginning.

Bringing the power to the panel box is by far the most difficult part of wiring. You may want to hire a pro just for this part of the job, but it's not easy to find an electrician who is willing to do only this unpleasant part and leave the rest to you, so you'll probably have to do it yourself. There are so many variations in rules and power-company practices that what follows can only be a rough outline.

Usually, the power company will bring the power to the meter, which you have to wire, although it belongs to them. Nowadays meters are almost always outdoors, on a pole you own or on the side of your house. Cable coming out of the meter that a person could touch will be encased in PVC (polyvinyl chloride) pipe.

You can bring the power from a meter on a pole to your house overhead or underground. You'll have to erect at least one pole in any case, and more, of course, if you choose the overhead route. For several

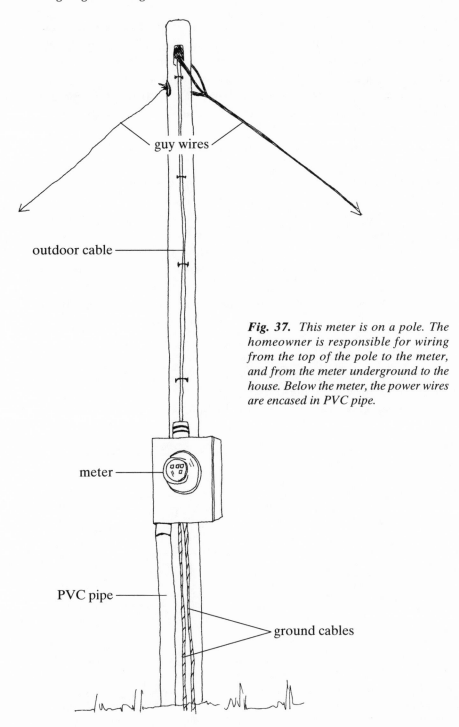

guy wires

outdoor cable

meter

PVC pipe

ground cables

Fig. 37. *This meter is on a pole. The homeowner is responsible for wiring from the top of the pole to the meter, and from the meter underground to the house. Below the meter, the power wires are encased in PVC pipe.*

reasons we recommend underground installation. If an underground line is installed properly, and if you keep large trees from growing over or near it, it should be totally trouble-free, and impervious to windstorm or blizzard. In addition, there won't be any overhead wires near your house for someone to touch with a ladder or a kite string. If the meter is on the house, try hard to persuade the company to bring the power to it underground.

Run wires underground in a trench lined with sand. After the cable is laid, throw more sand in, so that when the trench is backfilled, sharp rocks won't fall directly on the cable. Digging, backfilling, and erecting poles, if any, are done by the excavation contractor.

The wiring from the meter to the house will require special very heavy gauge (00 or 000) aluminum wire, as well as PVC pipe. The wiring job is the same as any other, described below, but the wire is so heavy that it is quite a bit more difficult to work with. The hardest part of the job is bending this wire and feeding it around the bends of the PVC pipe, but it can be done, especially if you coat the cable with a lubricant that is designed to make it slide more easily through the pipe.

> **NOTE:** A feature of wiring that drives amateurs crazy is that lower-gauge wire is thicker. Standard house wiring is 12-gauge; the wire on a lamp may be 16. Number 00 wire is very thick indeed; it takes a strong person to bend it.

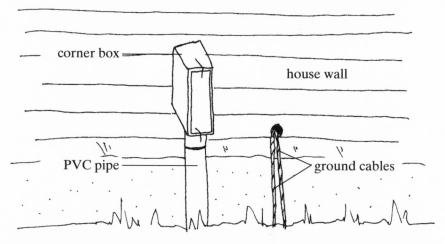

Fig. 38. *Here the power emerges from underground and enters the house. The cable is completely encased in PVC pipe. The PVC corner box at the top of the pipe is necessary only because it makes it easier to bend the heavy cable around a corner.*

There will be plenty of instruction sheets and wiring diagrams furnished by the power company and with each piece of equipment you buy, but in general, the cable leaves the meter inside PVC pipe and is carried to the top of the pole or underground. If the latter, make a large "frost loop" in the wire at each end of the trench to allow for expansion and contraction. In either case, drive grounding rods into the earth at the pole end and the house end; attach heavy copper grounding cable to them and to the appropriate connection inside the meter and the panel box.

The contractor will have left hundreds of steel fastening loops sticking out of the basement wall. Any that are in the way can be twisted and broken off; the others are great for hanging things on. Screw the panel box to a piece of plywood and hang the plywood on some of these loops, near the corner closest to the meter.

Connect the wires to the terminals inside the meter and panel box. It takes skill, strength, and the right tools to strip the ends of the wires, push them into the right slots, and tighten the connections. The two hot wires go into two slots in a device like a double circuit breaker, and the single cold wire goes to the ground bar to one side. One clue is that when the job is done, no part of the hot-wire connection can be touched, but the ground bar is out in the open. Three-wire cable in heavy gauges is clearly marked: One of the three, which is the cold wire, will be striped or otherwise differentiated. It doesn't matter which hot wire is which. The wire ends and the connections should be smeared with a special antioxidant grease.

NOTE: About forty years ago, aluminum wiring was all the rage. As it started to age and houses began burning down, it became less popular. Aluminum-to-copper connections can eventually cause a problem, which is why the above is the only place in your wiring that aluminum will be used. It is approved and safe for this use, especially if the antioxidant compound is used as indicated. If the 000-gauge wire were solid copper rather than made of small aluminum wires twisted together, you wouldn't be able to lift it or bend it. Or afford it.

To begin with, install one or two 20-amp circuit breakers as described in chapter 18 and connect temporary outlet boxes to them. Extension cords for saws and drills will be plugged into these. Leave the cover off the panel box and call the inspector. When he has approved your work, he will tell the power company, they will turn on the juice, and you'll have power.

ELECTRIC BOXES

Roughing-in is done after all the framing, including interior partitions, is done and the fiberglass insulation is put in exterior walls, but before Sheetrock or other paneling is applied. The first step in roughing-in is to fasten a "box" everywhere there will be any kind of switch, fixture, or electric outlet.

Most boxes are rectangular or octagonal. Some electricians call the rectangular ones "square," while some books call the octagonal ones "square." As if that weren't bad enough, there are truly square boxes as well. There are also double rectangular boxes, for putting two switches or a switch and a duplex side by side. Switches or duplex receptacles usually go in rectangular boxes, lighting fixtures in octagonal ones. For each octagon you use, you will probably use twenty rectangles. Purchase your fixtures or at least get a good look at them in the store before roughing-in.

Most electricians today use plastic rather than steel boxes. They are cheaper, probably safer, and easier to use, but they have one annoying characteristic: They come with two nails already inserted in them for driving into studs. If there is a knot in the wood where you want to put the box, you have a problem. If the nail bends, you'll probably have to throw away the box.

To add to your woes, all the boxes should be the same distance from the floor. Switch boxes are usually forty-eight inches high from where you think the finish floor will be, duplex outlets twenty-four inches, and counter outlets a few inches above the predicted countertop. (If you make counters extra high, don't put outlets at the conventionally recommended height or they'll wind up *under* the counter!)

Does that sound like enough trouble? You haven't heard the worst part. Electrical boxes are among those charming features of construction that have to be applied to conform to where you predict something else will come later. If you are going to apply 1/2-inch Sheetrock to the wall, the box should protrude 1/2 inch beyond the stud, or a bit more, since there may be a tiny gap between the Sheetrock and the stud. Bear in mind that it's easier to conceal the irregularity of a box that is a tiny bit too far in than one that sticks out too far.

Are you ready to send for the electrician? Don't. It's not that hard. In our house, out of well over one hundred electrical boxes, only one protrudes noticeably too far from the wall. It's in the kitchen, and apparently no one but us has ever noticed it. No part of our electrical work has ever caused any short circuit or other problem.

TYPES OF CABLE

The wiring you install will probably be "12-2 Romex with ground." This is cable with a heavy plastic outer coating, containing three (not two) 12-gauge wires—one with a black rubber coating, a similar white one, and a bare ground wire loosely wrapped in paper. Romex is one of those trade names everyone uses. If your code permits you to use 14-gauge wire, use 12-gauge anyway. For a few cents more, you'll buy a lot of peace of mind.

In some rooms, for example a laundry room, you may have to use very similar cable specially made for a damp environment. If you start with this, you have to carry it all the way to the panel box; you can't splice it to ordinary cable after it is well away from the damp area, unless you use a "junction box" (see below). A few codes still require BX (another trade name) cable, which is that metal-armored stuff, looking like an armadillo, that you see in the basements of old houses. Hope that yours doesn't.

> **NOTE:** Some old-timers refer to the Romex described above as "three-wire." While this seems logical, this term also refers to true three-wire, which has a black wire and a red wire, both hot, a neutral white wire, and a ground, and is used for 250-volt applications like your range. Don't worry about it; throw yourself upon the mercy of the guys at the electrical supply store. Unless they're unusually cold-hearted, they'll not only make sure you get the right stuff but also tell you how to perform the procedure.

ROUGH WIRING

Now you're ready for the actual wiring. Start at the last box (farthest from the service entrance) on a given circuit, and run cable from that through all the subsequent boxes to the panel. The route may be circuitous, but this is the easiest part of the job. When you get to the next box, cut the cable, leaving plenty of extra on both ends. Cable cuts best with a hacksaw or large, sturdy tin snips.

Few things are more annoying than having cut your wire too short. Buy a lot more cable than you think you'll need, and cut it plenty long. It comes in coils and in at least two colors. Try to get some of each; it will help you tell one circuit from another. If you have a whole coil left over, the store will probably take it back. It is infuriatingly determined to twist and tangle. Try not to uncoil more at a time than you need, and try to get it all straight and flat before you snake it around and staple it down.

Cable goes into boxes through "knockouts," potential holes covered by thin material (plastic or metal) already partially cut through. You knock out the ones you want with a hammer and screwdriver, sometimes assisted by pliers. Some knock out easily, others don't. If you know in advance where you want the holes, you can knock them out before you nail the box to the stud, but you don't always know this.

Cable is run through holes drilled in studs where necessary, or through the floor to the basement, which is preferable. In double-wall construction, wiring can very easily be run between the two walls. Don't be afraid to drill studs, but it's better to make holes in them (and especially in joists) near either end rather than in the unsupported middle.

Cable is fastened fairly tightly to wood with staples designed for this purpose. Code may require a staple every 18 inches or so; it usually requires a staple quite close to the box, which is irritating, because it gives you less slack to play with later. Inspectors don't like loose festoons of wire. Be careful; driving a staple *through* the cable is one of the few really dangerous ways you can screw up the job.

Switches require special wiring, using a different kind of cable. Read chapter 18 before roughing-in switch wiring.

When you finish roughing-in the first circuit, you'll have six or eight boxes, each (except the first) with two cable ends drooping out of it. The pro can save a few inches of cable here, but you can't. The pro will also, at this point, strip the wires in preparation for the finish job, but you should wait (if the inspector permits) until you've acquired some skill in estimating how much wire to leave and how much to strip. It's a good idea, at this point, to try finish-wiring at least one duplex and one switch, so you'll get a feeling for what's involved. As long as the cover plate is left off, the Sheetrockers can apply their panels over a couple of these, although they'll grumble about it.

In most cases, the last run of cable—to the panel box—will be much longer than runs between boxes. *Don't* run the cable into the box at this point; leave it hanging outside. *Immediately* attach a tag securely to this end of the cable describing in detail what items are on this circuit.

Soon, you'll have an octopus, in fact, several octopi, of cables approaching the panel box. It is necessary to *plan ahead* to have room for all of them to be stapled to the approach route and onto the plywood panel holding the box. Some will enter from the right, some from the left, but they can't all approach the service entrance along the same cellar beam; vary the route.

TESTING WIRING

Test the rough wiring now, and the finish wiring later, with an inexpensive doorbell or buzzer and the dry cell to operate it, both from the hardware store. You can probably figure out how to use it: One person at the outlet end of the cable hooks the black wire to one contact on the bell and the white to the other; his confederate, at the panel box, hooks the battery up similarly. If the bell goes off, bingo! Test the ground wire similarly, with either of the other two.

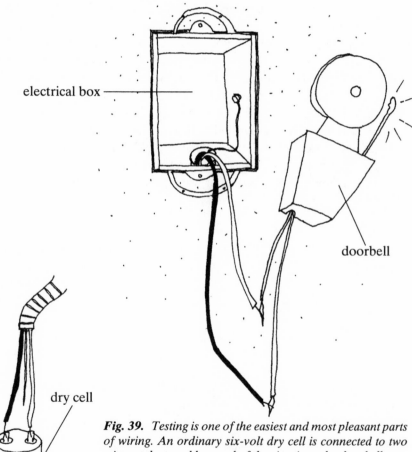

electrical box

doorbell

dry cell

Fig. 39. *Testing is one of the easiest and most pleasant parts of wiring. An ordinary six-volt dry cell is connected to two wires at the panel box end of the circuit, and a doorbell connected to the same two wires at the box. If the bell rings, the wiring is correct. To check for short circuits, the electrician would connect the bell to the white or black wire and to the ground wire, in which case the bell should remain silent.*

Also test for short circuits by hooking the bell up wrong. For example, connect the battery to the black wire and the white wire at the panel box end. At the other end of the circuit, connect the bell to the white wire and the ground. If the bell rings, the black wire and the ground are making electrical contact at some point. Try all the possible combinations; it is safer and more pleasant to find out the bad news now rather than when you throw the main switch on later.

JUNCTION BOXES

For safety reasons, there can never be a bare wire or splicing outside of a box. Instead of simply going from box to box to box, however, you can bring wires from two or three boxes together at a "junction box." Since junction boxes can't be covered by paneling, they can only be in a basement, crawl space, or similar area. It's a good idea to incorporate a few junction boxes into your plan even if you don't particularly need them. They have a metal cover, fastened with screws, that comes off easily later on, and more room inside than other boxes. That makes it a lot easier to add that one more fixture, later on, that you didn't anticipate needing.

Usually, 250-volt appliances are roughed-in and finished all in one operation. Hooking up the range or water heater is described in the next chapter.

Finish Wiring

MOST OF THE FINISH WIRING will be done later, after the Sheetrockers have departed, but let's discuss it now. Whether Sheetrock or some other paneling is used, the installers will have cut holes in it in exactly the right places (theoretically) to fit over all the electric boxes. You are now faced with a blank wall holding an occasional box, from which wires dangle. You can't see the cables behind the walls, but you know they're all right because you put them in and tested them.

Your first few attempts may be sloppy; start in the basement where they won't show. Eventually you will acquire the necessary skill, which involves twisting wires and fastening them in a very small space. It helps to have small fingers.

Many people seem to think that they are likely to electrocute themselves if they do their own wiring. This could only happen to you if you were dumb enough to start wiring at the panel box end, instead of leaving that until last, and work with the main switch in the "on" position. A master electrician is more likely to get a shock than you, because he hasn't your healthy fear of it. Wiring can't hurt you, *as long as the main switch is definitely in the "off" position.*

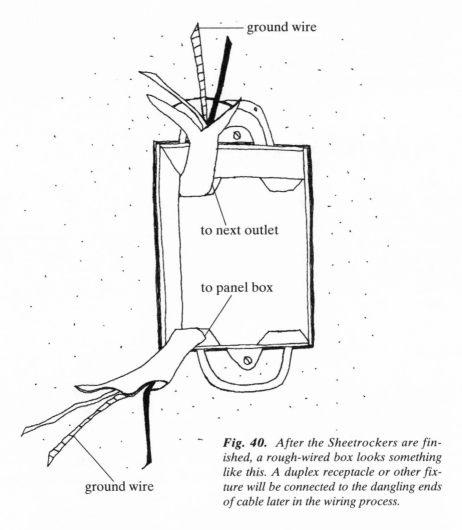

Fig. 40. *After the Sheetrockers are finished, a rough-wired box looks something like this. A duplex receptacle or other fixture will be connected to the dangling ends of cable later in the wiring process.*

DUPLEX RECEPTACLES

Start at the box farthest away from the panel. Mostly you'll be installing duplexes; other items are similar. At the end box, only one cable end is hanging out, rather than two. Cut it off as short as you dare, knowing what's ahead of you. Slice through about four inches of the outer covering and remove it, then strip each wire an inch or less (the ground will pretty much strip itself). Nothing seems to work as well as a jackknife for some of the cutting and stripping, although an electrician's wire stripper, which can be adjusted to any wire gauge, is also good.

Connect the wires to the appropriate terminals on the duplex receptacle. (Duplex outlets, which have three holes, should go right side up, so they look like a little face with two eyes and a mouth.) Always connect black wires to gold (brass) screws, white to silver (chrome), and bare ground wires to green (except for three-way switches). A useful mnemonic device for remembering which wire goes to which screw is the term "black gold." Figure out which way the screw is going to turn, and bend the wire in a small loop in that direction with a pair of electrician's long-nose pliers. When you've made all the connections, you should have no bare wire (except ground wire) showing; you should have stripped just enough. That's the ideal.

Now push the receptacle firmly into the box, forcing the wires to give and bend a little. When it is in the right position, screw it to the box, using the top and bottom screws between the places that look like Mickey Mouse ears. Don't put the cover plate on yet; the inspector will want to check your work. (You might be able to get away with covering all but a dozen examples, which of course will be your most successful attempts.)

The beginner often nervously leaves too much wire hanging out, which makes it hard to push it all into the box. You'll soon acquire the knack of cutting it just short enough, bearing in mind that if you really cut it too short, there is almost no way to solve the problem.

Now go to the next box on this circuit. Using the bell and dry cell, test what you have just done. Connect an old plug to the bell, push it into the duplex, and connect the battery to the appropriate wires at the other end. Then install the second duplex. Now there are six wires, instead of three, which makes the task twice as hard, especially since the duplex has two gold screws, two silver, but only one green. With practice you can get two wires on one screw, but if all else fails, get one ground wire on the screw and the other twisted around the first.

> **TIP:** The screws will back out just so far, then you meet with resistance. Never back them out farther than that, or you'll wish fervently that you hadn't.

Some duplexes, switches, and the like have a quick-connect device in addition to the screw. Pros sneer at them; you'll love them. Strip about 3/4 inch of wire and push it into the appropriate hole as far as it will go. That's it. If you have followed the strip gauge on the item, there will be an excellent connection and no wire showing. Sometimes it is easier to make the wires bend and fit into the box if you connect one wire to the screw and put the other in the quick-connect device. One drawback: Although there is theoretically a way to get the wire back out of the hole again if you've made a mistake, it's very difficult to do.

Continue in this fashion from box to box, testing as you go. You can wire one whole room before leaving, dealing with two circuits, as long as you remember what connects to what.

LIGHTING FIXTURES

Lighting fixtures and similar devices are child's play compared with duplexes and switches. Follow the directions on the package. Usually lamps have two wires hanging out the back, which may need to be trimmed back. Here you'll learn splicing. Put the black wire together with one of the wires from the light and twist a "wire nut" (solderless connector) of the appropriate size down over both of them. Do the same with the white wire and the other lamp wire; with lights, it doesn't matter which wire is connected to which. The chief difficulty may be the small gauge of the fixture wire compared to the supply wire.

When the connection is tight, wind black electrician's tape thoroughly and securely around nut and wire. It is unlikely that code will require you to solder these connections, but if it does, that's not difficult either. Connect the ground wire as the directions suggest. If there is no suggestion, use your own judgment, remembering that ground wires should be in contact with metal but of course not with black or white wires.

Old-fashioned cheap ceramic (now often plastic) bare lights such as are used in basements are the devil to wire. These are the ones that may or may not have pull chains and/or an incorporated side outlet. The cheaper and older kind have two screws, and it is sometimes well-nigh impossible to get two 12-gauge wires on each screw. Get the newer, more expensive kind that have wires hanging out the back.

SWITCHES

It is possible to figure out logically how switches work, even three-way switches. It is also possible just to follow directions to the letter without worrying about why. Regular (two-way) switches aren't too difficult. They're the ones that say "off" and "on." They are connected only to one wire, the black one, and have only gold screws (and maybe a green one). This means that when the switch is all connected up, two white wires are left over. Splice them with a wire nut. If there is no green screw, splice the two ground wires similarly.

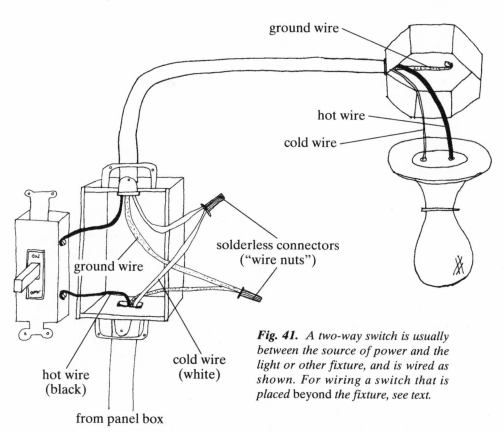

ground wire

hot wire

cold wire

solderless connectors
("wire nuts")

ground wire

cold wire
(white)

hot wire
(black)

from panel box

Fig. 41. *A two-way switch is usually between the source of power and the light or other fixture, and is wired as shown. For wiring a switch that is placed* beyond *the fixture, see text.*

A switch normally comes between the source of power and the light or lights or other items it operates. If it is necessary to put a switch beyond the fixture—that is, with the light between the switch and the panel box—the light is connected to the white wire from the source and the black wire from the switch. The black wire from the source is spliced to the white wire from the switch. At the switch, one white wire and one black wire are connected to two gold screws. Since in any other case splicing a white wire to a black wire is a no-no, electricians sometimes cover the end of the white wire with an inch or two of black tape.

You may want to use fancier switches. Mercury switches are silent and last much longer. There are also dimmer switches, which use a rheostat; "tap" switches, which respond to a touch; and of course, "clap-on-and-off" switches. All of these are as easy to install as regular switches; follow the instructions that come with them.

Now we come to the dreaded three-way switches, the kind that are located at the top and bottom of a flight of stairs. These don't say "on" and "off," because either position can be "on." After you learn how to wire them, you may be able to figure out the logic of it. The cable that runs between the two switches and the fixture is true three-wire: It has a red wire, a black wire, a white wire, and a ground. Each of the two switches has three screws: two brass ones on one side, and one, sometimes colored black, on the other. The red wire is attached to the single screw, which is called the common terminal. Stores that sell three-way switches will give you a set of instructions, which you can compare with the following.

Let's call one the upstairs and one the downstairs switch; it makes no difference which is which. The red wire connects the two common terminals. The black wire connects the two lower terminals, the ones opposite the common terminal. From the upper terminal of the upstairs switch, a wire leads to the power source; from the upper terminal of the downstairs switch, a wire leads to the light or other fixture. One wire from the power source leads directly to the fixture. As a practical matter, wires usually lead from one switch to the other through a splice at the fixture, but the principle is the same. Finally, there are three ground wires to splice together or hook to a screw at the light, but it actually can be done.

Nothing in wiring is as confusing as directions for a three-way switch. You may find some that disagree with those above, but if you study them closely, you will probably find that the disagreement is largely over the color of wires; electricians have a built-in aversion to connecting a white wire to a gold screw. Most of the time this is a healthy prejudice. You will note that the description above deliberately fails to specify the color of certain wires. Once again, the electricity doesn't know which color wire it is passing through, but if it makes you feel better, you can make a white wire "black" by putting a piece of black tape at its end.

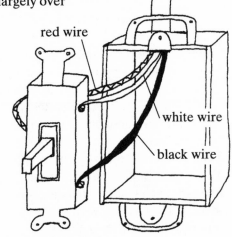

red wire

white wire

black wire

downstairs switch

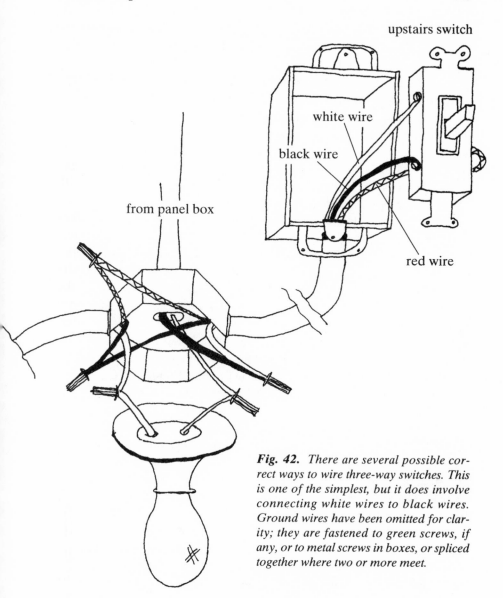

upstairs switch

white wire

black wire

from panel box

red wire

Fig. 42. *There are several possible correct ways to wire three-way switches. This is one of the simplest, but it does involve connecting white wires to black wires. Ground wires have been omitted for clarity; they are fastened to green screws, if any, or to metal screws in boxes, or spliced together where two or more meet.*

JUNCTION BOXES AND PANEL BOX

You now have the knowledge and skill to wire in a junction box. Since there is no fixture, all identical wires—for example, all black ones—are spliced together. Ground wires can be spliced together or fastened to the box, if it is metal. Remember that all ground wires eventually go to ground where you drove that rod into the earth outside your house. It doesn't matter if they touch metal; in fact, they should wherever possible. It is the other two wires, particularly the black one, that should never touch anything except the appropriate contact.

Now you can wire the circuits into the panel box. Throw the main switch off. (Use a flashlight if there is not enough natural light.) Take the cover completely off the panel box. Start at the bottom. Each cable goes through a knockout hole into the box and is fastened there with a cable clamp, with a couple of feet of cable left over inside the box. Peel back quite a lot of the outer cable covering. Cut the black wire to the appropriate length, strip it about 3/4 inch, and fasten it to the screw in a circuit breaker, 20-amp for small appliances, 15-amp for lights.

Run the white wire and the ground wire around the top or bottom of the panel, cut them to the appropriate length, and fasten them to the ground bar to one side of the panel, where the main ground and the cold wire from the power source are fastened. Knock out the bottom metal rectangle of the panel box and install the circuit breaker. It pivots into position and snaps down over the contact. Label the circuit immediately and permanently.

Continue as above with each circuit. When you have finished, put the panel box cover on and throw the main switch. If any circuit breaker pops open, close it. If it instantly pops again, that circuit is defective and you'll have to find the trouble and fix it, but that is most unlikely if you've tested each circuit as you wired it.

You could do the job one section at a time, but it's better to do it all at once. For one thing, if you made a mistake at the panel box, you might later be working on a live wire. Furthermore, it's not a good idea to take the panel box cover off and put it on too many times, because the threads on the screws that hold it may strip. It's a much worse idea to leave the cover off when the main switch is on.

Does it trouble you that, in the end, all the white wires and the ground wires go to the same place? It troubled me, too. Every expert I have talked to has assured me that this is the correct procedure, but none has been able to explain it in terms I can totally understand. GFI circuits are a minor exception to this.

GROUND FAULT INTERRUPTER (GFI) CIRCUITS

The electrical code in most areas requires GFI outlets in certain places, such as in bathrooms, in garages, and near kitchen sinks. All you need to know about them is that they provide an extra measure of protection in places that are more likely to become damp. They also cost more and are slightly harder to wire.

There are two ways to achieve this protection: with a GFI duplex outlet or with a GFI circuit breaker. We strongly recommend the latter; it is easier to wire, works better, and costs about the same. The usual disadvantage cited is that the entire circuit will go out if water gets in the bathroom outlet. That seems a small price to pay, especially since, in seven years, this has not happened to us once. On the other hand, we had to rip out and replace the GFI outlet in the garage because it malfunctioned and could not be made to operate correctly.

The only difference between wiring in an ordinary circuit breaker and a GFI circuit breaker is that with the GFI, the white wire from the cable is connected to the breaker, and another white wire leads from the breaker to the ground bar. Whether the GFI device is a breaker or an outlet, it has a button marked "test," which you are supposed to push once a month, and a chart you are supposed to put up beside it and mark monthly. Although the inspector will never come back to your house after it is completed, there is no recorded instance of a householder who has failed to do this.

WIRING 250-VOLT APPLIANCES

Surprisingly, connecting up a 250-volt appliance such as a range or water heater is generally easier than doing 125-volt wiring. Each item is different, but this description of wiring a range will suffice. Since each appliance has a circuit all to itself, the cable is simply connected to the range, usually underneath, in the back, according to clear directions that come with the appliance. The cable is then led to the panel box. Since it is a heavier-gauge wire, as recommended by the range manufacturer, it is a little harder to bend and staple, and you'll use one of the larger knockouts near the top of the box.

There are two hot wires in this cable: a red and a black. The 50-amp circuit breaker looks and functions like two ordinary circuit breakers fused together. You connect the red wire to one terminal, the black to the other, lead the white and ground wires to the ground bar, pivot the breaker and snap it into position over two adjoining contacts. In effect, you get 250 volts by adding 125 and 125.

SERVICE DISCONNECTS

You may not need service disconnects, but there's nothing much to wiring them. As explained to me, the electrical code states, "If a person can't see the panel box from a position in front of an appliance such as a water heater, a service disconnect must be installed immediately over that item."

A service disconnect is a miniature panel box for just that one appliance. It is placed as close to the appliance as possible, the theory being that if the item begins to malfunction, you can throw the cutoff switch instantly without wasting time looking for the panel box. Like most parts of the code, the theory doesn't say what happens if you are visiting Bermuda when a malfunction occurs that doesn't cause the circuit breaker to open. It's usually easier just to do it, however, than to argue with the inspector.

The hot, cold, and ground wires entering the service disconnect are wired up appropriately, as are the similar wires leaving it, and a circuit breaker of the correct size is inserted. There are now two breakers in this circuit, one at the disconnect and one at the panel box.

TELEPHONE WIRING

If you can electrify your own house, you also can save money by installing your own telephones. The procedure is exactly parallel to that above, with roughing-in and finish wiring, but much easier and more casual, partly because the electric current in a phone line is minuscule. In most places, the telephone company is responsible for bringing the wire to a point inside your house; from there on it's up to you. You can get all the equipment and advice you need in an electronics supply store.

Your house is now totally wired. The inspector made sure the job was done safely. In the unlikely event that anything ever goes wrong, you will know how to fix it.

19

Roughing-in Plumbing

WIRING AND PLUMBING are similar. Each is done in two steps: roughing-in and finish work. Each involves a circuit of sorts. In each case, the supply originates outside and the first step is to get it to the house, from the power company or from a well or municipal water supply. Finally, wiring and plumbing are "cookbook" skills that are easily mastered, although most Americans believe otherwise.

The two ends of the plumbing circuit are the well or a municipal water source and the septic tank or municipal sewage main. If you have access to city water and sewerage, all that is necessary is to make the hookups, but you probably won't be able to handle these yourself. The city may require you to hire a plumber from its recommended list to do this; it's a good idea in any case. The water comes in and the sewage goes out through breaches in the concrete wall of the basement. The plumber should coordinate with the foundation contractor, who will embed the pipes in the correct places and dig the necessary ditches.

SEPTIC TANKS AND DRY WELLS

If, like most, your passive solar house is in the country, you will have to hire a well driller, as well as someone to put in the septic tank and leach field. (The leach or drain field consists of many feet of branching perforated pipes that allow the liquid effluent of the septic tank to sink harmlessly into the ground.) In most cases, the septic system is installed by the foundation contractor, who will see that the tank and leach field are in the right place at the right depth and that the necessary connection is in place through the basement wall. Your blueprints will suggest the best place for this, in keeping with the placement of baths and kitchens in the house, as well as with code requirements. The tank usually must be two hundred feet or more from the well, preferably downhill. This generally will place the tank a short distance in front of the house and the well a long distance behind it.

You should understand how a septic tank works. Human waste and various other unpleasant materials, like hair and dirt from showers and sinks, mixed with a vast quantity of water, flow through pipes into a large tank. Here bacteria go to work, breaking them down and "digesting" them until, at least in theory, most of what remains is liquid. This liquid passes out of the pipe at the other end of the tank and into the leach field. A series of baffles prevents solid material from reaching this exit pipe.

In the digestion process, sewer gas is given off. This gas, primarily methane, is both smelly and combustible. If your plumbing vent smells awful, the system is working perfectly.

In practice, as opposed to theory, any number of things can prevent the bacteria from functioning perfectly. Detergents, cleaning compounds, drain cleaners, or other chemicals can kill bacteria. If necessary, you can buy a bottle of sewage bacteria in liquid at a plumbing supply store and pour it down the drain. If you spill it, you'll wish you hadn't.

It is sometimes necessary to have the tank pumped out. This is an expensive and messy operation, but it's best to plan for it by making sure that it will be possible for a large truck to reach the tank. How often your tank has to be pumped out depends on how well you treat it. I know of one that was installed twenty-five years ago and has not yet been pumped out, and of others that are pumped out regularly every two or three years. It depends on how many people live in the house, how big the tank is, and what bacteria killers in what quantity go down the drain. The first item is probably out of your control; the second and third aren't.

NOTE: If you think you have to have a garbage disposal unit built into the kitchen sink, so be it. You'll pay for it many times over in bills for pumping out the septic tank and/or dry well. Of course, if you're hooked up to city sewerage, it becomes the city's problem, which you pay for in increased taxes. A sewage treatment system, whether it's your septic tank or the Indianapolis municipal plant, would have far fewer problems if nobody ever put anything down the drain except what's supposed to go there. The place for garbage is the compost heap.

The best and easiest way to keep detergents and similar materials out of the septic tank is to have only toilets empty into it. If this is not practical, it is often possible to have only drains from bathrooms empty into the septic tank and to have greywater empty into an old-fashioned cesspool or dry well. Many codes allow this, although, curiously, local plumbers and builders often think it is forbidden. You may even have to argue a bit, but there is no good health reason against this arrangement. It's a good deal healthier than constantly digging up septic tanks.

If a dry well is permitted, you can have the contractor install a concrete one or have him dig the hole and do the rest yourself. Here's one way to proceed:

Locate the hole as far away from the well as possible and near the kitchen and laundry. Have the contractor embed the appropriate pipe in the appropriate place in the basement wall and dig a ditch for a 3-inch pipe from there to the hole.

Obtain an empty 55-gallon drum, preferably plastic. Make about a thousand holes in it with a 1/4-inch drill or large nail or punch. Line the bottom of the pit with rocks, first fairly large ones (perhaps three to six inches in diameter), then heavy gravel. Then put the drum into the hole, upside down, with the top (now the bottom) totally open. Fill the large space around the drum with more rocks and gravel, right up to the top (formerly the bottom) of the drum. Cut a hole in this new top and fit a drain pipe into it, with a 90-degree elbow at the start. The fit should be tight enough to keep dirt from getting into the drum, but it need not be watertight. Make the necessary connections back to the pipe the contractor embedded in the basement wall.

To allow for overflow, which may never occur, cut another hole, near the top, in the side of the drum opposite the house. Run a piece of perforated drain pipe from there, in a trench lined with gravel. Extend it twenty feet or more. Cover everything with more gravel and rocks, then with earth. In the future, be sure that heavy vehicles never pass directly over the dry well. Some kind of reinforcement, like a large steel plate, is good insurance.

Unlike supply pipes, which are always full of water, drain pipes don't necessarily have to be below the frost line. In fact, most codes require that a septic tank be only a foot or so below ground. The depth of the dry well will be determined by two factors. The first is whether you plan to have the laundry or similar facility in the basement, in which case the pipe must exit the basement fairly low in the wall, and the second is the length of the run of pipe. The standard practice is to slope "horizontal" drain pipe at least 1/4 inch per foot.

NOTE: Many people find it convenient to have a toilet or "half bath" in the basement, which makes a backup from a city sewerage connection into the basement a possibility. With a septic tank this won't happen, but it's hard to have a toilet in the basement that drains downhill into a septic tank. There is a device on the market that will pump waste from a basement toilet up to the height of the normal drain pipe; you can decide if the cost of installation and maintenance is worth it to you.

SOURCES OF WATER

Unless you have city water or a really good spring, stream, or pond, you'll have to hire a professional well driller. Drilled wells are often called artesian, although technically they are usually not. Shop around; get estimates and references as with the hiring of any other contractor. The price usually includes the drilling, pump, pressure tank, and all the materials and work necessary to get the water into the basement.

Well drilling is the only part of house construction where you're buying a pig in a poke. Most drillers will quote a price per foot, plus the extras outlined above. It's impossible to guess how many feet down, if at all, there will be a vein that will provide the necessary amount of water. The experience of neighbors is usually helpful, but it is by no means certain that you won't be luckier or unluckier than someone a quarter mile away. This is a fact that there is no getting around. Most people aren't too unlucky; they wind up paying less than $5,000, sometimes quite a bit less, for the whole job.

Most authorities, especially well drillers, believe that a modern household requires a water supply of five to seven gallons per minute. Even one gallon per minute provides 1,440 gallons per day, far more than you need. The problem is a place to store it, and you have one—in the well. The average drilled well will have a column of water in it 125 feet tall and 6 inches in diameter, about 188 gallons. You probably won't be able to persuade your driller to settle for a flow of one gallon per minute, but you may be able to persuade him to quit when you have three.

Get your water tested for coliform bacteria. At about the same time, you should get it tested for "hardness." Water from a drilled well may contain any of a variety of naturally occurring chemicals, such as calcium salts. Most of them won't hurt you—in fact, some of them are good for you—but certain ones, if present in more than minute quantities, will make beverages such as coffee and tea taste bad, leave deposits on tubs and inside teakettles, and worst of all, ruin your water heater and dishwasher in a short time. Have a water softener installed if necessary; it will pay for itself many times over. In this case, the best-known trade names aren't necessarily superior. One of your prime considerations in choosing a water softener should be how near you the serviceman lives or works.

ROUGHING-IN DRAIN PIPES

In the roughing-in stage, supply and waste pipes are installed in the walls and under the floor and are brought to the point at which they will pass through the Sheetrock and other paneling. Unlike an electrical box, a pipe may protrude a few inches after the paneling is installed. At this point, you may want to go back to your friends' houses to study the plumbing.

It is customary to install waste pipes first, beginning with the "soil stack," a column of 3-inch pipe that rises vertically from a horizontal connection with the sewer exit to the roof or an inconspicuous point high on an exterior wall. This is the "main line" of the drainage system. It serves two purposes: Waste water goes down it, and sewer gas comes up it and is vented to the outdoors.

> **NOTE:** Some codes require a separate vent pipe and drain pipe, close to and parallel to each other. The vent pipe is connected to the soil stack with a T at the top (well above where any waste enters) and a Y at the bottom. Such a system, while it seems to many plumbers redundant, poses no particular construction problem.

Older books on plumbing discuss how to work with cast-iron pipe, including melting lead to seal certain connections. ("Plumber" essentially means "one who works with lead.") It is doubtful, however, that there is any municipality left in North America where the use of PVC drain pipe is not standard. Working with it is child's play; in fact, putting the various Ts, Ys, elbows, and straight lengths together is something like playing with Tinkertoys.

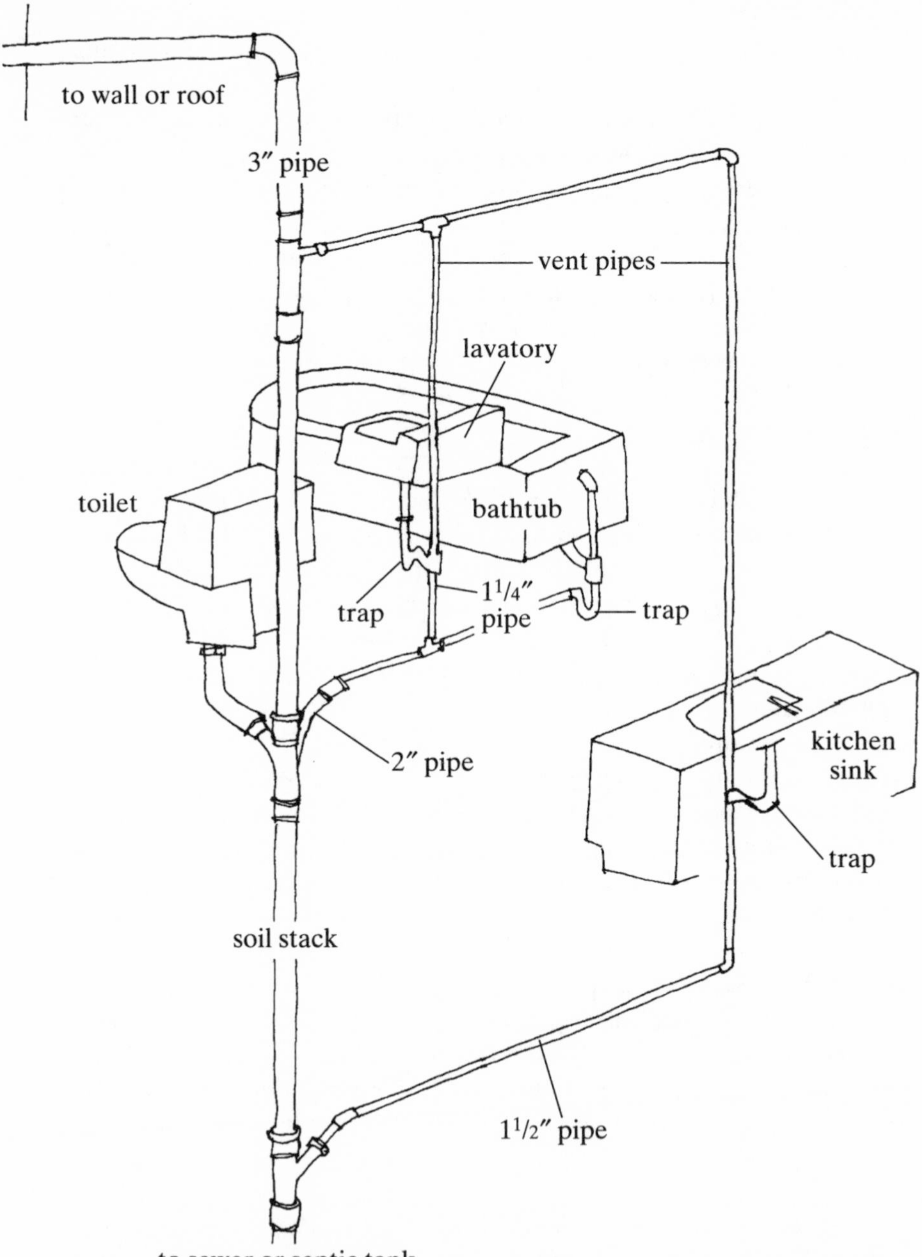

Fig. 43. *This stylized diagram of a typical plumbing system shows only drains. Note that each fixture is plumbed with a trap, except the toilet, which has a built-in trap. The entire system must be vented by an open pipe that passes through the roof or a wall, near the top.*

PVC pipe comes in 10-foot lengths and in various inner diameters (ID). You will probably use 3-inch ID for the main drain and toilets, 2-inch for the drain from the kitchen sink and dishwasher, 1¹/₂-inch for tubs and kitchen sinks, and 1¹/₄-inch for lavatories. It can be cut easily with almost any kind of saw. For each diameter, you will need a number of Ts and a few Ys (connections shaped like those letters), some 90-degree elbows, possibly some 45-degree elbows, couplings to join two pieces, and a large number of connections that join different-size pipes. The manufacturer has anticipated your every desire: You can buy a straight connector that joins 1¹/₂-inch to 3-inch, a T with two 3-inch legs and a 1¹/₄-inch leg, or anything else you could imagine.

In the design stage, you planned carefully the location of the toilets, lavatories, bathtubs, showers, kitchen sink, dishwasher, and clothes washer in relation to the septic tank (and possibly dry well) so that the soil stack would be as straight as possible and the connections from these items to it as short as possible. It is more important for toilets to be placed reasonably close to the soil stack than for lavatories.

Remember that horizontal drain pipes should slant ¹/₄ inch per foot. If you have to run a pipe fifty feet from the kitchen drain to the soil stack, it will be a foot lower at the soil stack than it is at the other end, which is why even the most modern basements often wind up with overhead pipes to duck.

Begin at the end. Run a line up vertically from the sewer exit to the desired height near the top of the basement wall, then over to where it will meet the vertical soil stack. En route, there may be one or more connections to showers or lavatories. At the sewer exit, there will be a clean-out T, one leg of which has a threaded stopper that can be opened to clean out any blockage. Put these in at the ends of horizontal runs everywhere they could be useful; if you need one, you'll be glad you have it.

Figure out exactly where everything goes, allowing the necessary slope, then carefully cut whatever lengths you need. You do have a little leeway, though not much, in how far the pipe slides into a connector. Use a jackknife first, then emery cloth, to smooth all cuts, and use emery cloth on both parts of any connection, inside and out, whether or not you cut the pipe there.

Put the pipe together for a dry run. Study it long and carefully. Have you forgotten any connector? Are the Ts backward? (Most Ts have a curve on the middle leg indicating the direction of flow.) If you're sure you're all set, glue the first connection. First, clean both parts with pipe-cleaning fluid; after that dries, apply glue to both parts, push and twist the pipe into the connector, and move it to exactly where and how you want it. For a minute or two you can move things around easily. Once the glue sets, the deed is done. Now the only way to correct a mistake is to saw it apart and start over, hoping there is enough pipe left to work with. Since drain pipes are never full of water under pressure, leaks are not as great a concern as they are in supply pipes.

> **TIP:** Until the glue hardens, it acts as a lubricant, permitting you to slide the pipe farther into the connector than you could before. You'll learn to allow for this.

Continue working slowly from the sewer exit toward the top of the house. Make one connection at a time, except for those cases where it is obvious that two or more must be made simultaneously. Where a pipe goes up vertically through two floors, use a plumb bob to get one hole directly above the other. Pause and think after each connection. Planning in advance is all-important in plumbing.

In the basement or crawl space, you generally will not cut joists to run pipes through them but will instead run the pipes under the joists and use pipe hangers. These can be bought to fit smaller pipe; for larger pipe, buy a roll of metal tape with holes cut out of it, sold for this purpose, cut off what you need, and nail it with roofing nails to wooden members.

You can't conceal 3-inch pipe in a 2x4 wall. Frequently partitions are built of 2x6s for the sole purpose of concealing plumbing. Even then you can't cut a hole in a 2x6 that will accommodate a 3-inch pipe and expect the stud to do much to hold up the house, although holes in toe and top plates won't weaken the structure. It will take all your ingenuity to plan the concealment of pipes, especially if you follow our advice and do not place them in exterior walls.

There is no particular problem with first-floor fixtures: All the pipes for tub and toilet simply go through the floor into the basement. You still have to conceal the vent pipe, however, and any second-floor plumbing gives you a lot of pipes to conceal. Plan one or more clothes closets in strategic places, perhaps one directly above another.

> **TIP:** All pipe expands and contracts with temperature. Don't drill holes that are so tight that the pipe has to be forced through, and don't make hangers too tight. If they are a bit loose, the pipe will still have enough support, and you will be less likely to hear it squeaking or "ticking" as it expands and contracts.

TRAPS

Every item of plumbing has to have a trap in its drain line. The trap is a U-shaped piece that is always full of water and thus prevents sewer gas from passing through and emerging into the house. Its secondary function is to stop a diamond ring that is accidentally washed down the drain. For this reason, among others, don't use the cheaper traps that have no clean-out, or you may have to saw the trap out of the line just on the off chance that Aunt Bessie's ring *might* be in there.

Toilets have built-in traps. Sink traps are part of finish plumbing, but bathtub and shower traps are placed in the drain line during the roughing-in process. As a matter of fact, tub and shower drains, which pass through the floor rather than through Sheetrock, can be connected to the fixture now. If they are on the second floor, this must be done before the first-floor ceiling is applied.

If anyone is going to live in the house before the finish floor is down, you just about have to connect up a toilet, then rip it up and reconnect it later. This is no fun, but if you try to cut underlayment and vinyl flooring and tuck it around an already-installed toilet, you will never be satisfied with the results. Perhaps the best way around this dilemma is to live with only one toilet at first and/or to delay moving into the house until at least one bathroom floor is completely finished, even if nothing else in the house is. Neither a tub nor a lavatory causes any similar problem, because finish floor customarily is laid down after tub and shower structures and lavatory cupboards are completed.

Eventually all the drains are roughed in, with a few inches of pipe protruding from walls where sinks will be and the proper connections sticking up the right distance from the floor for toilets. Tub and shower drains are connected. You'll have to purchase all the plumbing fixtures, read the directions, and study the parts before you finish this process. Tubs and toilets are pretty standard; sinks can vary somewhat.

Everybody's plumbing system is different (except in housing developments). It is not possible to give specific directions here for yours; you'll need to look at the locations of the various plumbing fixtures, the sewer exit, the water entry, and the girder, joists, studs, closets, and other places to conceal pipes, and plan the route of each drain and supply pipe for your own individual needs.

In practice, you won't rough-in all the drains before starting on supply pipes, since it may be easier to do all the work in one bathroom before starting on the next. As indicated above, you also may finish some plumbing fixtures before roughing in others. For clarity, however, we are treating each topic separately here.

ROUGHING-IN SUPPLY PIPES

Roughing-in supply pipes is easier in some ways and harder in others. You don't have to worry about vents, but almost every fixture requires two pipes, one for hot and one for cold water. There are no traps and far fewer bends and connections, and the pipe is more flexible; on the other hand, there is a far greater prospect of leaks. If none of your connections leaks the first time, you are far luckier or more skillful than most.

Presumably you will be using plastic pipe. This is connected just like the drain pipe, using emery cloth, pipe cleaner, and cement. Use 3/4-inch pipe for most long lines, 1/2-inch near the fixture. For example, the larger-diameter pipe runs from the source to the second-floor bathroom; from that point, side lines going to the individual fixtures are 1/2-inch.

Supply pipes in older houses are "lead" pipes, which really means they're galvanized steel. Newer ones may be copper or plastic. Plastic pipe is vastly cheaper and easier to work with than copper. Although some plumbers will disagree, in our opinion modern plastic pipe is just as effective as copper, even with hot water; in fact, it's better, because it is a much better insulator. The label on plastic supply pipe says something like "100 PSI at 180°," which is to say that at over 180 degrees, the pipe loses some strength. Since water heaters shouldn't be set above 180 degrees and most water systems, especially rural ones, have much less pressure than one hundred pounds per square inch, you are taking no risk whatsoever by using plastic pipe, which is why code permits it in most parts of North America.

This is one topic that is worth arguing, even pleading, with the code enforcement officer about. If all else fails, you can learn to sweat copper pipe. It's a skill like any other. One last statement on this subject: Recent studies indicate that copper pipe may affect health adversely. In fairness, we may learn soon that this is also true of plastic.

The actual supply plumbing follows roughly the same pattern used for the drains. Start at the source. If you have a well, the water comes into a pressure tank, and a pipe emerging from that already has a tap (faucet) on it and a fitting at which the entire supply system begins. You've been using the tap for some time, or at least the stonemason has. Don't connect your entire water supply to that, but rather to the fitting.

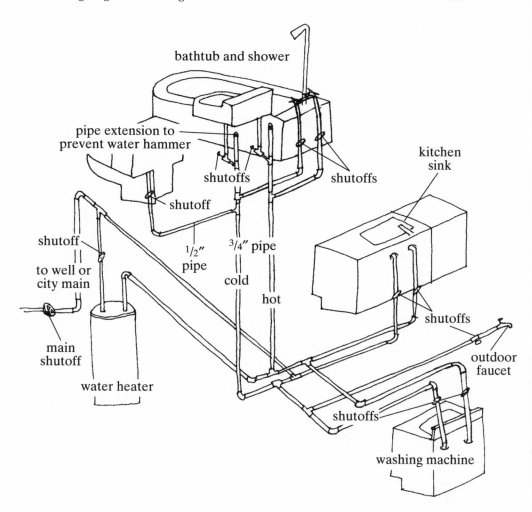

Fig. 44. *This stylized diagram of a typical plumbing system shows only supply pipes. A shutoff at every fixture makes life much simpler when there is an accident or a need for repair.*

The first line runs to the water heater, with possible side lines from Ts to some fixtures. The water heater has to be in place at this point. You may be able to figure out the most logical place to put it, although in most cases, "the farther off from England, the nearer 'tis to France." Unless the kitchen, laundry, and baths are all juxtaposed, placement that makes some hot-water lines shorter makes others longer.

Proceed just as with drains: Drill studs and toe plates, hang pipes from joists, and so on. It is customary and probably easier to run cold and hot water lines close to and parallel to each other. Bear in mind that in any pair, the hot-water faucet is customarily on the left (from the point of view of the consumer, not the installer).

I like to plumb part of the job as far as shut-off valves (see below), be sure they're all closed (don't miss one), then turn on the water. (Wait twenty-four hours to be absolutely sure the glue is dry.) It's too depressing to wait until the job is finished, then count twenty-three leaking places.

Have a confederate turn on the valve while you watch closely. It's easy to be mistaken about exactly where the water is leaking from. If you have a leak in the middle of a run, the pipe has a hole or split in it. You may have done this, or it may have come from the factory that way ("Monday-morning pipe"). Sometimes you could have prevented this by careful examination beforehand; in many cases, however, the defect is invisible.

If the leak is at an elbow, T, or coupling, you didn't get a complete glue (or solder) bond. When you are sure where the leak is, the remedy is just what you think: Cut out the offending part and try again. If it is a defective pipe, be sure that you have cut out absolutely all the split part before installing another piece of pipe and two couplings. In any case, the pipe must be totally, absolutely dry before it is glued.

Put shut-off valves everywhere, on every hot and cold water pipe before it enters a fixture, and anywhere else you think they might be handy. They cost little and add great peace of mind and convenience. It's your house, and you may have to repair or change the plumbing someday. In most cases shut-offs are applied during the finish stage, but some, like those in the basement or for bathtubs, may be installed now. Long after the plumbing is completed and you are living in the house, make it a practice to close and open these valves a few turns every now and then so that they don't seize up.

Most builders act as if no one ever will have to get at the plumbing to fix it. Be sure to build in big panels that can be opened behind tubs, and large cabinets with big doors under sinks, so you can crawl in there, close the shut-off valves, and install new faucets or whatever.

In city apartments, if you shut off a faucet fairly quickly, you may hear a loud bang. This is called water hammer. It is not usually a problem in areas where water pressure is not high, but its prevention is so simple that it's worth doing. As a pipe reaches its ultimate destination, for example at a second-floor lavatory, you would normally install an elbow and lead it out through where the Sheetrock later will be. Instead, put on a T and add about a two-foot extension above this point, with a cap on the end. When the faucet is turned off suddenly, any sudden pressure surge will harmlessly and noiselessly compress the column of air in this extension.

Don't worry about the water softener. The man who sells it to you will install it, and he'll be able to cut it into supply and waste pipes at the right place no matter what your plumbing is like.

Finish Plumbing

AFTER THE SHEETROCKERS HAVE LEFT, the mess is cleaned up, and the bathroom wall tile, if any, has been installed, finish the plumbing. In general, the technique is to unpack the fixture, read the directions, and try to figure them out and make the connections.

BUYING FIXTURES

Don't save money by buying cheap lavatories or kitchen sinks. With toilets, however, although the more expensive ones may have low profiles, come in colors, or claim to flush more quietly, they all work about the same way and last just about as long.

For bathtubs and showers, you have an almost infinite number of choices, from an inexpensive enameled steel tub to a molded fiberglass or plastic tub-shower enclosure that costs almost as much as a small car. The larger and heavier items have to be in place before the partitions are up and are so heavy that they can be difficult for two workers to handle without the help of equipment.

Faucets are extra, and even the shoddiest of them can be surprisingly expensive. The cheaper ones look like metal but actually are a very thin plating over plastic; this corrodes, bubbles, and peels after a few years, sometimes a few months. If you can afford it, buy solid metal.

CONNECTING FIXTURES

Each manufacturer seems to delight in a different complex system for connecting the supply pipes and drain to the fixture. About all I can do is suggest that you read the directions several times over, lay out all the parts, try to figure the thing out, and begin. You sometimes will be connecting plastic to metal, or quasi-metal. This is not difficult; the metal connector has a plastic sleeve inside it. Just clean and glue as before.

Toilets

Toilets are unique—not difficult, but sometimes irritating. To seat the stool, use a wax seal according to the directions, no matter how bizarre they sound. How the toilet bolts work is obvious. Don't feel that you have to clamp the bowl down too hard. In all finish plumbing, too much force is worse than too little. Toilets have only one supply pipe, a cold-water one, which can come up from the floor or out from the wall with an elbow. You'll definitely want a shut-off on it.

Connecting the tank to the bowl and the pipe to the tank requires a gentle patience. In both cases, too much force will ruin the job. Make the connections less tight than you believe necessary, then turn on the water. If there are leaks, finger tighten until they disappear. If you have to use pliers or a vise-grip to tighten enough to stop the leak, proceed very slowly and carefully. It is possible to crack either the plastic supply connection or the entire ceramic tank by using too much force.

> **TIP:** As you will discover, a leak can be so tiny that the difference between leaking and not leaking becomes metaphysical. In such cases, sometimes (though not always), if you go away and come back much later, the leak will have stopped, because minute particles in your water have plugged it. In the meantime, a rag will absorb the small amount of water. In my experience, leaks that cure themselves never open up again.

Bathroom and Kitchen Sinks

Most sink and lavatory connections are quite similar to toilet connections, and all the above suggestions apply. Here you will encounter threaded connections. Use Teflon tape, rather than pipe joint compound, on them, and don't use too much. Finger tighten at first; if you must use a tool, use it gently.

Tubs and lavatories have overflow drains. Kitchen sinks do not. I don't know why. Kitchen sinks have been known to overflow, and it is physically possible to design an overflow drain for a kitchen sink. Overflows in lavatories are usually cast right into the ceramic fixture; the drain installation is obvious. A tub overflow is a piece of plumbing attached later; how to attach it also is obvious. A tub and shower combination has a slight supply complication, which allows water to flow to the shower when the right lever is thrown. The better ones go back to normal tub supply the moment the pressure is off, which prevents the experience we have all had of leaning in fully clothed to turn on the water to fill the tub, and getting an unexpected drenching from overhead. The connection is not difficult if you read and follow the directions.

Dishwashers, Washing Machines, and Other Items

A built-in dishwasher can be hooked up at any point in the plumbing operation, following the directions. It will require rough-in and finish wiring (a simple 125-volt connection) as well as plumbing. Directions often suggest connecting the supply pipe (hot water only) to the existing sink pipe. If the dishwasher is installed with the rest of the plumbing, it is better to connect it to a separate supply pipe with its own shut-off. If the time ever comes when the dishwasher is out of service, not having a hot water supply to the kitchen sink can turn an inconvenience into a disaster.

The dishwasher drain is connected to a sink drain, above the trap. The drain connection is usually a rubber tube and the final supply connection a flexible copper tube, since the final plumbing and wiring connections have to be made with the machine pulled out a few inches. The tubing will flex that much when the job is completed and the dishwasher is pushed back into place.

> **CAUTION:** If your kitchen faucet has an attached spray and you install a portable dishwasher later, the hose will probably burst if it is not disconnected. It's far more satisfactory to build in a dishwasher when the house is built.

Washing machines have built-in rubber hoses; you will need to prepare supply pipe connections ending in a threaded fitting. Don't forget the shut-offs. A washing machine drain is a large-diameter rubber tube, which fits easily into a vertical 1 1/2-inch pipe, open at the top. This line runs through a trap to the general drain connection.

Connections to other items of your choice, such as a hot tub, sauna, greenhouse water supply, darkroom sink, wet bar, refrigerator, or outdoor faucet, are made similarly, according to directions, common sense, and what you have taught yourself about plumbing by now. Any outdoor faucet, except in an area where it never freezes, should be provided with a shut-off and drain arrangement so that there will be no water in it in winter.

Now you can relax and enjoy hot and cold running water at the turn of a tap and electricity at the throw of a switch, secure in the knowledge that your plumbing and wiring were done right and that you know how and where the jobs were done. If you ever need repairs or additions to either system, you won't have to call in outside help to get them done.

Insulation and Vapor Barrier

THE TWO MOST IMPORTANT DIFFERENCES between your passive solar house and conventional houses are the placement of the windows and the amount and type of insulation. Any contractor could build your house and put the windows in the right places, but no one else would do as good a job on the insulation as you will.

Carefully read chapter 24 in conjunction with this chapter.

TYPES OF INSULATION

There are many kinds of insulation. Three common kinds are spun fiberglass, a woolly material that is often pink; panels of foamed polyurethane or polyisocyanurate, called by various trade names such as Hi-R or Tuff-R; and polystyrene, known by the trade name Styrofoam. Styrofoam is usually blue or white and comes in 1- or 2-inch thick 2-by-8 panels, often tongue-and-groove. Hi-R comes in 4-by-8 sheets of various thicknesses with foil backing on both sides.

Fiberglass is sold in a wide range of sizes and kinds. Rolls, faced with kraft paper or foil or unfaced, are $14^{1}/_2$ or $22^{1}/_2$ inches wide to fit between studs 16 or 24 inches OC. They may be about 3 inches thick to be used with 2x4 studs, 5 inches thick to be used with 2x6s, or thicker. Ceilings are often filled with 9-inch "batts," which are like large pillows, rather than rolls. All of these sizes and shapes can be fluffed up or compressed slightly when installed.

All insulating materials are more or less toxic and/or allergenic. When you're working with them, especially with fiberglass, you should wear long pants, long sleeves, a hat, gloves, and a mask. This may be a hard rule to follow in hot weather. Some people are more allergic than others, but it's a bad idea to have these materials come in contact with your skin, and it's a very bad idea to breathe in their dust.

Fiberglass is the most unpleasant to work with; Hi-R sheathing is faced with nonallergenic aluminum foil on each side; Styrofoam is the least allergenic. On the other hand, fiberglass is fireproof, but the other two give off highly toxic gases when burned. Code requires that Styrofoam and Hi-R be covered with fireproof material. Smoke inhalation kills more than half of all people who die in modern fires. (That's why this book talks so much about Sheetrock and so little about lovely wood paneling.)

Every material has an R-factor, which is an indication of how slowly heat passes through it. All you need to know about R-value is that it's an approximation, and the higher, the better. It's all relative; a handy thing to remember is that four inches of air space has an R-value slightly under one. If your ceiling insulation is R-19, it's vaguely like having eighty inches of air between the ceiling and the roof.

Most insulation is based on pockets of trapped air, like those in the "spun wool" of fiberglass or the rigid foam of insulating board. Next to a vacuum, air is the best insulator—air trapped in pockets so that it can't circulate. Air circulates from a warm surface to a cold one, which is why eighty inches of air, if such were possible, wouldn't really have twenty times the R-value of four inches of air.

RADIATION AND CONDUCTION

Heat leaves your house, or cold enters it, in three ways: through radiation, conduction, and air infiltration. Heat is prevented from radiating out of your house by the shiny foil facing on insulating sheathing, and also by painted surfaces or anything else that reflects light and heat back into the room. (Foil surfaces buried under Sheetrock still work.)

Conduction refers to this well-known phenomenon: If you put a silver spoon in hot coffee, the handle will soon be extremely hot. If your house were built entirely of high-quality steel, it would always be almost exactly the same temperature indoors as out. Wood conducts heat more slowly than steel, while fiberglass is vastly better than wood.

INSTALLING FIBERGLASS

Aside from itchy skin and coughing, installing fiberglass is easy. For a double 2x4 wall, buy rolls of 5-inch material and roll them out horizontally, weaving them between the inner and outer studs. For single 2x6 walls, use the same material installed vertically between the studs. Under the roof, between the 2x12s, install 9-inch-thick batts designed for this purpose. This is much harder, because there is initially nothing to hold them up but staples, which they tend to tear away from. If you have other kinds of walls or ceilings, put in the appropriate fiberglass as recommended by your lumberyard.

Fiberglass batts and rolls often come faced with aluminum foil or kraft paper, which is designed to function as a vapor barrier. Try to buy material without this; it is of no use to you. You may not be able to get batts without this facing. If this is the case, install them with the paper facing toward the inside of the house, then, just before you cover it with another vapor barrier, like the foil on Hi-R sheathing, or polyethylene film, slash big *X*s in the kraft paper. I know it sounds crazy, but it's the recommended procedure. This is to prevent moisture from becoming trapped between two layers of vapor barrier. You want no moisture to penetrate the innermost barrier, but some will. If it does, you then want it to have an unhampered path to the outdoors.

Around windows and doors, stuff odd pieces of fiberglass into all the cracks. Don't compress it much. The harder you pack it in, the more you reduce its R-value. In all work with fiberglass insulation, the art is to pack it in just tight enough. If you are in the house on a cold day before the vapor barrier is applied, you will be able to feel the places, if any, where the insulation is too thin; add a bit more.

Five inches of fiberglass insulation in the walls is sufficient because the double-wall construction is so efficient as a heat retainer. If you have used a conventional wall built of 2x6s, you should add Hi-R inside of it. *Don't ever* let anyone talk you into putting this on the outside of your house!

INSTALLING INSULATING BOARD

A long time ago, you put a double layer of 1-inch Styrofoam outside the foundation walls, and the same under the basement floor. Above the basement floor Styrofoam, you rolled out a vapor barrier, which you hope wasn't breached much when the concrete was poured. You could have used Hi-R instead of Styrofoam, but it would probably have been overkill.

If you have a roof supported by 2x12s, you shouldn't cram the spaces between the rafters with more than nine inches of insulation, because you need a space above the insulation through which air can pass from the front vents to the rear ones. In fact, you probably should buy thin Styrofoam "troughs" made for this purpose, and staple them in place before you install the insulation. If air cannot pass freely through here, there will be a condensation buildup under the roof deck.

If the climate in your area is colder than New York City, you need more insulation under the roof. Nail Hi-R to the underside of the rafters. Although it makes little difference, the side with the advertising should go up. Before you do this, slash the kraft paper on the batts. This is easy to forget, but you can't do it far in advance, because the fiberglass inside will begin oozing out. The technique is to slash a row, then apply a row of sheathing, then slash the next row. If you forget, you probably won't want to go back and rip off all the Hi-R. We certainly don't advocate forgetting, but it may be some consolation to you to learn that we forgot for nearly one entire room, and we have not discovered any dire consequences.

Installing Hi-R sheathing on the ceiling will give you an increased respect for Michelangelo. The job is downright impossible without retainers you can buy for it. These are circles of thin, shiny metal, about 1 1/2 inches in diameter. Drive an 8d nail through the center of one of these, then through the sheathing into the rafter. Of course, you have to know exactly where the rafter is after it's covered. Now you begin to understand how important it is to have rafters exactly sixteen inches OC. Insulation board will pull right over a nailhead; hence the circles.

Since the foil facing becomes your vapor barrier, cracks where two panels come together are covered with an aluminum foil tape. Some use much cheaper duct tape, especially if the ceiling will be finished with paint that acts as a vapor barrier. (See chapter 23.) Inquire around and use your own judgment, remembering that the makers of duct tape don't claim that it will serve as a vapor barrier.

AIR INFILTRATION AND VAPOR BARRIER

As an owner-builder, the greatest advantage you have is in the prevention of air infiltration. Your house should be so airtight that when you close a door, you'll feel the pressure go up slightly. That's another reason to use sliding glass doors. Having such an airtight house has some disadvantages, but they are not nearly so great as your friends would have you believe. For one thing, no matter how hard you try, there will still be some leaks. For another, you can always open a window, and you will, on sunny February afternoons. Owners of conventional houses never open windows during the winter. They don't need to; experts estimate that all the air leaks in the average conventional home add up to an opening two feet by four feet.

There is a device called an air-to-air heat exchanger. In theory, stale air passes out of the house as fresh air comes in; through a complex series of tubes, channels, and baffles, all heat energy is transferred from the outgoing air to the incoming air. In practice, air-to-air heat exchangers are extremely expensive and not very efficient. One authority states that the best of them is only slightly better than opening a window.

You pays your money and you takes your choice. We can assure you that if you follow all of our advice, the smell when cabbage is being cooked will permeate your house in a way unknown in conventional homes. You can either live with the smell, open a window and burn a bit more wood, or live in a conventional home and pay thousands of dollars for heat every year, secure in the knowledge that the cost will be ever-increasing.

The basic weapon against air infiltration is the vapor barrier. A modern home is sealed inside an envelope of clear polyethylene plastic, the usual thickness being "six mil." This does not mean that it is six millimeters thick, but something much less, about six times the thickness of a sandwich bag. This material comes in various widths; ten feet is wide enough for the average room. The plastic goes inside (that is, toward the center of the house) everything except the Sheetrock and surrounds the entire living area. Staple it to the studs, overlapping widths where necessary and sealing the overlap with duct tape. Do this only after you have filled the space with fiberglass and put in the rough wiring.

You will do this far better than a contractor, because you will take infinite pains with it. In a conventional house, after the carpenters have more or less carefully put on the vapor barrier, the plumbers' and electricians' apprentices make huge, jagged holes in it to install the wiring and plumbing.

Installing the various kinds of insulation and vapor barriers is fussy, tricky, painstaking work, which is why you wouldn't trust it to anyone but yourself. Your pains will be repaid a thousandfold in years to come.

22

Exterior Finish

EXTERIOR FINISH CAN BE APPLIED at almost any time. The rough sheathing is often applied before the walls are erected and will certainly be on before insulation, wiring, and plumbing are done. Many owner-builders, however, move in long before the outside of the house is finished, feeling a greater need for plumbing and other amenities than for a pretty exterior.

ROUGH SHEATHING

Most builders use 4-by-8 sheets of 1/2-inch CD plywood or wafer board for rough sheathing. Try to get a material that is reasonably permeable to moisture, so that it will allow dampness in the wall to pass to the outdoors. Sheathing can be applied before the roof is constructed or afterward. There is probably no house construction job more simple. If you have some skilled workers and some unskilled, put the unskilled to work on the sheathing.

The task does require moderate strength, especially in nailing on the first piece. Start from the bottom and work up; the second course rests on the first while you're nailing it on. The job is like rough flooring: Joints are staggered, which means the second course starts with a panel cut in half. You shouldn't need to bend the studs into perfect position; your hard work and fussiness in selecting straight studs, putting the crowns out, and making the corners just right pays off here.

Run the panels horizontally rather than vertically, and nail them with 8d common nails four to six inches apart. Since you want the wall to breathe, don't work hard to keep the cracks between panels tight. You'll probably have to cut the topmost panel to fit. When you get farther up on a high wall, you'll need ladders or scaffolding. Be careful.

Wall right over all the window and door openings. Cut them out afterward with the reciprocating saw. The bits and pieces of sheathing material you would save by careful planning and cutting around doors and windows beforehand wouldn't be worth it. Of course, if you have an 8-foot-wide door opening, you don't have to cover the whole thing.

BUILDING PAPER

A building paper is applied over the rough sheathing. "Tar paper" used to be used for this; now a number of companies, such as DuPont and Georgia-Pacific, produce a white, paperlike product that is far superior to tar paper for this purpose. DuPont's is called Tyvek. It is a semipermeable membrane—it lets moisture out but won't let it in, which is exactly what you want.

Tyvek comes in 3-foot and 9-foot rolls and is expensive. The process of applying it is simple to understand and hard to do: Pretend your house is a Christmas package and wrap it totally in overlapping white swaths. Use a staple gun and the ever-useful duct tape in the task, and work, as always, from the bottom up. Push the paper a short distance into window and door openings for better waterproofing; you can always remove the excess much later, if any shows. Cut Tyvek with a razor blade knife. Be sure to put it on right side out, remembering that the manufacturer always wants his name to show. If you put it on inside out, it will let moisture *into* your walls and not let it out again.

> **CAUTION:** Papers like this should never be used for roofing paper; they are far too slippery.

WINDOW AND DOOR TRIM

Factory-made doors and windows come with trim. Before applying siding, put trim around "homemade" windows and doors, on the top and sides, but not under the sills. Use a good grade of 1x4 pine, cut to fit and nailed with 6d or 8d galvanized finish nails. Countersink the nails slightly with a nail set. The trim corners may be mitred (cut diagonally), but if they aren't, the finished effect will be the same unless guests scrutinize the frames from closer than five feet. Caulk countersunk nails and any cracks, and apply two coats of paint. You may also want to widen the trim around ready-made windows by adding 1x3 or 1x4 boards as above.

Over the top trim of each door and window, apply aluminum flashing to shed rain. The flashing is bent roughly into a Z shape (in cross-section). It goes under the Tyvek and bends down over the trim.

SIDING

You may put the exterior finish on the house immediately after putting in windows and doors, or you may wait until much later. Eventually, high winds will tear Tyvek off the exterior, but some people feel that having to make repairs to the paper is worth the trouble if it enables them to move into the house sooner.

There are hundreds of possible exterior finishes. We strongly do not recommend vinyl or aluminum siding, because they are difficult for the layman to apply; they never look as good, to our eyes, as wood; and worst of all, they lock moisture into the wall. You may choose wooden shingles, which are relatively expensive and difficult to apply but look great; wooden finish sheathing, which is quite cheap and easy but not quite so attractive; bevel siding; clapboards; or other materials, such as shiplap. All of these materials are often referred to as siding.

Sheathing

Wooden finish sheathing comes in 4-by-8 sheets in a variety of colors and patterns and is usually put on as a "board and batten" finish: The vertical cracks between the sheets are covered with 1x2s or similar lumber. The panels are applied vertically; horizontal cracks are made as tight as possible, then caulked.

Shingles

Wooden shingles come in bundles of various widths; the widths should be alternated. A small vertical crack is left between shingles for expansion; the width of the crack varies with the dryness of the material. Horizontally, wooden shingles should overlap 1/2 inch more than half their length; that is, with 18-inch shingles, each course should have 8 1/2 inches showing.

To apply, start with the bottom course. Snap a chalk line on the wall where the top of the course will come. Using specially designed galvanized nails, nail above the halfway point, so that the next course will always cover the nails, and stagger individual shingles so that the cracks never come at the same point from course to course.

Clapboards and Bevel Siding

Clapboards, like shingles, give a nice old-fashioned look to a house, but are cheaper and easier to apply. True clapboards, which are the same thickness throughout, are seldom used today; bevel siding is more common. This consists of long boards much narrower at one edge than the other, made of cedar or a similar wood that is by nature highly rot-resistant. It comes in at least two grades. You will probably be satisfied with #2, which will save money, but not as much as you think, because you'll have to cut out a lot of bad places, including knotholes, and throw them away.

Cedar and other bevel sidings come in lengths ranging from eight to twenty feet. Buy some of every length; it's worth your while to go to the lumberyard and select the pieces you want, rather than having them delivered. Not only does #2 siding contain many knotholes, but many pieces are cracked, gouged, or dirty. No amount of work, paint, or stain will cover up dirty lumber, but you can salvage some of it by applying it with the other side out.

Applying bevel siding is easy for anyone who has shingled a roof. Begin by nailing 1x4s vertically on exterior corners, then apply siding. Stagger the lengths so that one crack doesn't come immediately above another. Start at the bottom and work up.

Never use plain steel nails where they will be exposed to weather. Not only will they rust and deteriorate, they'll leave rusty streaks on the finish. Special galvanized nails are available for applying bevel siding. Place the nail in the thick part of the board, not too close to the end, to minimize cracking. If you have to put on very short pieces, for example between two windows, you may have to drill each piece for the nails.

Corner boards and bevel siding are often stained rather than painted. Use caulk the color of the stain between the siding and the corner boards and the siding and the window trim.

FASCIAS AND SOFFITS

If you look at other people's houses, especially conventional ones, you will notice that the parts of the rafters that extend beyond the house are totally boxed in. We don't recommend that you enclose the spaces between rafters with soffits, but they look neater and are protected

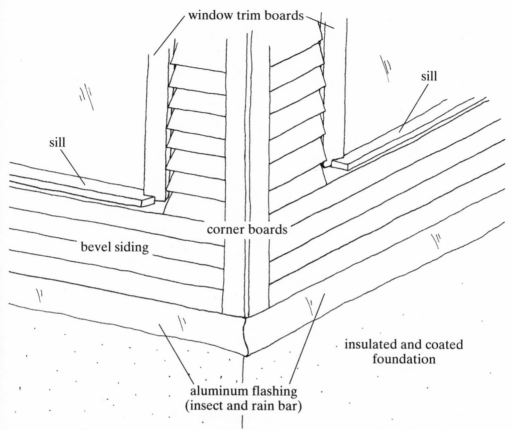

Fig. 45. *Before an exterior wall is finished with clapboards or bevel siding, corner boards are nailed on. These are usually 1x4 pine and are stained the same color as the siding. Window trim, usually painted a contrasting color, is also applied before the siding.*

against rot if the ends are covered with pine boards called fascias, painted in your trim color.

It's easier to cut rafters for fascias before the rafters are in place. Make a plumb cut on the rafter five inches long. From this point, cut back (toward the house) at about a 135-degree angle. This will provide a plumb face the right size for a 1x6 board. Water will drip straight down from the fascia.

Fascia boards can be nailed on from ladders or scaffolding, but it is easier to do the nailing from the roof, lying on your stomach. They must be cut to meet at a rafter face. As with any exterior trim, use galvanized finish nails, countersink, and putty.

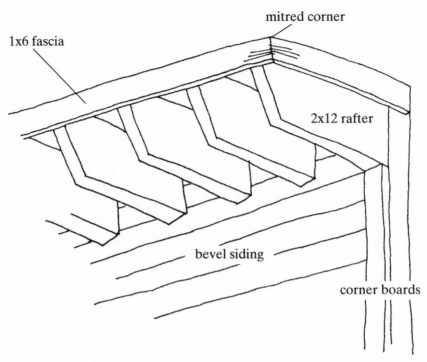

Fig. 46. *Rafter ends look neater and resist rot if covered with a fascia board, but if rafters are 2x12, 1x14 fascia boards are not practical or attractive. The problem is solved by cutting the plumb cut back toward the house as shown. Five inches of the rafter, which is hidden under the fascia, are cut plumb; the rest is cut at a 135-degree angle.*

FOUNDATION FINISH

After your house is otherwise finished, you will notice that the part of the foundation that shows, which is probably covered with blue Styrofoam, is the least attractive part of the exterior. There's a better reason than appearance for covering it, however. In time, sunlight will cause uncovered Styrofoam to deteriorate. In addition, ants and bees like to make nests in the cracks or tunnel into the material.

The standard way to cover Styrofoam is with a thin cement, which comes in a five-gallon pail. The pail contains everything you need, including powder, latex liquid, and a brush, but you should have a trowel handy, too. Mix according to directions; it's better to start with it too thick than too thin.

It is not easy to apply, and it doesn't stand up very well, but we haven't found anything better. The chief difficulty is with the tape that comes in the package, which is supposed to be applied over the seams, cracks, and small holes in the Styrofoam. The best technique is to supplement its feeble self-sticking action with light staples from a staple gun, and cover the tape fairly quickly.

Other than that, there isn't much difficulty in applying the glop as long as it's neither too thin nor too thick. Like all such materials, it will thicken up as the liquid evaporates. It should be applied when the outdoor temperature is neither too cold nor too warm, and preferably not in direct sunlight. There must be all of three or four days a year that meet these criteria; fortunately, you can stretch the rules a bit. You can wait a year or two before doing this, and if you can't do it all at once, you can wait quite some time before doing the back of the house, where the sun never shines.

After a while, this coating will get nicked and cracked, so you should save a small amount of cement to mix up a couple of years later in order to repair the cracks. The finished product looks so much like concrete that people don't realize it's fragile. Hitting it with a lawnmower will cause a big gouge. This all sounds rather depressing, but the truth is that after a few years, with plantings around the foundation, you won't notice it any more, nor will the sun get to it.

You've probably noticed that we are suggesting you take more care with exterior finish than with any previous task—countersinking nails, for instance. Unless you finish the interior first, the exterior finish is the first job you'll do that will always be there for people to see, so you'll want to make it as near perfect as possible.

Interior Finish

THIS CHAPTER DEALS with the interior finish details that make a house a showplace. (Well, a home, at least.) There are a few ways in which the interior finish of a passive solar house might differ from that of a conventional house; these will be mentioned as they come up. If you're like most owner-builders, you'll finish the interior of your house a little at a time after you move in.

Interior finish is like all other construction tasks: Everything has to be done before everything else. Usually, wall finishes come first and wood trim last, but you may decide to vary the order. It is difficult to do painting or cabinetry above a finished floor and not mar it, but you may decide to have the floor extend into a cupboard and therefore build the cupboard last. Closets are constructed like tiny rooms: Partitions are erected early on, and flooring is put down much later.

Constructing stairs on a finished floor may mar it, but if the stairs are done first, it is necessary to allow for the thickness of the floor to come when calculating the height of risers.

WALL FINISHES

Paint
While they may be nervous about wiring or shingling, most homeowners know how to paint, and many have done wallpapering. For this reason,

this section will not go into great detail about brushes, rollers, and technique. Purists still feel that oil-base (or rather the modern equivalent, alkyd) paint gives a nicer finish, especially if gloss is desired. Most people choose latex, because the ease of using water for cleanup outweighs all other considerations.

We repeat the good advice everyone gives and no one takes: Buy expensive brushes and rollers and take good care of them, cleaning them thoroughly immediately after use and storing them properly. Buy the best paint for the job; ask a professional painter what he would recommend.

Start with the ceiling and work down. For a really high ceiling, use scaffolding. For standard ceilings, you might consider renting plasterers' stilts and painting all the ceilings before doing any of the walls. Plan to apply at least two coats, perhaps three, especially over wood with knots.

One difference between this and previous painting jobs is that you've probably never before had the luxury of being as messy as you wish. If you're working above subfloor and there is no furniture in the room, you probably won't need dropcloths, and you may want to try a paint sprayer, perhaps the kind that attaches to your vacuum cleaner, although I've never had much luck with them. Use a roller on large areas.

A second difference has to do with condensation. In a passive solar house, you may want to use a primer that is especially designed to be impervious to moisture, such as Benjamin Moore's alkyd primer-sealer. (Other companies make similar products.) Such paints will aid greatly in keeping water vapor inside the house. (See chapter 10 for a possible disadvantage of such paint.)

Wallpaper

With the advent of self-pasted wallpapers, the homeowner can hang wallpaper that will look almost as good as if a pro had done it. The secret, besides following directions to the letter, is an infinite capacity for taking pains. Buy all the necessary professional tools, like brushes and rollers, where you buy the paper. Get a pattern that is not too demanding in terms of making the edges match. Buy a lot more than you think you need. It is easier to buy paint that matches what you have previously applied than it is to do the same with wallpaper.

Moisture may cause wallpaper to peel or bubble in a bathroom, especially if lots of people in the household are given to long, steamy showers. Buy wallpaper that is specifically designed for bathroom use.

NOTE: Wallpaper has a very definite shelf life. Don't buy bargain wallpaper if you think it's been lying around the store a long time. More important, don't buy wallpaper months before you can apply it. This is probably the most common cause of peeling.

Wood Paneling

Wood paneling like knotty pine is attractive in a den or other special room but may be too expensive to use throughout. Installation is simple for someone who has successfully built an entire house.

CAUTION: Applying wood or other combustible paneling over polyisocyanurate or similar sheathing is dangerous and contrary to most building codes.

Tiles

Tiling a bathroom or kitchen wall is not as difficult as most people think. If you want tiling, you shouldn't have to resort to fake tile, which comes in sheets and always looks like fake tile. All tiling, whether floor or walls, is a two-step process. First, mastic or cement is applied to the surface and the tiles are embedded in it. After the mastic is thoroughly dry, the cracks between tiles are grouted. The only really suitable implement for the application of the grout in tiny cracks is the human finger, which should be protected by a rubber glove.

The most important part of each step is wiping excess mastic and grout off the tiles with a damp cloth or sponge. This must be done over and over until the surface sparkles. Tiling is vastly easier as a two-person job, with one wielding the sponge.

Tile must be cut to fit at corners or where pipes come through the wall. Cut it with a tile cutter that the tile store will rent or lend you, or score the surface with a glass cutter, then break the tile. Straight lines can be broken, after scoring, by putting the tile on a pencil, then stepping on it. More complicated cuts, such as those around pipes, can be scored with a glass cutter and broken with pliers, a bit at a time. Special glass pliers are useful, but a vise-grip will do the job. It's hard to make a neat job of this, but your mistakes will be hidden under the decorative trim around bathtub or shower faucets. At corners, hide the surface you cut under the adjoining surface. Very few construction jobs will give you as much satisfaction as your own wall tiling.

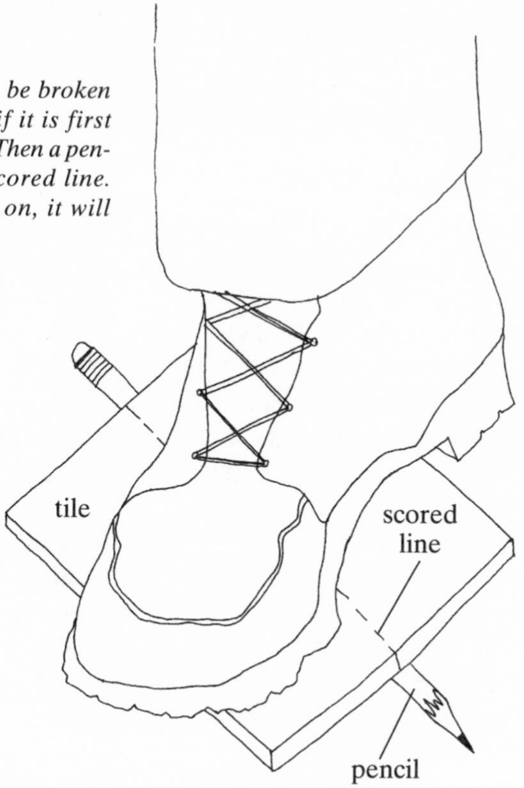

Fig. 47. *Ceramic tile can be broken fairly neatly and easily if it is first scored with a glass cutter. Then a pencil is placed under the scored line. When the tile is stepped on, it will break along the line.*

tile

scored line

pencil

CUPBOARDS, COUNTERTOPS, BOOKCASES, AND CLOSETS

You may choose to hire a cabinetmaker for cupboards, countertops, stairs, the fireplace mantel, or other parts of the interior finish. You can make these yourself, but they will look better if you hire a professional. The decision depends on how finicky you are. You can make cupboards that will function adequately and look decent if they're painted, but if you want perfect countertops or doors that are totally symmetrical and look good varnished, better hire a pro.

Cupboards are not limited to the kitchen; they go under sinks or elsewhere in bathrooms, and you may want a row of them against the north wall of the living room. You might find someone who will hang doors and put on a countertop after you build the rough interior frame of a cupboard.

Building supply stores sell ready-made kitchen cupboards in a wide range of sizes, styles, and prices, but they never fit perfectly into the spaces in your house, and they aren't designed specifically to accommodate the length, width, height, and weight of your own treasures, such as your particular stereo system. Even if you don't use ready-mades in the kitchen, you may want to buy a countertop cut by the supplier to fit your bathroom sink. You'll probably be satisfied with the appearance of the cupboard you can build in under that.

There are several different ways to build cupboards, all of which seem to work about equally well. A cupboard may be built entirely of 3/4-inch plywood pieces glued and nailed together, or it can have a framework or skeleton made of 2x2s or even 1x2s.

A novice might overlook toe space; when you stand facing a kitchen or bathroom cupboard, there should be a space under the bottom shelf your toes can go into. To accomplish this, start with a rectangular frame of 2x4s (turned sideways) topped with a shelf of 3/4-inch plywood that extends a couple of inches out over the framework in front. Build up from this base. Even if the cupboard is built on subfloor, this will allow for the thickness of the finish floor added later.

All supports and crosspieces must be identical so that the cupboard will be perfectly level and plumb. Since the floor is not perfect, total perfection is impossible, but strive for it. All members should be glued, then nailed with finish nails, except for shelves that you might someday wish to remove to gain better access to plumbing or for some other purpose. Some shelves may be made of 1/2-inch plywood, but if the shelf is to bear much weight, use 3/4-inch.

When the doors are closed, they'll cover cupboard imperfections, but nothing will cover imperfections in the doors. Doors should be made of cabinet-grade plywood, often birch, which costs two or three times as much as softwood. You'll need chisels, sanding tools, a coping saw, and incredibly careful measurement and patience to do even a journeyman job of cutting the little spaces for the butts (hinges) and hanging the doors. When they are finished and covered with two coats of paint, you'll still see the imperfections, but no one else will. Look into the fancy, expensive hinges that are available to cabinetmakers. These make the job a great deal easier. Some have several sets of screws that can be adjusted to move each door slightly in or out or to the left or right.

Countertops are also fussy. Build them of plywood and apply the "Formica" material, following the directions carefully. Once the two

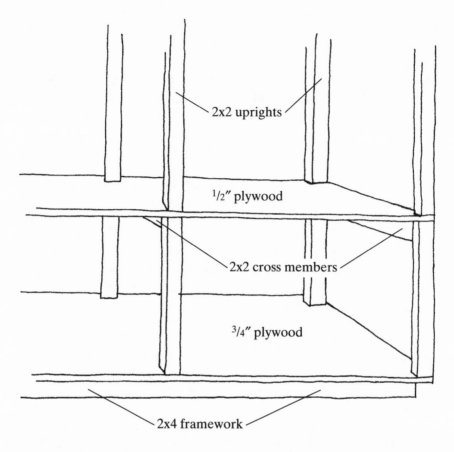

Fig. 48. *There are many ways to build cupboards, but all floor cupboards need a toe space. A framework is constructed of 2x4s on their sides; then a sheet of ³/4" plywood is laid on this, extending a couple of inches out into the room. The cupboard framework is erected from this.*

coatings of contact cement touch, you won't be able to budge the surface, so it had better be right. Borrow or rent a router for the edge trim.

Bookcases, especially painted ones, are no reason to call the cabinetmaker. The books will cover 90 percent of the mistakes. Buy some 1x12 clear (best-quality) pine, measure the heights of a few of your books, and go to work. Support the shelves on 1x2 strips screwed through the Sheetrock into the studs, as well as on vertical pieces of 1x12 at regular intervals. Even though you know where the studs are, use a stud finder. You can pay up to $50 for an electronic one, but a $2 magnetic one will do the job. Build a lot more bookcase space than you need; it will get filled eventually, and in the meantime you can use it for knickknacks.

Closets aren't beyond your powers either. Whether they are big walk-in ones or smaller, they are essentially small rooms, with either a regular interior door or ready-made folding, louvered ones. Make closet shelves like bookcases, and cut them to fit around pipes, if the closet conceals any.

STAIRS

Probably no aspect of home construction is more difficult than stairs. You might do the basement stairs yourself, because you're not so fussy about how they look, and hire a good finish carpenter to build the main staircase that is the centerpiece of your living room.

Stairs come in a dizzying array of styles. They can be open or closed (inside an ascending hallway, so to speak). One side can be open and the other closed, or the bottom can be open and the top closed. Really grand ballrooms have a magnificent flight of totally open and apparently unsupported stairs. Don't try to do that yourself.

They can be open in another way, consisting of treads fastened securely within uncut stringers, and no risers. This style is often used for basement stairs, but if made well of hardwood and finished nicely, it can be attractive as your main staircase, especially if the general style of your house is rustic or colonial rather than formal.

No matter what style you choose, your stairs will be almost identical to everybody else's in the angle at which they ascend and the length of treads and height of risers. If you had lived two hundred years ago, when stairs were built any old way, that might not be true. Over the years, builders have discovered what height of risers and angle of ascent feel "right" to most people, and these data have been incorporated into building codes.

Let's build a flight of basement stairs. Your mistakes will be hidden away, and all the skill acquired can be applied to building the main stairs later on. Start with some terms: The part you step on is called the *tread;* the part your toe bumps is the *riser;* the sidewalls that support the treads are *stringers.* Stringers may be solid, with the treads nailed and glued within them, as in the basement stairs described here, or cut in a large sawtooth pattern, with the treads fastened on top of the *teeth.* Fancy treads for main staircases will have *bullnosing:* The front edge of the tread will extend out a bit and be nicely rounded. Bullnosing doesn't count in measuring tread depth, called *run.*

Let's suppose that the distance from the basement floor to the top of the finish floor will be 100 inches, which is the likely distance in most houses for either story. Divide this number by 7 or 8, to get somewhere between 12 and 14. Whatever you get, round it to a whole number. This is the number of risers you will have. There will always be one less tread than riser, since you don't count as a tread the floor you start from or the floor you reach.

If you have 13 risers and 12 treads, your house is like most. To find the height of each riser, divide 100 inches by 13 and get 7.7. The closest you can come to that on the carpenter square is 7¹¹/₁₆ inches. Since that isn't exactly as much as 7.7, when you lay out the stair, you will have to fudge a very small amount as you go along, or the last riser will be noticeably taller than the rest.

Make the 12 or 13 treads you need from 2x10 stock. Cut them the width of the available opening less the thickness of the two stringers, which will be very close to 33 inches. Use 2x10s because the builder's rule of thumb is that two risers plus one tread should add up to 2 feet or a bit more. Two times 7.7 (the total distance of the riser) plus 9¹/₄ (the width of a 2x10) equals a bit more than 2 feet. Obviously, the shorter the riser, the longer the tread, but you will find that any dimensions that vary greatly from those given here are uncomfortable, impractical, and not in conformance with code.

The depth of a tread times the number of treads is the total "run," the horizontal distance taken up by the staircase. If the run is too long relative to the rise, the angle will be too shallow. Twelve treads 9¹/₄ inches long add up to 111 inches. Add 9¹/₄ (include the space at the bottom, but not at the top, as a "tread"; you'll see why) and you get a space about 10 feet long that the staircase will take up. Recommended width for a stairway is about 3 feet, so when framing the floor you should have framed a hole about 3 feet by 10 feet. You could have made it a bit shorter, since there would still have been sufficient headroom above the first step, but it's best to be on the safe side.

Recommended headroom is 6 feet, 4 inches for basement stairs and 6 feet, 8 inches for main stairs. You may want to allow more room if someone in the family is quite tall. Calculating headroom is difficult; as one climbs the stairs he gets higher and higher, of course. Sometimes the clearance is close at the bottom of the stairs, and sometimes at the top.

Some problems can be solved by landings or winders, which allow the stairs to make a 90-degree turn at some point. You know what a landing is. Winders are treads that are triangular rather than rectangular, so that two or more of them enable the staircase to turn, usually 90 degrees. Code enforcement people frown on them. You probably won't get away with them in a main staircase, but the officer may permit them in a basement stair.

To build winders, think of them as a landing cut into parts, and design the main flight to just reach the lowest winder. At midpoint, where people usually step, the winders should be the same width as the other treads, in the above example 9$1/4$ inches. They will be wider at the outer edge and narrower at the inner, but they should not come completely to a point. Risers for the winders will be the same height as those on the main flight.

Now that you have mastered all these arcane details, select two good, straight pieces of 2x10 about 13 feet long to be the stringers. Use the square to mark where the treads will go. Lay it on the stringer in such a way that one leg touches the edge of the stringer where the scale reads "7$11/16$" (the rise) and the other touches it where it reads "9$1/4$" (the run). Use the outside, not the inside, scales. Now draw a pencil line around the outside of the square, and you have laid out the position of the first tread and riser.

Move the square along the stringer to the point at which the run line intersects the edge, and repeat the procedure until you have laid out 13 run lines (if you have 12 treads). These are where the treads will go, except for the bottom run, which is where you will cut the stringer to rest on the basement floor. The top rise line will be cut to rest against the joist or header where the stair reaches the first floor. The completed stringer will be almost exactly 12 feet, 7 inches long. Make two identical stringers.

It is necessary to be very accurate, using a sharp pencil and making the lines meet exactly at the edge of the stock, but it is easier to perform the above procedure than to describe it. One trick that will help is to buy clips that you can fasten to the square at exactly the prescribed distances. If you think it necessary, you can check your work by tacking the treads in place, *below* the lines, to see if the completed stair is as you wish. Don't cut until you're sure you're right. You may have to do the layout more than once to get it just right, so don't make the pencil lines too dark. A common error is to forget that the treads have thickness.

When you're sure the pattern is right, while the stair is tacked together, glue and nail 2x4 blocks to the stringers just below the treads, to help support them. Then take the stair apart and make the top and bottom cuts on the stringers. These cuts will be at right angles to each other. Then glue and nail the treads in place. This alone might not sup-

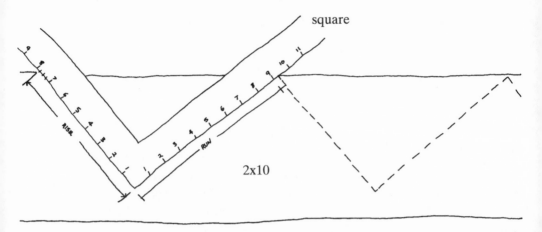

Fig. 49. *A stair stringers may be laid out fairly easily with a carpenters square. The square is placed against the 2x10 in such a way that the rise distance on one leg of the square and the run distance on the other exactly intersect the edge of the plank. The lines are then drawn along the* outside *edges of the square. The task is made easier through the use of clips, not shown here, which are fastened to the square at precisely the correct distances.*

port all the weight the stairs will take, but with the addition of the blocks, the stair will be strong enough. Put it in place and fasten it securely.

After reading the above, you may well decide to hire an expert to build all the stairs in your house. That might be a good idea, but you probably could manage the basement stairs, and if you can build them, you can make the main stairs. You can make stairs very similar to the above but better looking by using oak or other hardwood, sanded to a smooth finish. Since blocks supporting the treads don't look as elegant, cut a dado (slot) in the stringer to help support the tread, or fasten the treads with heavy lag bolts concealed with wooden plugs.

There are a great many possibilities: Your plan may call for a pre-built spiral staircase or a loft reached only by a permanent ladder (either of which will have to be approved by the inspector). You may use oak treads bought from a supplier and fastened on top of stringers cut out in the sawtooth pattern. You may have the stairs manufactured by a mill-work factory to your specifications, but put them together yourself. You can buy newels, balusters, and other parts at the yard and put them together to form a railing, technically called a balustrade.

If the main staircase is not enclosed, it will be one of the focal points of your home. If you aren't sure you can build it yourself in a way that will satisfy you for years to come, you'd better hire a pro.

FLOORS

There is no end to finish floor materials: hardwood (including parquet), softwood, slate of various kinds, vinyl flooring in rolls or squares, tile, brick, and others. We hope you won't have a cement slab floor and wall-to-wall carpet. It is curious that building codes require insulating panels like Hi-R sheathing to be covered with fireproof material but allow furniture and carpets that give off approximately the same noxious fumes when they burn. We are hearing more and more about "building disease" caused by, among other things, synthetic carpet materials.

Wood Flooring

Most of the floor will probably be wood, which is usually put down before slate or vinyl. Hardwood is more expensive and harder to lay down than softwood, but it will certainly stand up to traffic better, and many people find it more attractive. The most expensive type is probably parquet, which comes in preformed and prepasted squares; follow the directions on the package.

Ordinary hardwood strip flooring is tongue-and-groove. To lay this, rent a floor-nailing gun, which will hold a strip firmly against the last one and nail it simultaneously. Beware of having your finger in the line of fire! Special flooring nails, which (theoretically) won't split hardwood, are used. They are driven in just above the tongue and at an angle, so that no nails will show when the work is finished.

Start at one side of the room, with the groove side of the flooring strip toward the wall, and work toward the other side. Put the strips perpendicular to the joists underneath, and try to nail directly into the joists, although it may not matter if you miss occasionally. Cut the last strip lengthwise to fit. Don't worry about gaps at the edges; the baseboard, which is the last item added, will cover them. Try to have all your errors where the baseboard, or something else, will cover them. By now, you probably know where the sofa, bed, or another large piece of furniture will go. If you have to use an inferior piece of wood, try to put it there.

Leave a 1/4- to 1/2-inch space on each side between the wall and the flooring for possible expansion, but avoid expansion and contraction by storing materials inside the house as long as possible before using them; a week is the minimum time for this. Unless the wood was terribly green, by that time it will have reached the temperature and humidity of its surroundings. It is unnecessary and undesirable in a house like the one you are building to put a layer of tar paper between the subfloor and finish floor.

If you like the knotty pine look of old colonial floors, you can duplicate it easily and cheaply with "shiplap," which is usually used as an inexpensive exterior wall covering. It has a sort of tongue and groove and comes in various widths. Buy some of each width, and vary them as randomly as possible. Fasten them with Sheetrock screws; when the floor is finished, these black screws will look remarkably like old-fashioned hand-cut nails.

The boards will not want to go together snugly, and they will be wavy in both dimensions, but you can force them to fit. As you did with the siding, cut off and throw away some of the worst knotholes and bends. Follow the basic procedure for hardwood strips. Pick a nice straight piece to start. Screw it down (you will need a power screwdriver), but not quite tight, especially on the outer edge. Now put the next piece against it. If it doesn't want to go in tight, make a device to force it, as follows:

Cut two large triangles of scrap wood. Nail the outer one to the floor. Then drive the inner one between it and the board you're trying to coax into place. The rubber hammer is useful here. Of course, the whole rig has to be organized tongue to groove. When this section of board is "persuaded," screw it down, move the triangle, and repeat. You won't have to use the device on every part of every board. (See figure 50.)

Finish such a floor with two coats of polyurethane varnish, after first filling and sealing the knots with a thick, clear plastic filler. This makes an attractive effect, but any softwood floor will scratch and dent more than hardwood.

Slate Floors

Slate floors look attractive, are impervious to spike heels, and form part of the heat sink in a solar house. They have one major drawback: If you drop a cup, it's gone! Presumably you won't want slate everywhere in the house, but you may want it at heavy traffic areas like entrances, in a wide area around the fireplace or woodstove, and in a damp area like a greenhouse. Use standard precut 1/4-inch slate tiles in the house, and rougher flagstone in a greenhouse. The technique for laying either is basically similar to that described above for wall tile.

You must plan ahead; otherwise, the slate in the living room or the bathroom vinyl will be much lower than the adjoining wood floor. If you

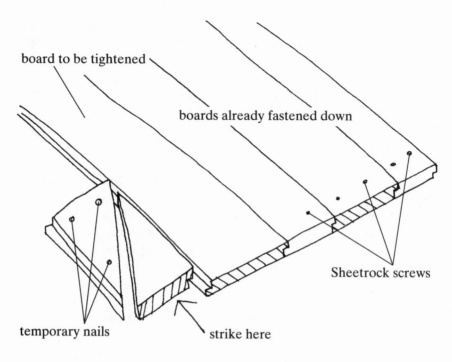

board to be tightened

boards already fastened down

Sheetrock screws

temporary nails   strike here

Fig. 50. *In this simple system for forcing any tongue-and-groove floorboards tightly together, two triangles are cut out of scrap flooring material and placed as shown. The tongue of the inner triangle engages the groove of the board to be "persuaded." The faces of the triangles that touch each other are cut; they have neither tongue nor groove. Pressure is applied where indicated, preferably with a rubber hammer. It helps* not *to finish nailing or screwing down the outside edge of the previous board until after the next one has been forced into place.*

plan correctly, when you add the 1/4 inch of slate and about 1/8 inch of cement to the plywood underneath, it will come to just the level of the adjoining wood floor. It can be about 1/4 inch off; any more will have to be compensated for in advance by adding underlayment.

Laying slate isn't any more difficult than putting down wooden floor. In fact, in some ways it's easier, although it's dirtier and messier. Slate tiles 1/4 inch thick can be bought in packages containing 10 square feet. Buy at least 10 percent more than you think you need. This is a natural material, and it varies a bit in color and thickness.

Lay out the slate, dry, in the opening. Leave a 1/4-inch space between tiles. Juggle them a bit until you get the sizes and colors where you want them. It's unlikely that the pattern will come out just right; you'll probably have to cut one or two. Cut slate with a hacksaw. This is slow work; don't try to rush it, or you'll break the slate.

> **TIP:** Where slate meets wood floor, butt the tiles flush to the wood. Don't use grout between slate and wood; it will crumble, because the wood flexes more than the slate.

When you're satisfied with the arrangement, number the pieces with chalk; otherwise you won't remember where each one goes. Now take them all out of the opening, and put down the mastic. Use a toothed trowel, and follow the directions on the package. Do a few square feet at a time.

Place the tiles about where you want them, and move them gently into place. Then bear down hard on each, and hit it repeatedly with the rubber hammer. If it's going to break, it's better if it breaks now. If you leave an air space under it, it will break later on, and you'll have to replace it then. The tiles will move easily for about ten minutes, until the glue starts to set; trying to move them after that will break the bond. Clean constantly as with wall tile. Grout after a day or so; rubber kitchen spatulas and human fingers are the best tools. Wear rubber gloves for all parts of the tile-setting activity.

Setting inch-thick flagstones on a concrete base is very similar, although the cement and grout have a different chemical makeup. If it's warm and dry, keep wetting the stone and cover the job to permit it to dry more slowly. Finish slate with a liquid like Thompson's Waterseal. Let that dry overnight, and follow it with a hard acrylic liquid wax such as Future. We learned this from a stonemason. No other finish will look as good and stand up as well. You'll like the look and feel of your handiwork, even if it does have a few nicks and cracks.

> **NOTE:** Where you live, slate may be scarce and expensive and "quarry tile" or some other material may be abundant. Laying such material is similar to laying slate. Half the fun of building your own house is choosing the materials *you* want, especially materials native to the area.

Vinyl Flooring

If you say "linoleum" in a floor-covering store, they'll throw you out, but the material found on most modern bathroom and kitchen floors is the twenty-first-century descendant of linoleum. Vinyl flooring comes in rolls for professionals or prepasted squares designed for the household handyman. Use the squares. We tried both. Trust me on this one.

Vinyl squares are easy to put down, look good, and stand up well. The chief problem you'll encounter is in bringing the surface below the vinyl up enough so that the vinyl will be level with the adjoining wood floor. You'll have to put down one or more layers of plywood underlayment with a special surface designed for this purpose. Even then, you may have to plane or sand the wood a little before placing a metal strip to cover the joint where the two floors meet. For some reason, no matter how you jockey things around, wooden floors always wind up higher, never lower, than tile, slate, or vinyl floors.

To install vinyl flooring, follow the directions on the package. It's easy. Most vinyl floors need no finish whatsoever, which is another nice thing about them.

INTERIOR DOORS

By now you have all the skills necessary to install doors and apply wood trim. You can buy "prehung" doors at the building supply store, but unless they are very expensive, their construction is sleazy, and although the door openings in the house are standard size, the doors still have to be cut. A common standard for interior doors is 2^1/$_2$ by 6^1/$_2$ feet. Prehung doors will be the right width but not the right length, so the first thing you'll have to do is cut them to the desired length. Since they are not solid (far from it), you'll have to remove the "plug" from the bottom, make the cut, then reglue the plug in place. Next, fasten the frame in the opening, shimming as necessary to make everything nicely level and plumb. Finally, put on the hardware, which costs extra, and cover up any mistakes with the trim package.

By the time you're through, you've done about the same amount of work as if you'd bought an old-fashioned door and hung it yourself. In most localities, you can buy doors in a secondhand building supply store. You'll have to do some planning and use a chisel to get the hinges in the right place, but it isn't that much harder. Watch out, though, for old doors that have about seventeen coats of paint. Not only is it a lot of work to strip them down, but you may be surprised at what's under there.

Whichever kind of door you choose, you'll probably have to fuss a bit with it to get it to hang straight, shut tight, and not touch the floor at any part of its swing. It is usual to have to take it off the hinges several times and plane or sand the bottom just a bit more. An interior door needn't fit very tightly at the bottom—most people won't notice a 1/4-inch gap there—and the door may sag slightly over time.

WOOD TRIM

The final step in finishing the house is the application of wood trim. This is the last and best way of covering up mistakes. Prehung doors come with trim, which you'll still have to cut to fit. Lumberyards sell other trim in a great variety of sizes and shapes.

In modern houses, trim is usually restricted to door frames, mop boards or baseboards, and (sometimes) quarter-round applied at the bottom of the baseboard. Measure carefully, and make mitred cuts with a power saw or in a mitre box. Fasten with finish nails, using long ones to nail the baseboard through into the studs and smaller ones elsewhere. Use a nail set and putty the holes.

Take great care, but if you just can't get the slanted cuts to match perfectly, conceal the imperfections with putty and paint. Afterward, examine the trim done by pros in a couple of new homes. This probably will make you feel better.

Your home is finished. Now you have to learn to live in it. A solar house is a machine for living; learning to operate the machine is a necessary and enjoyable experience.

Part Three

Solar Living

Condensation and Ventilation

NOTHING IN LIFE IS PERFECT. There are drawbacks to living in a solar home. Only you can decide whether they are outweighed by the advantages. Some people don't like being conspicuously different from their neighbors. Others don't like the low sun in their eyes in winter. Still others object that the sunlight that permeates a solar home fades drapes and carpets. The greatest disadvantage of passive solar construction, however, lies in the relatively airtight quality of the building.

CONDENSATION
The air in the average American house in winter is drier than the air over the Sahara desert. This dryness causes many problems, ranging from furniture falling apart to serious respiratory infections. Most Americans, however, are used to dryness and never think about it; some use humidifiers, which breed algae and bacteria.

The first winter we were in our solar house, we borrowed our neighbor's dehumidifier. He said, "I use that in the summer. You're confused. What you want is a humidifier." We didn't, but we decided that we didn't want his gadget either. Dehumidifiers work by cooling, which we didn't need; besides, we liked having the health advantages of high humidity.

Any passive solar house, if it is built right, will have massive condensation problems, in the form of water running down all the windows and making pools on the sills. We're not talking here a little moisture, but pints of water. On a very cold morning, the windows will be covered on the inside with a complete glazing of ice. This is easier to clean up than water, because you can hold a pan under it and scrape it off with a windshield scraper.

There are things you can do about condensation. First of all, if you do nothing, it will get better with time. I was a basket case two weeks after moving into our new, unfinished house. Not only were the windows all wet, but water was dripping from the unfinished ceiling. Not much, and not every morning, but there was water. We consulted an expert, who said, "It will get better." It did. After that week, water never again dripped from the ceiling, and now, seven years later, we get little or no condensation on the windows.

Other solar homeowners we've talked to have had very similar experiences. Everything in a new house, especially the framing lumber and the concrete, is drying. The concrete, I am told, will continue to dry for twenty years or more. In drying, it releases water into the atmosphere. This is true in any new house, but in your house, because you constructed the vapor barrier so well, the moisture doesn't leak to the outdoors as fast.

As the house dries out, particularly in the first summer, the condensation problem will lessen. If you could finish your house completely before moving in, preferably in April, it would help, but most owner-builders move into an unfinished home in late fall. Time helped a lot with our condensation problem; so did getting all the walls covered with Sheetrock and painted.

Although it may not seem so, the humidity outdoors in winter is very low, because cold air holds far less moisture than warm. As heat energy seeks to travel from warm to cold, moisture seeks to travel from inside your house to outside. If it can, it will take heat with it. The solution to the condensation problem is not a leakier house any more than the solution to fleas is to set fire to the cat.

When warm air hits cold glass, it cools and deposits its moisture. There are two possible solutions to this problem. One is to reduce the moisture content of the air inside the house. The other is to keep the inside of the windows warm.

You may be willing to take some of the following actions: Use a dehumidifier in winter. Open windows whenever possible. (You'll be surprised how often it's possible; if you have six dinner guests, they'll heat up the house a lot and put out a lot of humidity. That's the time to open a window.) Burn wood in the fireplace; this sucks moisture out of the house like crazy.

CAUTION: Don't have fires in a fireplace and a woodstove simultaneously; the draft of one may suck the smoke of the other down the chimney and into the house.

Take baths instead of showers. Don't take long, hot showers. Try to avoid simmering liquids on the stove, uncovered, for a long time. Hang laundry outside, or if you have a dryer, vent it outdoors. Never hang laundry, or wet mittens or parkas, indoors. Don't store green firewood inside the house. Don't let the kids in the house in winter (just kidding).

Most of the humidity in your house comes from people or their actions. If you have a lot of company over Christmas, you'll have a lot of condensation. You can't stop breathing and you may not want to give up winter company, but anything you can do to cut down on the moisture they create, or to let this moisture out of the house, will help.

The best way to cut down on condensation is to keep your windows warm. The only practical way to do that—and it is extremely practical—is with outside shutters (see chapter 26). Shutters not only keep the windows warm, they keep the whole house warmer, saving you fuel and making the house cozier when you get up in the morning. They will work so well that if they have any holes or cracks, there will be small spots or streaks of moisture on the inside of the window opposite them.

VENTILATION

There is probably no aspect of modern home construction so much disagreed about and so bitterly fought over as ventilation. You will encounter people, many of them in the building trades, who will tell you that it is a great mistake to make your house too tight, that it's unhealthy and unnatural. From the beginning of civilization until about the middle of the twentieth century, houses were built that leaked air like sieves, partly because no one knew any other way to build them, partly because "we've always done it this way," and to a considerable extent because heating fuels were relatively cheap. In a typical house built before 1950 and never renovated, the entire air content is exchanged with outside air every four hours or so. This gives a whole new meaning to the term "heating all outdoors."

Many people in the building trades now understand how to seal and ventilate a house; some do not. The technique has two parts: The vapor barrier, usually a polyethylene film, should be as complete and lacking in holes and cracks as possible; but any moisture that passes through this barrier, or reaches the interior of the wall or roof in any other way, should be totally unimpeded in its journey to the outdoors.

In other words, it's all right to have a fairly high humidity level inside the house, but in the middle of the walls (where the insulation is) it should be dry, at least as dry as outdoors. This doesn't sound very difficult, and it isn't, provided that in the course of construction you don't create anything that would impede the progress of moisture to the outdoors, like a second vapor barrier.

How could you do that? One way is to nail Hi-R sheathing, which has a built-in vapor barrier in the form of an aluminum foil surface, on the outside of the house, outside the studs and the other insulation. Now you have a polyethylene vapor barrier on the inside and a foil barrier on the outside, with moisture trapped in between. Another way to achieve this undesirable effect is to finish the exterior of your house with a material like aluminum or vinyl, which unlike wood is impervious to water vapor.

In certain houses, it is possible to tear open the walls and squeeze quarts of water out of soaking-wet insulation. This causes two problems: Wet insulation has an R-factor of about zero, and wet studs will eventually rot.

Water vapor will move from a wetter to a drier environment, just as heat energy will travel from a warmer to a colder spot. As long as you provide it with an exit route, water vapor within your walls will move outdoors. In summer during a rainstorm or on a foggy day, moisture may gather in the walls, but it will always move out as the weather gets drier. Particularly in cold weather, when the outdoor relative humidity is quite low, there will be almost no moisture in the walls of your house, and that is just when you want them dry.

NOTE: If you live in a desert or semidesert area, moisture in your walls may not present the problem that it does in most parts of North America. Consult several local building experts. If their advice makes sense, take it.

It's important to provide ventilation just under the wooden deck of the roof, because the tar paper underlayment above is a very effective vapor barrier. If a house has an attic, it is customary to put insulation in the attic floor and ventilate the attic through louvres. Such an attic, in winter, is just about the same temperature as outdoors, and it is not uncommon to see frost on the underside of the roof.

If you have built a house much as described in this book, by creating large vent holes in each piece of blocking between rafters and by making sure the insulation doesn't block the airstream, you have created a current of air under the roof that will remove moisture successfully. You can prove this by holding your hand in front of one of the vents at the upper end. Regardless of wind direction or temperature, there will usually be a faint but discernible current of air moving from the lower to the upper vent.

There are various venting devices, usually metal or plastic, which can be used on other than shed roofs that are open at both ends. All are designed not to let in rain or snow but to let the roof "breathe." One type goes on the peak of a conventional roof; another goes at the upper end of a shed roof that joins a house wall, a common problem with sunspaces attached to the south side of a solar house.

After you have been living in the house for two or three years, you will occasionally, after a bitter night, have to mop condensation off a sill where a shutter blew off or where there is a window you can't reach to put a shutter on. While you're doing this, say to yourself, "We have fewer colds; we have fewer colds; we have fewer colds. . . ."

A Short Course in Woodburning

THICK BOOKS HAVE BEEN WRITTEN on cutting and burning wood. This chapter will teach you the fundamentals; experience will do the rest.

OTHER KINDS OF BACKUP HEAT

Many people choose electric baseboard heat for backup in a solar house. It is clean, neat, and convenient, and the initial installation cost is low. The cost of the heat per BTU, however, is greater in most parts of North America than with oil, gas, or wood. This doesn't make much difference in a house heated 90 percent by the sun; in other words, electric heat is cheap if you almost never use it.

Not many solar houses have an oil or gas furnace. It is usually not practical or economical to fill your basement with a furnace and your house with ducts or water pipes just for occasional use. Heat pumps are said to be practical in milder climates; I don't know anyone who uses one in the frozen north.

ADVANTAGES OF WOOD HEAT

There are basically two things to be said for wood heat: It is free if you cut your firewood on your own or a friend's land and it is environmentally the most sound. There are those who debate this, but the fact is that the wood you cut and burn would have put the same amount of carbon dioxide and other gases into the air sooner or later anyway, in what Robert Frost called "the slow smokeless burning of decay." If you harvest only dead, dying, or unhealthy trees, you can keep your house warm forever and always leave the forest better than you found it, or at least neater. A dying tree is said to be a haven for squirrels, woodpeckers, and the like, but we find no shortage of squirrels on our seven acres.

There is one other advantage to wood heat. In the event of a power failure, a not-unheard-of happening in cold climates, your house will still have heat. Not only will electric heat stop during a power failure, but also most oil or gas furnaces depend on electric thermostats and/or other electric devices. Design your wood-burning system to be simple and not dependent on electric fans or other gadgets.

DISADVANTAGES OF WOOD HEAT
Wood heat is dirtier than electric, and it takes up a lot more of the householder's time. Couples both of whom work full time probably shouldn't use it. For retired people, people who work at home, and/or people who like to putter, wood is ideal. The wood necessary to provide backup heat for a 2,000-square-foot solar house can be cut, split, stacked to dry, and carried to the stove area in about eighty man- (or woman-) hours. Unless you're Arnold Schwarzenegger, you won't do it all at once but will put in two to four hours at a time on pleasant afternoons or weekends.

SOURCES OF FIREWOOD
Four acres of hardwoods, reasonably well managed, will provide four cords of firewood a year forever. You can get by with less, because your neighbors or town will have trees they want to get rid of. If you have access to a truck, people will give you good firewood for the hauling away. Don't be afraid to ask.

You don't need to worry about whether ash is better than maple. You don't even need to know how to tell ash from maple, because you'll burn whatever you have. Don't burn too much softwood, like pine, or too much "punky" (semirotten) wood. You'll soon learn to tell both of these from good quality hardwoods; your saw will tell you the difference. Softer woods provide much less heat while gumming up your chimney faster. Even so, an occasional piece of pine mixed in with the hardwoods won't hurt. Many people in the southern Appalachians burn nothing but pine and make out fine.

There is no excuse, however, for burning green wood. Once you get your operation in full swing, you will do what our ancestors did: have next winter's wood all cut and stacked at the beginning of this winter, or at least by spring. (Winter is the traditional woodcutting season, because it is actually easier to get logs out of the woods then, and woodcutting is hot work.) If you can't tell any other way, you'll know green wood when you get it in the stove. It pops and steams, sap comes out of it, and it hates to burn. It also fills your chimney and stovepipe with creosote faster than you can say "chimney fire."

If you have to buy wood, don't buy it "seasoned." Although most firewood purveyors are honest in measuring a cord, almost all of them consider that wood that has lain in the wet forest for two weeks is "seasoned." Buy green wood six months to a year in advance, and stack it and dry it yourself.

A cord is a stack 4 by 4 by 8, 128 cubic feet. That's much more than will fit into an ordinary pickup truck. A "face cord" is defined as a stack that would be a cord if the logs were 24 inches long; instead they are "stove length," 20 or 16 or even 14 inches long. Another definition: "A face cord is something the country seller hopes the city buyer will be confused about and pay too much for."

CUTTING YOUR OWN FIREWOOD

Tools

Cutting your own wood is vastly better than buying it. You'll need a chain saw (two is better), an ax, a hatchet, one or two pulpwood saws, a splitting maul, a ten-pound sledge, and at least two wedges (three would be better). In addition, you'll need accessories: gasoline, oil to be mixed with the gas, bar and chain oil, the wrench-cum-screwdriver that comes with the chain saw, some small funnels, some rags, and a measuring device. Don't use chain oil in the gas or gas oil on the chain; in the long run it's better to pay the price for the right stuff.

Pay for a good-enough, big-enough gasoline chain saw. Ask around; some are much better than others. To supplement it, get a small, inexpensive electric saw to work up big pieces after you drag them home. Take everything into the woods with you; no matter how close it is, you'll get sick of running back to the garage for a wedge, gasoline, or the ax.

To get firewood home, you need a lot more equipment: stout rope, wire cable, a small tractor and trailer, a toboggan, and a Come-along. ("Come-along" is another of those trade names everyone uses. It is a wonderfully handy gadget like a compact block-and-tackle, involving steel cable, a ratchet and pawl, and a long handle. You could probably move a house with it, if you had something sturdy to fasten the other end to.) An extension ladder can also be handy.

Felling Trees

In looking for wood, look first at the logs lying on the ground. Make a test cut; if the tree seems reasonably solid, cut it in lengths and drag it out. But sooner or later, you'll have to cut down (fell, or as loggers say, fall) a tree. First, look up at the top to see which way the tree seems to lean and if there are any dead limbs that are likely to fall. Don't take dead limbs lightly; they have been known to loggers, since time immemorial, as "widowmakers." Wear a hard hat. Sometimes you can throw the rope over a dead limb and pull it down; sometimes it's best to find another tree.

A good time for felling is a couple of days after a big windstorm; chances are that all the widowmakers will be down. A terrible time is when anything greater than a gentle zephyr is blowing. Look up at the tops; it's blowing harder up there.

Trees mostly grow straight up, and they compensate for more weight on one side than the other by bending. Your tree probably has no more desire to fall one way than another. Still, you might as well let it fall the way it appears to want to, as long as there's nothing major in the way. If the tree is leaning the way you don't want it to fall, find another tree.

The traditional way to fell a tree exactly where you want it is to cut, with the saw, a large notch on the side facing the desired direction of fall, then cut through the trunk from the other side, starting somewhat higher up and cutting down on a slight slant to engage the notch. You know what? It works! The first time you try this and succeed, you'll consider yourself a real woodsman, but take out some added insurance.

Whenever possible, lug the extension ladder to the site, go up the tree as high as you can and tie a rope around it, using a bowline or other knot that you'll be able to untie after the operation. Take the rope (200 feet of 1/2-inch manila is good) away in the desired direction as far as it will go. If possible, fasten it to the back of a truck or tractor and have a skilled operator simply keep tension on the rope as you cut.

Sometimes you won't be able to use a vehicle. Then use the Come-along. Find a second tree the right distance away in the right direction to serve as an anchor, and take the rope to that. Loop a length of stout wire or cable around this anchor tree, and fasten it with a square knot tied with pliers, or with a cable clamp. Hook one end of the Come-along to it, pull the Come-along cable out to its full length, and hook the other end to the rope with a bowline. Have someone take up on the Come-along until it just maintains tension on the rope. Now fell your tree.

Both of you should move smartly away, in a direction perpendicular to the expected fall, as soon as the tree starts to move. I would say "run like hell," except that that's more likely to cause you to trip. Trees generally fall with a slow, awesome majesty; you'll have time to get away, *if* you have made absolutely certain of a clear escape route ahead of time. If you want to yell "Ti-i-mberrrr!" go ahead. You've earned it.

Cutting Up, Splitting, and Stacking

It sounds sensible to cut, split, and stack the wood in situ and come back for it later. Professionals don't do that; they employ giant, noisy skidders to drag huge logs out of the forest to a woodyard. It's a lot more convenient and efficient to work up logs at your leisure and stack them only once. Woodcutting has this in common with house building: Moving the materials around is more than half the work. Cut logs two to four times the desired length, then move them with horse, truck, tractor, or manpower to where you want them. You'll learn that wood near a road of some kind is more desirable than wood in the heart of the forest, and you'll find yourself constructing roads into the heart of your woodlot. It's a lot less work than you think.

Measure carefully the inside of your stove, then cut logs at least three inches shorter, or some multiple of that length. Use a tape measure, yardstick, or a stick cut to exactly the right length. If you use a stick, paint it fluorescent orange, or you'll soon put it down on the forest floor and pick up one of nature's by mistake, and all your logs will wind up three inches too long. If you try to eyeball the length, you are sure to fail. Professionals put a mark on the saw. My marks keep coming off, or the saw has so many nicks and scratches that I use the wrong one.

Few people do the final cutting up in the woods; no one does splitting there. For that, you need a woodyard, which might be a corner of the driveway, with a surface that is not too soft like lawn or too hard like asphalt, but just right, like Goldilocks or gravel. Split all logs that are more than eight inches in diameter. Even though your stove will take a 12-inch log, smaller ones are easier to handle, and split wood will season much faster.

You can go halves with your neighbor and rent a splitting machine, but it's not necessary. Most wood splits fairly easily, once you get the hang of it. The trick is to hit it with the maul, harder than you believe possible, exactly where you want to. It is simply a skill you will acquire. Try to split toward the direction that was up when the tree was growing. Be sure there is nothing overhead, like a tree branch or clothesline, to impede your swing and cause the maul to bounce back and bop you in the forehead.

Wood that is hard to split, like elm, is easier on a frosty morning. If you simply can't split the piece with the maul, make a crack with the ax, put a wedge in, and hit it with the sledgehammer. When that wedge is all the way in, put in another farther down the crack and start again. Eventually you'll be able to split 90 percent of your wood with the maul and most of the rest with the wedges, but terribly gnarled and knotty pieces may have to be cut vertically with the chain saw or used in the fireplace at yuletide.

Stack firelogs with the bark up. Make some kind of open shelter for your drying wood, like a plastic tarp securely fastened to poles, so that rain and snow don't fall on the top of the stack but sun can get at the sides. It will dry eventually in any case. Good wood can be left out a year or two; wood that is punky should be burned as soon as possible.

Insects

Some of your firewood will have insects in it. Spiders (all right, so they're not insects), sow bugs, earwigs, and the like won't really hurt anything inside your house, even if you do find them unattractive. The only creature you're likely to carry in that could do damage is the carpenter ant. Splitting logs in freezing weather will discourage most of the ants. Wood should be stored indoors only in a basement or other area where there is nothing but masonry and treated wood. Insects will greatly prefer the shelter of the log to the outside ambience until the log is in the stove, and then it's too late. Never spray firelogs with insecticide; when burned, it is far worse for you than the insects would be.

Safety

I am tempted to recommend that you cut yourself deliberately the first day you get your brand-new chain saw, since sooner or later everyone who uses a chain saw gets cut, after which he treats the tool with more respect. *Chain saws are horribly dangerous!* Read and follow all the directions. Wear long, heavy pants, a long-sleeved shirt, heavy boots, gloves, and a hard hat. That's right, I mean it—a hard hat. You should also wear safety glasses and earplugs.

Never work with a chain saw unless someone else is around to help if you get hurt; however, that person should not come within six feet of the sawyer when the saw is running. Don't for a minute use a saw that is malfunctioning so that it doesn't go immediately to idle speed (chain not moving) when you take your finger off the trigger. Clear away all brush from anywhere around the tree or log you're working on. Never cut anything higher than chest level, and don't work on lightweight branches that aren't securely fastened to something.

There are a million ways to cut yourself with a chain saw, but the most common is from a kickback. The saw is designed to function very well when it is snugly against a log, on the top, with the front end of the bar sticking out beyond the log. The trouble is that sometimes you will find it necessary to use the nose or top of the chain and bar. Logs will almost always bind the saw when you have cut halfway or more through them. You'll learn to feel this coming and pull the saw out before it is thoroughly stuck. If you don't, you'll have to drive in a wedge to open up the cut to pull out the saw. Now you should roll the log over, if possible, or attack another section that won't bind, but at times you'll be tempted to cut up from the underside the short distance remaining. As soon as you use the saw like this, the direction of the chain motion is not pulling the saw into the log but kicking it back toward you. Avoid this at all costs!

If you still aren't convinced that chain saws are dangerous, send a stamped, self-addressed envelope to the author for a free copy of "My Trip to the Emergency Room."

STOVES

Buy an airtight stove that is not too big. You will be surprised at how small a stove will heat your house; a large one will just overheat it and will burn too much wood in the process. A firebox that holds two cubic feet or a bit more is big enough for a 2,000-square-foot house. You will be running about two cords a year through your stove; the dealer is used to people who consume five times that much and will try to sell you too much stove.

Most well-known brands are satisfactory; cast iron is probably better for your purpose than sheet steel or soapstone. Front loaders are easier and safer than top loaders. The ideal location is in the basement, with nothing around but masonry. The stove must not be close to a combustible surface in any direction; stovepipe should go directly into a chimney and flue, not pass through a floor or wall. If the stove is in the basement, mount it well up on a base of concrete blocks, so you won't have to lie down to see into it.

Accessories

The most important accessory for your stove is an inexpensive stack thermometer that snaps magnetically to the stovepipe a foot above the stove. This will enable you, or even someone filling in for you, to keep the fire at the desired temperature. Most people run a woodstove too cold, which soon chokes the flue with creosote. If the chimney, flues, pipes, and stove are in good shape and clean, too hot is better than too cold, but the thermometer enables even an illiterate to keep the stack temperature in the orange zone, above the yellow and below the red. The stack temperature should rise as quickly as possible after the fire is started to above 240 degrees, the maximum temperature at which creosote condenses, and should stay there until the fire dies for good.

For either a fireplace or a wood stove, tools are necessary. The little bitty brass-knobbed ones sold in artsy stores are generally too feeble to do the job. The best tool by far is a pair of welder's gloves. With these on, you can reach into the red-hot stove and move logs around with your hands, or pull out that log that turned out to be too long and carry it out into the snow. If you don't have gloves, you'll need a huge, sturdy pair of tongs. Some kind of poker is helpful, as are a hearth broom and a shovel for ashes. Most shovels, however, like most tongs, are too dainty to do the job.

Disposing of Ashes

Speaking of ashes, they must, unfortunately, be disposed of. Don't clean out the stove or fireplace too often or too thoroughly, though; a shallow bed of ash makes a fire burn better. Put ashes in a totally fireproof container—even three-day-old ashes can contain live coals. Ashes will add traction to your driveway in winter if spread there; they will also track in all over your house. Dump them on your garden, but only within reason. Many home gardeners have put wood ashes in their gardens until the pH is as alkaline as the Arizona desert.

Never burn anything put plain paper and untreated wood. Colored or glossy paper or similar materials may contain toxic metals or chemicals, and most plastics give off toxic fumes when burned.

FIREPLACES

A fireplace (see also chapters 4 and 9) is never an efficient way to heat a house, but it's possible to design, build, and use one in such a way that it results in a net heat gain for the house rather than, as with many, a net heat loss. The basic theory is to keep heat, as much as possible, from going up the chimney, whether or not there is a fire in the fireplace. When there is not a fire it's fairly simple: Close the damper inside the chimney, the outdoor air intake, and the large opening in the front.

An attractive way to do this last is with glass doors. A more efficient way is with a large, square piece of thin galvanized steel, to which you attach some kind of feet (corner braces do nicely) and a handle. Have an artistic member of the family paint a sheaf of wheat or something on it, and keep it in front of the fireplace at all times except when there is a good fire going. Since steel, unlike glass, transmits heat but not light, you will still get something out of a dying fire with this device, and your guests won't have to look at a mess of ashes and charcoal.

When a fire is going, use some kind of heat exchanger to get heat but not smoke out into the room; a common kind is known as a Heatilator. Cold air goes in the bottom, is warmed by the fire through steel walls, and comes out the top. A better device is a series of metal tubes that are open at top and bottom and serve as a grate; the fire is built within them. Either of these devices should have the air driven by a fan; depending on hot air to rise under the influence of gravity is just not efficient. A fire-screen or glass doors will keep sparks in the fireplace; they will also keep the heat from getting out into the room.

CHIMNEY SWEEPING

Flues and pipes should be cleaned at least once a year. If you burn more than two cords or burn green wood or evergreens, clean them more often. There is no good reason not to do this yourself by getting up on the roof, with an assistant in the basement, and passing a brush on a weighted line up and down the flue several times. Most hardware stores sell chimney brushes in various sizes and shapes. The job is not danger-ous or difficult but is very dirty, mostly for the guy in the basement.

There is an old saying that wood warms you three times: when you cut it, when you split it, and when you burn it. Whether or not you find this to be true, you will find that heating your house with wood, espe-cially your own wood, is very satisfying to the spirit.

26

Shutters and Drapes

YOU CAN ADD GREATLY to the comfort, efficiency, and appearance of your solar home with coverings on the inside and outside of the windows. Drapes or curtains will add to the comfort and appearance without adding much to the efficiency; shutters will add greatly to the comfort and efficiency. Their beauty, if any, is in the eye of the beholder.

SHUTTERS

Windows were covered with shutters at night even before they were covered with glass. Earlier shutters were designed to prevent robbery, not to conserve energy; for this reason, they were barred on the inside. Even today it's easier to put shutters on the inside, but there they do more harm than good. The function of the shutters we recommend is to keep the cold on the outside and the heat on the inside—the outside and inside of the shutter, that is. Shutters inside the windows permit the inside of the glass to reach temperatures well below freezing. Moisture will condense on the glass, and in the morning, windows will have a coating of ice.

You will find it quite easy to make thermal shutters for the outside of your windows, moderately easy to keep them in place, and fairly difficult to make them attractive. The procedure described below is the result of a lot of trial and error.

Measure the inside of the external frame of each window very care-fully, more than once. Even the frames of identical windows will have tiny variations. If the frame is not perfectly rectangular, check each cor-ner with a square. Cut the shutter to fit as perfectly as possible, even, if necessary, by making the appropriate shutter corner slightly less or more than 90 degrees to match the window frame.

Buy 4-by-8 sheets of polyisocyanurate or similar sheathing (see chap-ter 21). This comes in various thicknesses. Use 1-inch for large, fixed win-dows. You may have to use 1/2-inch in your smaller windows, the ones that open, but don't try it for big sheets. The material is called "semirigid," and you'll find out what that means when it breaks of its own weight.

If you can find Styrofoam panels more than two feet wide, use them; the difference in R-value is not important here. Both these materials give off toxic fumes in a fire, and either can be allergenic. You may want to wear gloves when handling the material, and long sleeves are a must.

Use a felt pen, a square, a long straightedge, and a razor blade knife to mark and cut the shutter. It should be cut so that when it is in place the side with the advertising on it will be outside, but putting it up inside out won't result in much heat loss. You'll have to fight the tendency of the knife and the material to make wavy or tapered edges. As you make each shutter, try it in the window it was made to fit. If it's too big, trim it with the knife on site. If you try to force it, it will break. If it's much too small, recut it to fit another window. Fitting it is slightly easier because the sill slants. Put the top in first, then push the bottom in.

As soon as the shutter seems to fit, before pushing it all the way in, cut off at least one small lower corner, maybe both, to make a large enough space to get a finger into. Without this, every morning you will have to claw the shutter off with your fingernails or a jackknife, and soon it will look much worse than if you had cut the corner off.

It would seem that more attractive and sturdier shutters could be made by encasing the material in a light wood frame, perhaps with a fab-ric covering. This may be so, but it is preferable to work with lighter and softer shutters, so that when the wind swirls them into the window as they are being applied or removed, the glass won't break.

Although the shutters may seem to fit tightly, the wind will tear them off unless they have retainers. These can be made of wooden strap-ping (1x3) cut to fit horizontally across the middle of the shutter, pushed snugly down into L-shaped brackets made of two chunks of 3/4-inch ply-wood glued and screwed together, then fastened to the window frames with extra-long screws.

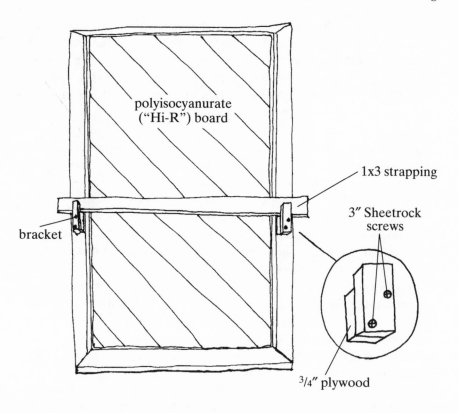

Fig. 51. *The shutter is cut to fit snugly inside the window frame. The L-shaped brackets, made of two pieces of ³/₄-inch plywood glued together, are screwed to the window trim boards, and a piece of wooden strapping is dropped down into them to hold the shutter in place.*

It is impossible to use this kind of retainer on some openable windows that have no additional trim (see chapter 22), because the frames are too narrow. In this case, a sort of elongated turn button made of ¹/₂-by-³/₄-inch parting bead can be nailed on each side, as well as the top if you can reach it. After the shutter is put on, these are turned to retain it.

Accessibility of windows varies. Those that can be reached from the ground, from a porch roof, or from a deck are no problem. Clerestory windows not accessible from a roof probably will have to get along without shutters; you'll get sick of using a ladder morning and evening all winter. Openable windows make it possible to put upstairs shutters on from the inside, if you're clever.

One way is this: After a shutter for an upstairs openable window has been carefully cut to size, make holes in it with a large nail, one hole in the center near the top and two near the bottom, about equidistant from the edges and from each other. Run a 12-inch length of strong string through each hole and through holes made with a center punch or nail in the centers of metal discs designed to support insulating sheathing (see chapter 21). You'll wind up with three pieces of string, each threaded first through a disc, then through the shutter, then through another disc. Keep the thread from coming back through the disc by tying it to a small washer. In place of the discs, you could use squares of 1/8-inch board. (See figure 52.)

Tape the outside discs to the shutter with duct tape, leaving the inner ones dangling. Open the top of the window slightly and the bottom as wide as possible. Put the shutter through the opening diagonally, and juggle it into place by using the upper string pulled through the top of the window and the lower two pulled through the bottom. (It may help to tie the lower two together to form a loop or have two people work together to do this.) When you have everything the way you want it, shut the window on the strings, with the discs on the inside.

If this is too difficult, give up a small amount of R-value but retain your sanity by cutting one or two finger holes in the bottom of the shutter so that you can exercise more control. If the bottom of a window opens but the top doesn't, or if you have casement windows, you'll have to think of something else or give up. It is not as important to cover smaller windows, if you can get all the big ones covered. Don't cover difficult windows on the inside with insulation board; it's against the fire laws.

We recommend leaving sliding glass doors uncovered, for safety reasons. If all the other glass is covered, the house will stay warm enough at night to keep condensation to a minimum; if necessary, you can wipe the doors with a towel every morning.

Shutters have to be stored daily as well as over the summer. A nearby shelter is necessary; you don't want to carry them far each day. An alternative would be to cover them securely with a big sheet of plastic or a tarp, weighted down with flat stones. If they are not protected somehow, sooner or later they will blow around and break. Another unpleasant possibility is that they would be wet when you put them on, then freeze into position and be totally immovable the next morning. Shutters put up clean and dry will rarely freeze on, no matter how hard it snows or rains; the roof overhang keeps this from happening.

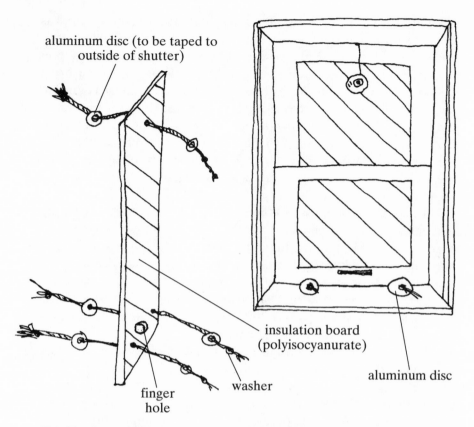

aluminum disc (to be taped to outside of shutter)

insulation board (polyisocyanurate)

aluminum disc

finger hole

washer

Fig. 52. *One possible way to put a shutter on the outside of a window from the inside is to open the top of the window a small amount and open the bottom wide, put the shutter diagonally through the larger opening, use the strings and finger hole to work it into position, and then hold the strings tight while closing the window on them.*

As soon as a shutter is fitted to a window, label it, stating which window it covers and which way is up. Label it on the inside; writing on the outside will fade in sunlight. Use a really indelible felt-tipped pen and write directly on the shutter; any paper label will eventually come off.

After the shutters have been put up and taken down a few score times, their edges will erode to the point where they fit more loosely. At this point, bind the edges with duct tape. This will keep them from eroding further, keep your hands from coming in contact with the actual polyisocyanurate foam, and make them generally sturdier. At the same time, paint them or cover them with self-sticking shelf paper to make them more attractive, if you wish. Duct tape can also be used to effect repairs, even on badly broken shutters.

DRAPES

Drapes without shutters will not add much to the heat-retaining quality of your house, but they have other merits. Most solar home owners feel that the vast expanse of glass on the south side is prettier when framed by drapes. Closed at night, they keep the full moon from waking you up when it shines in your big bedroom windows, the neighbors from seeing in through that vast expanse of glass, and your guests from reading the labels you wrote on the insides of the shutters.

In ordinary houses, drapes cut down on drafts. Your window frames don't have any air leaks, but drapes do help slightly to keep the cold air between them and the glass, which is particularly useful on those cool but not cold spring and fall nights when you don't put the shutters on.

You can buy drapes or make them, if someone in the household has the necessary skill. Drape material is available that is already lined with a special insulating fabric; the R-value is not great, however, so if something else is cheaper, you might as well buy it.

In keeping with the spirit of this book, consider using 1 1/4-inch wooden closet poles and 1 1/2-inch wooden rings to support the drapes wherever possible, opening and closing them entirely by hand. You can design and build painted plywood brackets to support the poles. Where the windows are too high, you'll have to fall back on expensive rods and drawstrings, or open and close drapes with a hook on the end of a pole.

It's possible to make or buy curtains, rather than drapes, for any windows in your house. Most people feel that drapes look better at very large windows and that a mix of drapes and curtains in one room is unattractive.

Drapes will make the inside of your house look prettier and more finished. Even at best, shutters made of insulation board won't make the outside look prettier, but when you learn how much they cut down on condensation and heat loss, they'll look beautiful to you.

27 ☼

A Solar Home Calendar

Obviously, solar home owners, like all home owners, rake leaves in the fall, plant gardens in the spring, and shovel snow in the winter; this calendar deals with those activities peculiar to life in a passive solar house. Not everyone is suited to this kind of life, but those who are love it. A dweller in such a house is closely in tune with nature. The outdoors, seen through an expanse of glass, is an important part of the surroundings. Cloudy days, rain, and snow, while less attractive, are all part of life. As all philosophers know, you couldn't appreciate the sunny days if there were no cloudy ones.

Most of us who dwell in such houses are constant putterers. There is always something to do: put on shutters, take off shutters, sweep leaves or snow off the deck, bring in wood, tend a fire, clean the stove and chimney, carry out ashes, open drapes, close drapes, open up the sunspace, close the sunspace, and so on ad infinitum. If that doesn't sound like your kind of lifestyle, you probably shouldn't plan to live in a passive solar house, at least not unless it has backup electric heat that is thermostatically controlled.

Solar home owners also get used to variations in warmth. In winter, it will usually be cool in the house when you get up; you may throw on a sweater in the morning. By afternoon on a sunny winter day you'll be dressed like a resident of a tropic isle. You could have electric heat set permanently at 68 degrees, but you'd miss some of the fun.

Especially if you heat with wood, you'll learn to plan ahead. You'll watch the TV meteorologists with rapt attention and probably buy a weather radio and listen to the NOAA forecasts. The massive heat sink in a solar house takes a long time to cool down, but it also takes a long time to heat up, so you have to make an educated guess about the weather to come. The most annoying forecast is the one that says it will be sunny tomorrow morning and is wrong. Then you wake up to a cold house that will take a long time to get warm. If you are away for a week at Christmas and you don't have automatic backup heat, unless there is a lot of sunny weather it is going to be COLD in the house when you get home. It's very unlikely that the pipes will have frozen, but it may be down to 48 degrees. Because you have to warm up all that masonry, rock, or sand, it will take a wood fire going for twenty-four hours to get the temperature back up to 68 degrees.

Inhabitants of solar homes own and study almanacs. From this study they learn, if they didn't already know, that long-range weather forecasting is seldom correct and that the traditional seasons don't match the observed behavior of the sun. For example, calendar winter begins on the shortest day of the year and lasts until the vernal equinox, on or about March 21, the date on which the days and nights become equally long. But the coldest day of winter usually comes long after the shortest. There's an obvious reason for this: The earth, or your part of it, has a heating and cooling time lag just as your house does.

Passive solar heating is more dependent on hours of sunlight than on outdoor temperature. For that reason, the solar home owner will find it useful to think about solar, rather than calendar, seasons. These are as follows.

SOLAR WINTER: NOVEMBER 6 TO FEBRUARY 5

If you think of this period as the winter, you won't be so disconcerted by your extensive fuel consumption, or large electric bill, by Christmas. Religious and family considerations aside, Christmas is the low point of the solar homeowner's year. Not only are the days shortest then, but in many parts of North America November and December have a great many cloudy days. This is also the period when you'll spend a lot of time each morning sopping up condensation from windows that were not shuttered. You will be surprised by how much less the windows steam up by mid- or late January.

If you use shutters, start putting them on each night during the first cold snap in November. At first, there will be nights when you leave them off; later you may leave them on for days at a time when the sun never shows its face.

Without a doubt you will discover the paradox mentioned in the Introduction: The warmer the winter, the more wood (or other fuel) you will consume. We have observed this for years now, and other solar home owners have noticed it. The reason is simple: When the weather warms up, it often becomes cloudy (or vice versa). Your heating system works much better on sunny days, regardless of the outdoor temperature. Pray for a cold, clear winter.

An old New England saying is that the farmer should have half his hay and half his wood left on February 1. I don't know about your hay, but a good deal more than half your wood or other fuel will be gone by then. Chances are that you'll use as much backup heat between November 10 and January 10 as you will during the rest of the calendar winter. Not only that, as you approach mid-February, the increase in insolation will warm your house, improve your mood, and make you less pessimistic about heating costs for the rest of the winter.

SOLAR SPRING: FEBRUARY 6 TO MAY 5

Everybody loves to see spring come. People who live in glass houses are no exception, but since a house with huge windows gives the inhabitants much less feeling of being cooped up in winter, they may not have been suffering as much from cabin fever. There is great pleasure in watching the sun climb higher and higher as the days grow longer, but there is also the frustration of a great many cold rainy spring days.

Nonetheless, this is the most pleasant time in a solar house. You and your cat will bask in the light and heat that pour in from the low sun. You will derive a great deal of admittedly selfish pleasure from seeing smoke emerging from the chimneys of your neighbors on days when you "have no heat in the house." You will enjoy the warmth of slate floors that have absorbed solar energy. Only on the very coldest and darkest days will a wood fire burn all day; in sunny weather, you will start the fire in late afternoon (if at all) and stop tending it when you go to bed.

In most climates the heaviest snow cover occurs in the first half of this period. You may want to remove the snow from your roof if it gets too deep. This is not too difficult nor dangerous, but it is hot, sweaty work. Search old-fashioned hardware stores in snow country for a long-handled snow rake. With this, you can stand under the eaves and pull the snow down off the roof, dodging to keep it from going down your neck.

You may also have to climb out on the roof and shovel or push the snow down off it. You are surprisingly unlikely to slide off a roof that is not steep, is not surfaced with slippery material, and has two feet of snow on it. After a good pile has built up under the eaves, you probably wouldn't get hurt too badly if you did fall off, but normal caution is still advisable. Sweep snow off porches, decks, and balconies. No matter how pretty it looks lying there, it can cause water to seep in under doors.

Snow has its advantages as well. We can't prove this statistically, but we're sure you'll use less fuel if there is a layer of snow. It reflects light into windows, banks the foundation, and instead of melting off heavily insulated roofs, adds another layer of very efficient insulation.

Don't store the shutters away for the summer too early, and don't be surprised if you have to have an occasional fire in the stove or fireplace in April or May. You may have to bring in a bit more wood from the supply you've kept dry in a shed or other shelter. Sooner or later warm weather will really come, and then you can store the shutters carefully, making sure their identifying numbers or labels are still legible.

SOLAR SUMMER: MAY 6 TO AUGUST 5

During the solar summer, there isn't much difference between a passive solar house and any other, except that your neighbors may have the furnace running in early May when you don't. This is the time to putter with repairs, adjustments, and improvements. Fix up shutters and make new ones, if necessary, early in this period. For one thing, insulation will be cheaper now. Caulk as necessary, and mend shingles and siding. Most years, however, such repairs won't be necessary.

Drag the screens out, wash them outdoors with the hose, and put them on. This is when you should clean the chimney. It's an unpleasant job, but it's more fun on a warm spring day than in cold drizzle in late fall. It doesn't really matter when you do it; you may hate having a fire one week after you clean it, but it doesn't make any difference to the chimney.

SOLAR FALL: AUGUST 6 TO NOVEMBER 5

If your house is ever too hot, it will be during the first half of the solar fall, when outdoor temperatures are at their peak but the sun begins to get lower in the sky and shine in the windows. Control this by drawing drapes (putting on shutters would be overkill), keeping windows open at night and closed in the daytime, and pushing up cooler air from the base-ment with the same duct-and-fan system that pushes warm air from the top to the bottom of the house in winter. If you have an extensive sand or rock heat sink with ductwork, you should be able to warm it up for the coming winter and cool your house in the same operation. You may not need air conditioning, but if you do, you'll enjoy knowing that your house will also be easier than most to keep cool.

This is your last chance to get ready for winter. You should have cut the wood you need, if any, last winter or earlier, or in the spring, but it's still not too late. Green wood cut and split in the heat of August will be dry enough to burn by Christmas, but *only* if it has been stacked in the sun in piles that allow air to circulate throughout *and* covered every time it rained. It would have been far easier and less sweaty to have done it when you should have.

Pull the shutters out of storage by late September and examine them. Be sure they are correctly labeled, repair those that need it, and make new ones if necessary. (Yes, I know, theoretically you did this last spring.) Check the brackets and retainers to make sure they are strong, tight, and all there; you might have inadvertently used a retainer in dog-house construction or some similar project during the summer.

If you are a gardener, this is the time for harvesting and storing. If you use homegrown vegetables, whether your own or those bought at a farmers' market, you can save a lot of wear and tear on the septic tank or dry well, kitchen floor, and nervous system by cleaning them as well as possible in a bucket of water outside the house, handy to the compost pile if you have one.

You're all ready for winter in your passive solar home. You know how well it's designed, since you designed it; how well it's built, since you built it; and how well it works, since you've lived in it. Sit back, put your feet up, and relax, without a worry about what the price of oil will go to next winter or whether the dealer's truck will be able to make it up the drive. You are entitled to feel a bit smug; you worked hard to achieve this state.

APPENDIX

THIS SECTION IS FOR THOSE who want to know why and how things work. If you are satisfied just to know that they do work, you can skip this part, although the information is handy for squelching those friends and acquaintances who will assure you that passive solar heating won't work in your climate.

Why your solar house won't overheat in the summer, even if you live in Orlando:

If you live in a conventional house in Orlando, it probably gets hot indoors in the summer. To combat this, you might open windows, especially at night; use air conditioning; or not leave the furnace running. It is curious that so many people firmly believe that you can't use the same techniques in a solar house. The first two techniques are discussed in chapter 27.

How do you turn off the furnace in summer in a solar house? For the most part, nature takes care of it for you. Because the sun is too high in the sky, it simply doesn't shine in your south windows in summer. In order to help this natural system to function, you design overhangs (mostly roof extensions) over the windows. (See figure 53.)

Astronomical explanation, for those who want to know:

The axis of the earth is tilted with regard to the sun—that is, the earth doesn't just go around the sun like a top on a table. If it were not tilted, we wouldn't have summer and winter; it would just get colder all year round the farther you went from the equator.

As most people know, the summer solstice—the longest day of the year in the Northern Hemisphere—comes about June 21 (occasionally a day earlier or later). On that day at midday in Minneapolis, the sun is 68 degrees above the horizon. At the winter solstice, about December 21, at the same place at the same time, the sun is 22 degrees above the horizon. If you're building a solar house in Minneapolis, which is at 45 degrees north latitude, you make sure your windows will be shaded by overhangs when the sun is at 60 degrees or so, since that's about where the sun will be in July. It will probably shine in the windows a bit in mid-August.

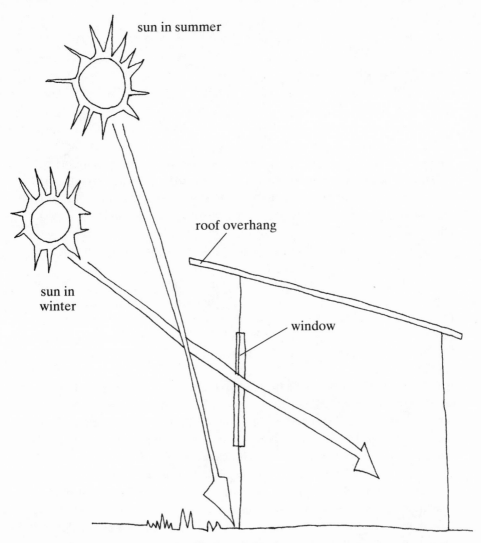

Fig. 53. *Passive solar houses do not overheat in the summer, chiefly because the sun is high overhead at that time. Roof overhangs prevent any direct sunlight from striking windows. Even if sunlight does occasionally shine on a window, it strikes at an acute angle, which cuts down a great deal on the light entering the building.*

It isn't nearly as difficult as it sounds; you can usually calculate the overhangs "by guess and by God." Fiddlers Green is at approximately 43 degrees north latitude, about the same as Milwaukee. Our roof is two feet above the tops of most of the windows, and it extends out 27 inches.

Since it is a shed roof, it also inclines upward at a slope of 3 in 12. We didn't calculate this to five decimal places; we just looked at where the shadow of a plank fell on about June 21. If the overhangs were half a foot longer or shorter, it wouldn't make a great deal of difference. The nicest part of this natural system is that the hotter it gets because you are farther south, the less overhang you need.

To make the same calculation for your house site: 1. Find a large city that is almost exactly due east or west of your site. It doesn't matter how far away it is. 2. Look up this city in a good almanac, like the *Old Farmer's Almanac,* to find out its latitude. That is your latitude. 3. Subtract that number from 113. That is how high in the sky, in degrees, the sun will be at your site at midday on June 21. Now subtract your latitude from 67. That's how high it will be on December 21.

Where did I get 113 and 67? Because of the tilt or wobble of the earth, the sun is at 90 degrees (directly overhead) with regard to the Tropic of Cancer on June 21, and in the same position with regard to the Tropic of Capricorn on December 21. These Tropics (imaginary lines like the equator) are at 23 degrees north and south latitudes, respectively. Therefore, you add 23 to 90 to get 113 in midsummer, and subtract 23 from 90 to get 67 in midwinter.

INDEX